"Seeing the Elephant"

D0863551

"Seeing the Elephant"

RAW RECRUITS AT THE BATTLE OF SHILOH

Joseph Allan Frank
and
George A. Reaves

WITHDRAWN

University of Illinois Press

Urbana and Chicago

First Illinois paperback, 2003
© 1989 by Joseph Allan Frank and Alice Reaves
Reprinted by arrangement with the copyright holders.
All rights reserved
Manufactured in the United States of America
P 5 4 3 2 1

♾ This book is printed on acid-free paper.

Library of Congress Cataloging-in-Publication Data
Frank, Joseph Allan.
"Seeing the elephant" : raw recruits at the Battle of Shiloh /
Joseph Allan Frank and George A. Reaves.
p.   cm.
Originally published: New York: Greenwood Press, 1989, in series:
Contributions in military studies ; no. 88.
Includes bibliographical references (p.   ) and index.
ISBN 0-252-07126-3 (pbk. : alk. paper)
1. Shiloh, Battle of, Tenn., 1862. 2. Combat—Psychological aspects.
3. United States—History—Civil War, 1861–1865—
Psychological aspects. 4. United States. Army—History—Civil
War, 1861–1965. 5. Confederate States of America. Army—History.
I. Reaves, George A. II. Title.
E473.54.F7   2003
973.7'31—dc21   2002032229

Contents

Illustrations follow page 86

Acknowledgments

The authors would like to express their gratitude to Anthony Kellett of the Operational Research and Analysis Establishment at the Department of National Defence, Ottawa, Canada, for his advice and interest in our project. We also wish to thank Professor Fred Caloren, Department of Sociology, University of Ottawa, for his help and judgment in preparing the manuscript. And finally, and above all, we wish to express our affection and appreciation to Alice Reaves and Brigitte Paquet-Frank for their support and patience during the eight years' research and writing of this work.

Introduction

At last Ambrose Bierce could hear it, "a dull distant sound like the heavy breathing of some great animal below the horizon" (Bierce 1966: I, 235).[1] It had a mournful, yet ominous groan, as it rose and fell on the wind. The column listened, shivered, and shook itself back into motion, plunging on. Bierce, an Indiana volunteer, was exhilarated and eager at the prospect of "seeing the elephant" (Bierce 1966: I, 235).[2] As he and his comrades approached Shiloh from the opposite bank of the Tennessee River, the moans of distant battle became more distinct, the muffled rumble became a continuous din. Reaching the bank opposite the battlefied, Bierce and his fellow Indianians rushed aboard the steamboat and were quickly ferried to the other side. They scrambled up the steep, muddy bank. Through the crowds of stragglers and their forewarning of doom, past the jumble of wounded strewn about, the novice warriors tumbled into their assigned position to await their baptism of fire. When it came the next morning, it was a frenetic rush of horrifying disjointed cameos.

Bierce was among thousands of men from Don Carlos Buell's Army of the Ohio rushing to support General Ulysses Grant's outnumbered forces who were staving off an attack by the Confederate army of General Albert Sidney Johnston. For Johnston, the battle was a desperate attempt to foil the impending linkup of Buell's and Grant's armies, a combination that would enable a renewed Union offensive against the Confederate base and rail junction at Corinth, Mississippi. The ensuing engagement, on April 6 and 7, 1862, was the largest battle in the West fought with raw recruits.

Not all those at Shiloh that day shared Bierce's proclivity for war. William D. Niles of the 16th Wisconsin emerged from the ordeal with a markedly different reaction. He wrote to his parents shortly after the battle that he had at last "seen the elephant." Yet, he did not mention the "heavy breathing" of Bierce's "great animal," but matter-of-factly stated that it had a "mighty big trunk" (Quiner, Reel No. 2, Vol. 5, pp. 251–52). On the other hand, Gunner George Levally was profoundly shaken by his first combat experience. He had seen his unit's horses butchered by counterbattery fire. Worse still, his outfit, Captain John B. Myer's 13th Ohio Battery, was overrun. And more intimately, he felt the whoosh of a ball virtually parting his hair as it snapped the kepi off his head. After such an unpropitious debut on the "field of glory," young George solemnly vowed that he did "not want to see [the elephant] . . . again" (To father, April 12, 1862).

Bierce, Niles, and Levally all underwent their baptism of fire at Shiloh, but they reacted differently to the experience: Bierce thrived on the drama of battle, Niles took it in stride, and Levally was traumatized. The differences appeared in the letters and diaries of several hundred new recruits who fought at Shiloh. Recent military sociology on combat motivation has introduced categories for assessing the sources of morale. This monograph will examine tactical preparation, political attitudes, logistics, and leadership as well as esprit de corps, comradeship, and officer competence that affect combat motivation. Information on these is available in soldiers' letters and diaries. This examination will suggest which factors were most significant at different moments in the Shiloh campaign, thus avoiding another anecdotal account. The soldiers' reactions will be presented in their own words regarding the morale factors as they appear at each stage of the campaign: enlistment and training, life in the field, approaching battle, combat, reactions after the battle, and so on.

Men may fight because of personal attachments to their comrades or their regiment. They may fight for patriotic motives such as flag, constitution, and country. Some contend soldiers are better fighters because of a particular cultural ethos such as heroic romanticism (Linderman: 1987). Others attribute fighter effectiveness to training and leadership (F. M. Richardson 1978: 4; Grinkler and Spiegel 1945: 37–38; Kellett 1982: 6, 292; Hauser 1980: 87).

The principal concern is with the human factor in war, specifically the attitudes of the common soldier and his immediate superiors, the company- and field-grade officers. Once "the ball opened," the rank and file took over. Shiloh was the archetypical soldier's battle, because the generals lost command and control early in the engagement. A veteran of Shiloh named Sam Watkins of the 1st Tennessee Infantry recalled, "I always shot at privates. It was they that did the shooting and killing, and if I could kill or wound a private, why, my chances were so much the better." He added that he "always looked upon officers as harmless personages" (Watkins 1962: 29). Our image of the campaign is "eye level," from man in the firing line, eschewing the wider horizon visible from the general's saddle.

Paradoxically, the attitudes and combat behavior of the Civil War soldiers have not received as much attention as the campaigns and battles. Among the few who have studied the soldiers are Bell I. Wiley (1978a, 1978b), Philip Van Doren Stern (1961), Pete Maslowski (1970), Michael Barton (1981), Grady McWhiney and Perry D. Jamieson (1982), Gerald F. Linderman (1987), and Reid Mitchell (1988). Maslowski's article took a look at Civil War soldiers' attitudes about various questions that were developed in Stouffer's study (1949) on combat morale in World War II. But Maslowski's survey was limited to a small sample of twenty-five Confederates and Unionists. Barton, and McWhiney and Jamieson dwelt on the soldiers' values and culture; they contended that there were differences between Northern and Southern troops and suggested that the latter were more motivated by chivalric traditions than the former.

The works of Wiley (1978a, 1978b) and a book edited by Van Doren Stern (1961) are general overviews of soldier life and provide little about the attitudes of the soldiers to combat. Linderman's recent work (1987), perhaps inspired by some of the points Marvin Cain (1982) and Richard H. Kohn (1981) have raised, addressed the problem of soldiers' attitudes toward combat. Linderman's account attributed their fighting morale to only one major source: the heroic culture of the Victorian era. He chose some fifty-odd soldiers' reminiscences, mainly published memoirs of upper-class, highly educated individuals such as Oliver Wendell Holmes, Jr., and Joshua Chamberlain to demonstrate how their idea of courage was corroded as the war dragged on. And most recently, is Mitchell's work, which is readable and well documented, although his description of the soldiers' attitudes makes no use of works on military sociology.

To avoid yet another anecdotal narrative, as large a body of evidence as possible on green volunteers was required. Information had to be organized according to sociological categories related to combat motivation, thus permitting the use of statistical analysis. The Shiloh campaign fit the bill; the largest contingent of green volunteers first saw combat in that battle. Eventually letters, diaries, and reminiscences of approximately 450 men who went through their baptism of fire at Shiloh were found. This information was then organized according to the elements that military sociologists frequently associate with combat motivation.

The research strategy was directed to men in some 160 green regiments and batteries, units that had never been in a brigade-level fight. They were selected after checking available adjutants' general reports, the records at the Shiloh National Military Park as well as the regimental histories. The vast majority of the troops of the Confederate Army of the Mississippi were green.[3] General Grant's Army of the Tennessee, was mainly green with only about thirty of its regiments having seen action either at Belmont or at Fort Donelson. As for General Buell's Army of the Ohio, it had been in some skirmishes, but the troops had been mainly engaged in garrison duty (Cunningham 1966: 168–69). There were a few individuals who were with veteran regiments, but who had not enlisted until after their unit's first engagement—men such as Augustus H. Mecklin, Company I, 15th Mississippi. Among the 450 men, the papers of 381 fighters included enough information on the points that were being studied to be put into a data set.[4] The scope is therefore strictly limited to only those soldiers who volunteered and fought at Shiloh. It is further restricted to only those among the Shiloh volunteers who had not seen action in previous battles. It makes no generalizations beyond this engagement.

The main source was the soldiers' correspondence. By an act of Congress, Civil War soldiers' letters were mailed free (*The Indiana True Republican*, August 8, 1861). The system was fairly efficient. It had to be, because a majority of the troops were literate and corresponded actively with their friends and relatives.[5] Feeling part of a great endeavor, many of them also kept diaries and recorded their reminiscences. As Edmund Wilson contended, never had there been an era in American history, when there were so many articulate people (1984: x, xiii). Some accounts were laconic, often reporting only the weather and merely sketching events. For example, Thomas Armes of Company A, 24th Indiana simply reported on the evening after the battle that "Walises [Wallace's] Brigad opend fire at day light driv the Rebils 6 miles seases firing at dark[.] Heavy & Cool rain all nite" (Diary, April 7, 1862).

Other sources were the published and unpublished reminiscences of the combatants. Finally, there were the letters to the editor and the letters home that were subsequently turned over to the town newspaper for publication. Local publishers solicited such letters and made arrangements with local men to serve as correspondents to keep folks at home informed about the doings of their regiment or their company. The editor of *The Dubuque Daily Times* advised his would-be military reporters, "What we desire is a simple narration of facts. All attempts at fine sentiments or funny nonsense are out of place here. . . . Crack jokes at one another and write sentiments to your sweethearts" (January 3, 1862). The local newspaper was the conduit through which information was exchanged and the "social contract" between the war front and home-front was maintained.[6]

To turn from sources to method, the list of seventy-six questions was built on works in military sociology and combat psychology written after World War II. Foremost among these are the studies by Samuel L. Stouffer et al. (1949), S.L.A. Marshall (1966), Robert L. Egbert et al. (1958), John Baynes (1967), Richardson (1978), Peter Watson (1978), Richard Holmes (1986), and above all Anthony Kellett (1982). The outline that was used to assess the manuscript collections included questions about the soldier's age, his profession, his unit and state, his branch of service, his rank, the losses that his regiment or battery sustained, and the reasons for which he joined and later fought as well as what he thought of his combat skills, his supplies, and his officers. The authors also looked for the soldier's assessment of the enemy as well as what he thought of support from home and his concerns with medical services. Finally, a series of questions about the soldier's reassessment of these factors after experiencing his first battle was devised and applied to the material. We limited the time frame of the analysis from June 1, 1861, during the initial mobilization, to the period ending with the Confederate withdrawal from Corinth, May 30 and 31, 1862. From then on a new campaign had begun, a campaign that was now being fought by different soldiers—they had become veterans.

To complicate the task, this study does not deal with living respondents, and thus unlike Stouffer and Egbert—we could not question the soldiers directly. Furthermore, the material was inchoate, spread throughout letters, diaries, and reminiscences. Given this situation, it was often necessary to infer their attitudes. To be included in the data set, a soldier's file had to contain ten responses out of seventy-six possible questions. This required the following basic information: his name or pseudonym and the type of source, its date, and the audience to whom his writing was directed (self, intimates, the public). It also required his army, his national affiliation, his state, his unit, his arm of service, his rank, and how long he was engaged in the battle.

Where there were enough respondents to a question, the data set provided us with information for assessing what the troops thought about various issues associated with fighting spirit. Problems such as whether there were any differences between Northern and Southern soldiers were also raised. National affiliation in Western armies, however, was often an accident of birth, families frequently moved from one side of the Ohio to the other as they migrated west. Nor was it possible to distinguish Confederate from Unionist by the style of their correspondence.

In assessing the sources of the fighting spirit of Shiloh's novice soldiers, this study will avoid one-dimensional approaches emphasizing, for example, a Victorian heroic ethos or a single factor such as comradeship. Many elements contribute to combat motivation and the purpose here is to provide a brief overview of some of the most important ones that were pertinent to this particular campaign. In this, the authors are particulary indebted to the work of Anthony Kellett, especially his book *Combat Motivation* (1982).

The fighting prowess of some Civil War armies is usually attributable to their commander's competence and to their long experience in the field. But there were armies that lacked both of these advantages, yet they, nevertheless, fought courageously. The Army of the Ohio, the Army of the Tennessee, and the Army of the Mississippi, the three armies that we will examine in their first campaign, are a case in point. Most of their enlistees and field-grade officers were total novices. Yet these brand new armies fought relatively well at Shiloh. This book will examine the reasons and sources of their fighting spirit and their resilience in facing the horrors of battle.

NOTES

1. At this point it would be appropriate to point out to the reader that all quotes have been left verbatim, often in the vernacular. Changes were only made to clarify a statement.

2. "Seeing the elephant" was a euphemism for experiencing combat. Conti (1984b: 19) suggests that the earliest possible source of the saying goes back to the third century B.C. when Alexander the Great's soldiers defeated King Porus' elephant-borne troops in the Indus Valley.

3. The exceptions were such units as the 2nd, 19th, 20th, 28th, and 154th Tennessee and the 15th Mississippi who had seen action at Logan's Cross Roads in January 1862 (also known as the Battle of Fishing Creek or Mill Springs, Kentucky). A few other Confederate units had been based at Columbus, Kentucky, and fought at Belmont, Missouri.

4. These files were used to carry out measurements of significance, cross-tabulations, measurements of association, and basic frequencies to assess the impact of various factors. Chi-square was used to measure the possibility that the sample's results were accidental and did not merit extrapolation. If the chi-square showed a low probability of chance, then the strength of the association between variables was tested using phi and Cramer's V for parametric measurements and the contingency coefficient for a nonparametric measure. The reader is referred to Hurbert M. Blalock's *Social Statistics* for more information.

5. Bell I. Wiley wrote that "the great majority of companies throughout the army had anywhere from one to a score of members who could not write their names" (1987b: 336–37). A company was 60 to 100 men. This would indicate a Southern literacy rate of 40 to 90 percent giving a mean of 70 percent for the South. For the Union recruits, Wiley found that "the average company in the Union Army had from one to a half dozen illiterates. Many had none" (1978a: 305–6). This would give the Union a rate of 90 to 100 percent and a mean of 95 percent literate.

6. The vast majority of the material was written during the first year of the war (91 percent). Among contemporary sources, 46 percent were personal let-

ters, 13 percent were diaries, 12 percent were reminiscences, and 29 percent were letters to the editor. Given the fact that officers were usually better educated and thus more politically articulate, one could assume that their response rate would be proportionally higher. But this did not turn out to be the case. Officers responded at the same rate as the enlisted men.

Shiloh Campaign Area

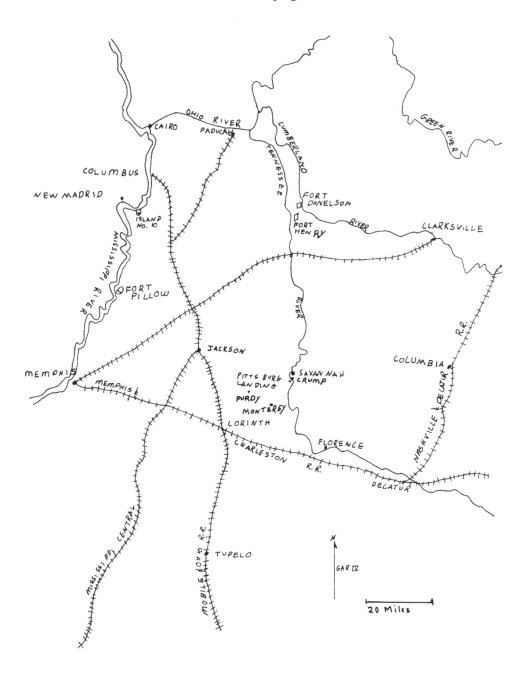

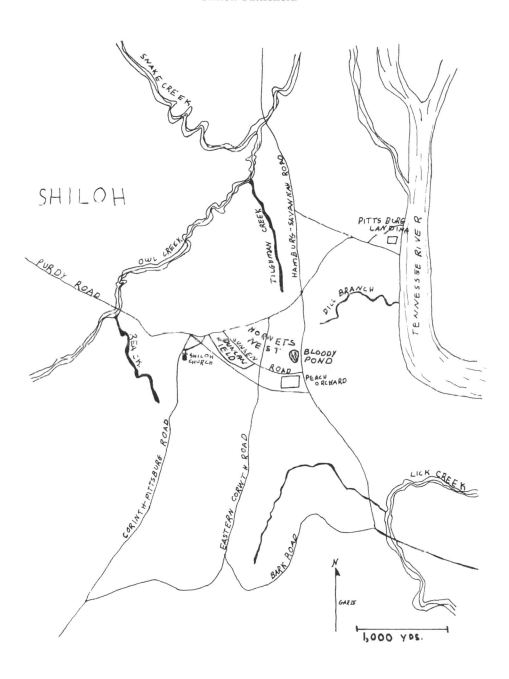

SHILOH

SNAKE CREEK

OWL CREEK

PURDY ROAD

TILGHMAN CREEK

HAMBURG-SAVANNAH ROAD

PITTS BURG LANDING

TENNESSEE RIVER

DILL BRANCH

BEA CK

HORNETS NEST

SUNKEN FIELD

DUNCAN ROAD

SHILOH CHURCH

BLOODY POND

PEACH ORCHARD

CORINTH-PITTSBURG ROAD

EASTERN CORINTH ROAD

BARK ROAD

LICK CREEK

N

GAR II

1,000 YDS.

Historical Prologue: The Shiloh Campaign

Major General Don Carlos Buell, who had commanded the Army of the Ohio, called Shiloh " 'the most famous and most interesting [battle] of the war' " (Nixon 1958: 144).[1] It is not hard to find reasons for its uniqueness: in numbers engaged, in intensity of fighting, and in the realization after the battle that the war would be fought differently than the volunteers had assumed. Rather than heroic brief engagements and grand strategic maneuvers, warfare had one objective: killing as many enemy soldiers as possible. In size and intensity, Shiloh signalled the change. In this respect, the clash at Shiloh dwarfed preceding battles. Major generals Buell and Ulysses S. Grant and General Albert Sidney Johnston together commanded over 100,000 men, and of these approximately 90,000 were actually engaged. As many were killed or wounded as all the previous major engagements combined.[2] Furthermore, there were more green troops in this battle than any battle of the Civil War. Three of Grant's divisions were raw, virtually all Buell's army had never seen major action before, and Johnston's Confederates were nearly all green as well. Some units got their weapons only when they disembarked at Pittsburg Landing. Leander Stillwell, a teenager from Otter Creek, Illinois, who joined the 61st Illinois and fought through all its campaigns, wondered back to his innocence before Shiloh, "What I didn't know about war, at that stage of the proceedings, was broad and comprehensive, and covered the whole field" (Stillwell 1920: 34). Considering that soldiers were new to the business, they inflicted enormous casualties, killing or wounding 23,000 people. Almost 25 percent of the troops engaged at Shiloh wound up casualties, as compared to an average casualty rate of 9 percent for preceding engagements.

The large numbers and the introduction of the deadlier weapons sig-nalled a change in the nature of war that many soldiers immediately grasped. And while tacticians such as William Joseph Hardee were aware of the implications of the increasing accuracy of rifles and cannons, many generals were still groping for a better doctrine to respond to the changes. For their part, the rank and file had already responded to the experience at Shiloh, learning to fight in looser formations and to use as much cover as possible. Paul Fussell's remarks about the First World War seem pertinent for Shiloh as well. In both, the prevailing image of war collided early on with its grim reality (1975: 7). And both would require an especially resilient recruit who by his ingenuity would bridge the gap between doctrine and the new weapons.

The battle at Pittsburg Landing, Tennessee, was part of the first great Northern offensive in the West. While General George B. McClellan led the Army of the Potomac against General Joseph E. Johnston's Confed-erates in the East, General Henry W. Halleck, in St. Louis, spent most of his energies securing his western flank in Missouri. Halleck's principal force east of the Mississippi was under the command of Major General Grant at Cairo, Illinois. In November 1861, Grant had led his men against the Confederate forces around Columbus, Kentucky, and fought a small action at Belmont, Missouri, just across the river. Other than that, he had devoted most of his efforts to training the recently mobilized green recruits.

East of the Cumberland River, the Union forces were commanded by Major General Buell. Buell's Army of the Ohio opposed the Confederate forces around Bowling Green, Kentucky. A small force under the com-mand of Brigadier General George Thomas operated in eastern Ken-tucky, but this detachment was under the control of Buell as well.

As can be seen, the command of Union forces west of the Appalachian Mountains was divided. Halleck lobbied for a unified command, with himself as the commander, but to no avail, because George B. McClellan, the Commander in Chief of the entire army, was not willing to consol-idate the Western command and thereby place his friend Buell in a subordinate position.

In the South, the command structure was clearer, but there were other problems. The commander was A. S. Johnston. He was in charge of the Confederate forces all the way from Arkansas to the Cumberland Gap in Kentucky. His principal army was stationed at Bowling Green, Ken-tucky. Johnston had a small force in east Tennessee, which was under the command of Brigadier General Felix Zollicoffer. In the western part of Kentucky, fronting on the Mississippi, Major General Leonidas Polk fortified the bluffs at Columbus. Finally, across the river there was a separate army under the command of Major General Earl Van Dorn, which—although technically under the command of A. S. Johnston—was operating independently in Arkansas and Missouri.

Johnston's problem was men and supplies. His total command in Kentucky and Tennessee numbered just over 30,000 men. By acting aggressively, he hoped to bluff the Northerners into delaying any advance until he was ready. This worked until February 1862, when Grant moved his army out of the Cairo area and, using the ironclad gunboats as an escort, advanced south up the Tennessee River.

Grant's targets were forts Henry and Heiman, Donelson's sister forts on the Tennessee River. If these installations could be taken, the Union would control the Tennessee River from its mouth on the Ohio River to Florence, Alabama. This would effectively cut west Tennessee off and force the Confederates to withdraw from Columbus, Kentucky, opening up the Mississippi River down to Island No. 10.

Due to bad design, Fort Henry was flooded and easily fell to the Union gunboats, but Grant decided not to waste time there. He marched across the spit separating the Tennessee from the Cumberland to besiege the Confederate bastion, Fort Donelson. Grant forced its surrender on February 16. With the Tennessee open to Alabama and the Cumberland open to Nashville, A. S. Johnston withdrew deeper and deeper into the South, ultimately taking up a new line that ran from Chattanooga, Tennessee, to Florence, Alabama, Corinth, Mississippi, and on to Fort Pillow on the Mississippi River.

All of these actions had been in response to Grant's moves, with Buell following A. S. Johnston's retreat into Bowling Green and then on to Nashville. In the meantime, Grant's successes brought good fortune to his superior. Halleck used the victories of his principal subordinate to claim command of all Union forces between the Kansas border and the Appalachian Mountains. This was granted by Abraham Lincoln, and Buell now suddenly found himself subordinate to Halleck, because of the victories of Grant.

In the South, General Pierre Gustave Toutant Beauregard, A. S. Johnston's second in command, urged a concentration of all Confederate forces in the Corinth, Mississippi, area. Even before Johnston agreed, Beauregard began to take what steps he could to hurry the concentration to meet the onrushing Union armies. A holding force was left at Island No. 10, and the remainder of the Confederate army west of the Tennessee River moved toward Corinth. Beauregard wrote to Van Dorn urging him to move his army to Mississippi. Furthermore, he contacted the governors of Mississippi, Alabama, Louisiana, and Tennessee for emergency levies.

The Northerners were also beginning to start their own concentration. Grant's army had advanced up the Tennessee River to Savannah, Tennessee. From there they moved nine miles upstream to Pittsburg Landing.[3] This was the closest all-weather landing place to Corinth, Mississippi, an important rail junction, which was Halleck's target. At this time, his Army of the Tennessee consisted of six divisions. The 1st, under the command of Major General John McClernand, had been in combat at Fort Donelson. The 2nd, led by Major General W.H.L. Wallace, had also fought at Donelson. The 3rd, commanded by Brigadier General Lew Wallace, had been created at Donelson but only some of the troops had fought there. This division was camped at Crump Landing, a few miles north of Pittsburg Landing. Brigadier General Stephen A. Hurlbut led the 4th, while the 5th, under the command of Brigadier General William T. Sherman, like the 4th, was also a green division. The 6th, under the command of Brigadier General Benjamin Prentiss, was still in the process of being created at Shiloh. On April 6, only two of its three brigades had been organized. The 5th and 6th divisions turned out to be the ones that had the misfortune of bearing the first rush by A. S. Johnston's attacking forces.

When he was given command of all the Union forces in the West, Halleck ordered Buell to move west from Nashville to join Grant at Pittsburg Landing. When the concentration was complete, Halleck planned to move to the landing and take command of the two armies. Buell was under no orders to move rapidly to join Grant, so he took his time so as to not wear out his men or equipment.

In the meantime, the Confederates were completing their concentration at Corinth. At this city, the Memphis and Charleston railroads crossed the Mobile and Ohio line. This facilitated the concentration. By the first week in April, the South had 44,000 effectives at Corinth. The biggest problem was that most of them were green and had never maneuvered in units larger than a regiment. Here they were organized into corps. The 1st Corps, under Major General Leonidas Polk, had been on garrison duty in west Tennessee and Kentucky. They had not maneuvered together except on the march. Some had been in combat at Belmont. The 2nd Corps was commanded by Major General Braxton Bragg. It was made up of troops that had been stationed along the Gulf Coast. They were well trained, but still mostly green. The 3rd Corps, led by Major General William Hardee, had maneuvered as a unit longer than any of the others, having been with Johnston at Bowling Green. The Reserve Corps, commanded by Brigadier General John C. Breckinridge, was basically a reinforced division, whose men had never maneuvered together.

Grant and his lieutenants viewed the Pittsburg Landing site primarily as a training area. They expected one more battle in the West at Corinth, assuming that the enemy would conform to these wishes. In fact, both sides' commanders were caught on the horns of a dilemma. On the one hand, they needed to whip their armies of recruits into shape, yet on the other, they wanted to gain the initiative and decisively defeat their opponents in one major engagement. Thus, the Union command also viewed training as paramount, yet it believed it had the time to train and hold the initiative. Because of this, it ignored all indications to the contrary and neither fortified the position at Pittsburg Landing nor even improved it with some basic fieldworks to slow an attacker down.

NOTES

1. The most recent works on the Battle of Shiloh are those of Wiley Sword (1974) and James Lee McDonough (1977). But the most detailed analysis of the campaign and the battle is O. Edward Cunningham's doctoral dissertation titled "Shiloh and the Western Campaign of 1862" (1966). We believe this dissertation deserves a better fate than remaining a manuscript on microfilm.

2. These engagements were Manassas, Wilson's Creek, Fort Donelson, and Pea Ridge.

3. Local people had told some naval officers that travelers usually disembarked at Pittsburg Landing to go to Corinth (Cunningham 1966: 113).

1

Mobilization

BECOMING A SOLDIER

The men who enlisted to later fight at Shiloh were swept up by patriotic fervor. "The Fort [Sumter] has surrendered. . . . We now have terrible times . . . the war feeling in the North is immense. We are United," wrote Saul Howell in his diary (April 16 and 25, 1861). Son of a Pella, Iowa, physician, Howell was about to get his degree at Central College, but after Sumter he was enlisting instead. In the South, the same atmosphere prevailed. Citizens everywhere were taking up arms. Militia outfits were being forged at town meetings throughout the land. Even little Arkansas, with its population of 60,000 voters, boasted that it fielded twenty regiments in the first four months of mobilization (*The Van Buren Press*, September 25, 1861).

The volunteers were quintessentially civilians; their offers of service were not open-ended and unquestioning. Their relationship with the government was, in their eyes, contractual. An officer joining the 6th Mississippi Regiment reminded his commander of the conditions for his enlistment, declaring that he could not serve on a regular basis, due to health reasons. The night air imperiled his condition, so guard duty after sunset was unfortunately out of question. Beyond this, however, he vowed that he was prepared to serve with equal diligence and risk all for Mississippi and the 6th Infantry (Thornton, "Statement by J.C. Cousins," December 3, 1861).

Dramatic accounts of the first engagement at Manassas poured from the local press. In Alabama, for example, *The Clairborne Southerner* described the uncontrollable martial impulse in a portrayal of a Mississippi outfit at Bull Run. The regiment was so eager to join with the enemy that it did not bother to reload and plunged on casting aside their firearms and resorting to the bowie knife when they closed with the Yankees. "Blood gushed from hundreds of wounds," *The Southerner* screamed histrionically (August 7, 1861). Reflecting the martial mood of the country, Captain John M. Coleman of the 15th Indiana Volunteers told his sister that "writing letters is like our fireside conversations, no matter *how* we *begin* it always *ends* on the *war*" (To Amanda, March 2, 1862).

James P. Snell, who joined the 32nd Illinois Infantry, declared that "when I hear of the fall of 'Fort Sumter' . . . I could not controll my own feelings . . . and would have shouldered my gun and started . . . had it not been for the earnest entreaty of my Parents" (To John G. Copely, June 2, 1861). In Michigan, Joseph Ruff, a German immigrant, "walked the eight miles to Albion impelled every mile by the desire to help . . . the saving of this great nation" (1943: 277). In Tennessee, much the same sentiment prevailed, Sam Watkins remembered how "every person . . . was eager for the war, and we were all afraid it would be over and we not be in the fight" (1962: 21).

The press stoked up the patriotic fires quoting an Oliver Wendell Holmes, Jr., poem:

> God of all Nations! Sovereign Lord!
> In Thy dreaded name we draw the sword,
> We lift the starry flag on high
> That fills with light our stormy sky.
> (*The Daily Steubenville Herald*, June 29, 1861)

The sheet music of patriotic songs was swept up, the choruses resounding from the marching ranks. Surgeon William B. Fletcher was waiting to entrain at Parkersburg (then in Virginia), when one of the men in Company A (6th Indiana) "Sung the 'Star Spangled Banner' with much feeling and the whole Company filled the chorus" (Memoirs, June 5, 1861).

The press bombarded those youths who were not answering the call to the colors with enough alacrity with castigations and summations to do their duty. In Tuskegee, Alabama, *The South Western Baptist* (February 27, 1862) berated the stay-at-homes, "Why do you stay at home while others are in the field? Are they not as good as you? . . . Examine yourselves and see if selfishness or cowardice or some unworthy motive is not at the bottom of all your excuses. If you have any mettle in you let it be seen now. The time has come and you know it. . . . Would you let the women and children hoot you into the army!" The pressure exerted by the press in the Southwest was probably more intense because of the threat of imminent invasion. Memphis was especially vulnerable as Grant's army swept into the interior threatening to cut it off from the rest of the country. The Yankee was at the door. A woman wrote to the editor of *The Memphis Daily Appeal* (February 20, 1862), "What are young men doing in Memphis at such a time as this?" She goaded them mercilessly, "Are you really willing . . . to be slapped in the face, snubbed, pricked with bayonets . . . and insulted by every epithet that a gloating, jubilant Yankee can manufacture?" Yet another excited matron, this one from Columbus, Kentucky, denounced those who "dare assert men able to be soldiers should stay at home to protect female relatives. Short-sighted vision! The best way to protect women," she declared, "is to slay the foe before he gets a foot-hold in our midst" (*The Memphis Daily Appeal*, March 1, 1862).

Henry Morton Stanley (the famed explorer) was a young immigrant in Arkansas when the war broke out. He delayed his enlistment until the female fire-eaters drove him to enlist. "I received a parcel," he recounted, "which I half suspected as the address was written in a feminine hand, to be a token of some lady's regard; but on opening it, I discovered a chemise and petticoat, such as negro lady's maid might wear. I hastily hid it from view, and retired to the back room, that my burning cheeks might not betray me to some onlooker" (Laurie 1985: 43).

Most of the volunteers shared this patriotic devotion. A young Confederate named Willie wrote to his brother urging him to sign up, "Every man who is not a producer, or who has not a family to support should rally in defence of his home and his kindred" (To Sister M., *The Republican Banner*, September 4, 1861). Like the generation of 1914–18, the men who marched off to Shiloh were not restrained by recent memories of war. Most were too young to have served in the Mexican War. The veterans from the 1845–48 conflict were already reaching middle age.[1]

The regiments that were being created were socially and politically homogeneous. The men were often friends, neighbors, and relatives enlisting together. The volunteers were careful about the comrades who enlisted with them. They wanted to make sure their comrades had compatible political views and that they could count on them when things got hot. Cyrus Boyd in Indianola, Iowa, had an acquaintance named Fisk who was forming the nucleus of a company that later was to become Company G, 15th Iowa Infantry, but a friend warned Boyd that Fisk might not be dependable. " 'Fisk,' " he warned, was a Democrat and " 'he may betray you someplace when you are in a tight place' " (Boyd 1953: 7). The social homogeneity of these volunteer regiments facilitated the development of unit cohesion during the early months of the war.

The quality of the recruits was probably higher than the regular army enlistees. A correspondent of the 15th Indiana wrote to the editor that the "war volunteers are usually men of much more education than those who enlist in time of peace" (*The Daily State Sentinel*, August 17, 1861). The average company in the Union army probably only had a half dozen illiterates (B. I. Wiley 1978a: 305–6). In the Confederate army, the portion of illiterates might have been only slightly larger. Wiley (1978b: 336–37) pointed out that "the great majority of companies throughout the army had anywhere from one to a score of members who could not write their names."

Physically, however, the volunteer army of 1861–62 in the West was probably of mixed quality as we shall see with the ravages of the first winter. Medical examinations must have been perfunctory to say the least—400 Union women managed to sneak through (G. W. Adams 1952: 12–13)! Part of the reason was that recruiters had a vested interest in enlisting as many men as they could in order to get their rank as early as possible for seniority purposes. This would have a corrosive effect on combat morale later on. Some regiments went into action at Shiloh with half their men on sick call.

The units were socially and economically homogeneous, composed mainly of farmers and men from small towns, coming from occupations that were associated with agriculture and the rural administrative and commercial activity that was auxiliary to it. Most, at least those on the Northern side, were recruited in rural townships where the principal economic activity was small grain farming, such as wheat, barley, oats, and corn. The small grain farming cycle engendered uniform social patterns that strengthened community bonds around similar harvest schedules and specific moments in the year requiring community cooperation. Most of the regiments at Shiloh came from such rural communities, rather than from the larger cities such as Chicago, St. Louis, Cincinnati, and Cleveland. Southern regiments, except for a few from New Orleans, were mainly from small rural townships as well. Less than one out of three of the recruits who gave their residence came from urban areas that were connected to the national communications network via rail and telegraph and had a population of more than 3,000 inhabitants.[2] They were not, however, technologically unsophisticated, being familiar with railroads, steamships, telegraph lines, and various types of machinery. They were early participants in the mechanization of agriculture. Their efficiency provided the excess capital to finance the war.

Besides being essentially rural types, the volunteers were quite young. Three-fourths of the new soldiers were under twenty-five years of age. Socially and economically, these volunteers probably represented a fair cross-section of their communities. They were hardly the marginal elements of society, what Lord Arthur Wellington called " 'the biggest scamps unhung,' " when he described his own army fifty years before (Moran 1966: 162).

Further reinforcing the cohesiveness of these territorially recruited regiments was their ethnic homogeneity. The overwhelming majority of the volunteers were native born. There were few among the troops who by name or writing style suggested that they were born abroad. Company E, 11th Iowa could have been typical; its ninety-seven–man roster included only twelve foreign-born soldiers: three Canadians, four Irish, two English, two Germans, and one Frenchman (Downing 1916: 13). The examinations of every tenth man of the six Iowa regiments showed that only 6 percent were native-born Iowans, which is not surprising in itself because the state was only recently settled. This very fact made Iowa a good sample to check, because virtually all its recruits would have been from elsewhere, and as a result, the recent pioneer population would be more heterogenous. Yet the foreign element was insignificant, making up only 14 percent of the sample, and half of these had English names, suggesting they came from Canada and England and were not linguistically and culturally very dissimilar. That left approximately 7 percent of the troops coming from culturally alien areas such as Germany. Among the Germans, few —perhaps 2 percent of the Iowa contingent—were old enough to have fought in the revolution of 1848, thus, even the German troops were not politically distinct. The largest group of the troops came from the old Northwest (44 percent), 23 percent came from the Mid-Atlantic states, and only 6 percent came from New England. Significantly, Southerners outnumbered New Englanders among the Iowans (7 percent), coming from slave states such as Missouri, Kentucky, and Virginia. This leads to the conclusion that the Western armies were generally far more ethnically homogeneous than their Eastern counterparts. Furthermore, most of Shiloh's regiments were not recruited in the larger cities where many of the Germans and Irish settled.

The new recruits were so similar that their family ties often overlapped the political boundaries that now separated them. This was especially true in the Western armies, whose volunteers came from counties of states abutting the Ohio and thus often had families who had settled alternately on the south side of the river in Kentucky or farther south in Tennessee. For example, Colonel Thomas Harrison commanding the 39th Indiana was of Southern ancestry and was perhaps typical of many others at Shiloh. Harrison's father had come to Indiana from Kentucky, following the same route as many other Southerners including President Lincoln (*The Howard Tribune*, September 19, 1861; Grant 1982: 124; Barton 1981: 15).

B. I. Wiley (1978b: 99) aptly described the Confederate army (and for that matter the Union army too) as a "neighborhood army." Regional recruitment cemented the early volunteer units and compensated for their lack of training. It was in line with the advice of the first-century Greek general Osnander who counseled that the leader should post " 'brothers in rank beside brothers; friends beside friends; and lovers beside their favorites' " (F. M Richardson 1978: 7). Osnander realized that local recruiting provided social compatibility, conformity, comradeship, tradition, and territoriality that were the major sources of cohesion during the first year of a campaign.

Effective recruiting also entailed emphasizing the community ties when advertising in the local newspaper. For example, John Keeper, seeking men for Company A, 53rd Ohio, promised that the company would be territorially homogeneous, with recruits from the same county (*The Ironton Register,* August 8, 1861).

Once a captain had signed up his quota of between eighty and one hundred recruits, the company was moved to a state reception center and combined with others into a regiment. There it was inducted into service, trained, and armed (Rudolph 1984: 10). But even after recruitment, politicking continued as each company and regiment held elections for lieutenant colonels, majors, and lieutenants. Even captains who had formed their companies might face elections, although colonels were usually appointed and not elected. Whereas professional armies invoke personal career incentives for drawing recruits, a mass army, mobilizing for a national emergency, recruits its soldiers with different inducements. Mobilizing a citizen army requires patriotic ideals. The mass army had to share prevailing ideas and understand the issues at stake. Thus, armies in the North and South were politicized because they were people's armies. Each army was composed of volunteer units that emerged from the bosom of their communities, sharing the same beliefs and opinions. The populace participated actively in organizing the outfits and in selecting commanders. An unwritten, but nevertheless binding, agreement came into place between the soldiers and their community. If either one failed in this mutual undertaking, the other quickly heard about it. As long as the bond remained strong, the community and its regiment were unified behind the cause.

Although the national authorities were obliged to share control of the armies with state authorities, they nevertheless gained from the partnership. The local leaders were instrumental in effectuating the mobilization. Their fervid support and active participation not only provided manpower, but the community also eased the financial burden for the national authorities. The people shouldered an important part of the costs of raising the regiments themselves. In the first month of the war, the citizens of the Northern states privately raised $23,777,000 (Hattaway and Jones 1983: 34). For example, it cost as much as $500,000 to organize and equip a cavalry regiment and there were units, such as the 1st Louisiana Cavalry, that were entirely funded by public subscription.[3] Other communities made more modest, but nevertheless important, contributions. They held fairs, organized dances, and staged patriotic plays to raise funds to equip their boys better than any other company in the army and outshine any other town. Such efforts demonstrated the intense community pride. Most typically, the ladies would sew a flag for the regiment or even, as in Grant's Galena, Illinois, make the company's uniforms (Grant 1982: 117). Such active local participation made state service more attractive than federal service (Mahon and Danysh 1972: 24). Federal infantry recruiters had a hard time getting men to fill their regiments. The 18th United States Infantry, which had a battalion at Shiloh, ran into this very problem. Lacking identity with any state, town, or county, it had a hard time getting volunteers and had to resort to paying a recruiter two dollars bounty for enlistees (*The Lima Weekly Gazette*, July 24, 1861).

As the enlistees boarded trains to their concentration points to be grouped into regiments, they participated in a ritual that embodied the mutual obligations binding the regiment and the community. It was the presentation of the regimental flag. The flag was made by the community and represented its presence when the unit went into battle. A Hoosier sergeant described how the ladies of Blackford County presented his unit with a hand-sewn flag. In reply, the colonel made a grand patriotic speech at the climax of which he is reported to have "called upon the whole Regiment to fall to their knees and swear that they would stand by our flag forever. When the Col. give the command 'down' every man fell to his knees as if one man" (*The Howard Tribune*, October 29, 1861). The speeches swore mutual fealty between civilians and soldiers.

Towns and hamlets throughout the region sent their men off bathed in adulation and patriotic nationalistic rhetoric. Their initial motivation echoed the high patriotism. Edward Reynolds, Company A, 2nd Illinois Cavalry, recalled bidding all good-bye "to put down the rebellion feeling a little uneasy for fear that it would be over before we reached the front" (Memoir-Diary, September 1, 1861). In neighboring Iowa, Saul Howell was elated by the cheering crowds that lined the tracks leading to his assembly point. "They yelled awfully at every station. Brass bands . . . played" all the way to Keokuk (Journal, May 31, 1861).

It was harder for some Southerners; Confederates in hostile parts of the border states had to raise their regiments clandestinely. Yet they went to great lengths to evade the authorities to enlist in the Southern cause. John William Green opted for the Confederacy, resigned his clerkship, and joined the Louisville Citizens' Guard. Green and his comrades smuggled their equipage past the federal sentries in a wagon covered with manure and hay. The unit eventually formed part of the 6th Kentucky Confederate Infantry and was brigaded under Colonel Robert P. Trabue at Shiloh (Green, Diary, p. 12).

Despite the military training, the men did not shake off their civilian outlook. They continued to envisage their commitment to fight in the light of a mutually agreed contract between community and soldier.

They were responding to a national emergency, which they believed would last only a few months. They saw no need for a prolonged open-ended commitment to national service. Often the men resisted enlisting for three years for fear that they would be stuck in the army after a short war. The first Union volunteers were ninety-day men and they often resented prolonging their service (Grant 1982: 125). Getting this acquiescence was one of the officers' first and most difficult tasks. They often reverted to the worst forms of hate mongering to stir up support for long enlistment. An Arkansan named Peter Hotze summarized the type of speech used to persuade the men to join for three years. The Razorback soldier declared that the "one subject they [the officers] all talked about in length was, how the Yankees raped the woman [sic] and the sisters" (Diary, March 20, 1862). The officers also played on patriotism to gain the men's acquiescence to three years' service. A solider-correspondent wrote to his hometown newspaper in Ohio that "our Lieutenant Colonel used very strong arguments to induce us to accept. He told us if we did we would get to go and fight the battles of our country; if not, we would have to serve the rest of our time in guarding the rail road switches, and then be hooted at when we returned home. [Nevertheless] very few offered to enlist" (*The Daily Steubenville Herald*, June 5, 1861).

At this stage of the war, it was not a question of lacking the motivation to fight, it was simply that many citizen-soldiers thought a three-year commitment was unnecessary. Balzer Grebe, an unemployed German housepainter from Springfield, Illinois, had joined for three months, thinking that by the end of his enlistment the health of the economy would have improved. When the choice was presented to him, he therefore declined three-year enlistment and requested a discharge (Diary). James Fee's company (Company G, 31st Indiana) was also split on the issue when its officers polled the men. Only one out of three of the volunteers was prepared to undertake such a long commitment (To Julius [brother], May 29, 1861). Some companies even mutinied. Jesse Connelley described one such affair at Camp Vigo near Terre Haute, Indiana. "Capt. Bladen of the Manson Guards from Greencastle took his company consisting of 25 men, and started for home without the consent of the Colonel. The result was that two squads of men with loaded muskets were sent after them on the quick under command of Lieut. Beadle. They arrested them just as they were stepping on the train and brought them back to camp. The captain's commission was taken from him and he was escorted out of camp by Capt. Harvey. . . . Capt. Bladen . . . sent a challenge to the Colonel, but it was not accepted" (Dairy, September 18, 1861). When persuasion did not avail, the federal authorities resorted to humiliation. Kenneth Mitchell described how a soldier was drummed out of camp for refusing to enlist for the period demanded. "The soldiers were formed into lines from the gate back into camp between which . . . the man was marched with four bayonets in his rear, and the bands playing. As he passed, each company bade him farewell with a groan" (K. Mitchell 1960: 1).

Despite the war euphoria, the three-year enlistment was not a decision to be made lightly. Thomas Honnell's 15th Ohio was confronted with the choice when this colonel tendered the regiment for three years' service. "I do not know what to do," he wrote to a friend, "I do not wish to go home & have it said of me that I am a coward & afraid to meet the enemy. . . . But if we enlist for three years. [sic] in all probability we would at the close of the war. [sic] be sent to guard some distant fort & for my part I do not feel like spending 3 years of my life in that way" (To Ben Epler, May 21, 1861). There were other things to keep in mind besides personal considerations. Payson Shumway responded to queries from his wife, Hattie, who wanted him to return now that his one-month stint with the Illinois militia was drawing to a close. The good soldier replied that he would nevertheless stay with his regiment (14th Illinois) when it was mustered into federal service for three years. "What could I do? . . . could you even *wish me* to come home under such circumstances with the double stigma of coward and deserter resting on me?" he asked (To wife, May 29, 1861). All in all, the majority of the volunteers ultimately enlisted for three years, fearing community disapproval. Peer pressure also played an important role. A soldier with the 3rd Iowa in Keokuk described how the men reacted when one man started to take the three paces forward signifying his opposition to being mustered in for three years. "[He] had not gone beyond one step when his comrade next to him hauled him off and dealt him a blow, and would no doubt have severly beaten him but for the interference of the others. . . . [I]t is needless say," wrote the Iowan, "that conscientious individuals became scarce" (*The Daily Democrat and News,* June 1, 1861). Jobe M. Foxworth in the 7th Mississippi was one of the many who probably typified those exerting intense pressure for longer service when he declared that "a man who is not willing to enlist for any length of time to serve his country has a soul small enough to rest on the head of a pin" (Diary, February 13, 1862). Such sentiments were echoed by Lunsford Yandell, an assistant surgeon from Kentucky who was serving with the 4th Tennessee Infantry. Young Yandell vowed, "may I never live to see the war ended, if it is to end in our subjugation. I would rather see it annihilated, than give up the cause. What are a few hundred—or thousands of lives, compared to the success of the nation" (To Sally [sister], January 27, 1862).

Citizens who volunteered to fight did so for a specific cause, they were not embarking on a lifetime career as professionals nor were they forced by conscription. Motivating them to fight well required more than just standard military discipline. First, there was not the time or enough competent officers to discipline them, and second, the totalitarian decision-making process of a military organization never did—and never would—sit well with Civil War volunteers. As John Ellis phrased the argument, "It is not enough to suggest that disciplinary threats alone could force men to obey orders, for what is the threat of ultimate sanction, death, in the face of another kind of death?" (1980: 315). Something more was needed to create and sustain the combat morale of citizen volunteers.

The recruits learned discipline through close-order drill. It instilled social cohesion as the new recruits came to know the comrades in front and behind them, as well as those on their right and their left. This had important advantages for the new army. As Kellett remarked, "close order formations such as the line and the square contained powerful coercive properties, both social and physical; men trusted each other to stand firm because if they did not, the consequences could be terrible" (1982: 137). By coincidence, the manual that was used by both armies was written by Major General William Joseph Hardee, who later commanded one of the Confederate corps at Shiloh. His two-volume work, titled *Rifle and Light Infantry Tactics*, was the best-known text on close-order formations. Hardee's training program provided for learning marching without arms such as position, facings, and speeds. It went on to explain the manual of arms, i.e., loading and firing. And finally, it outlined the tactical formations that were supposed to be used in combat, such as march by front, different speeds and steps, march by flank, wheeling, change of direction, and fire by rank. The men had to be well drilled to carry out the maneuvers under fire (Hardee 1855: I, 17, 61). The manual also laid down the structure of the basic unit of maneuver, the regiment. This unit was to be composed of ten companies with the flank companies (A and K) being the best trained and armed (rifles), because they protected the most vulnerable portion of the line. These companies were also to provide skirmishers to protect the front. The regiment was commanded by three mounted officers, first was the colonel who rode thirty paces in front of the regiment; second were his two subordinates, his lieutenant colonel and his major who would be slightly in back of him and in front of the right and left wings of the regiment, respectively (Hardee 1855: I, 5, 8). The whole formation was supposed to move and fire in unison despite the communication problems that were caused by the noise and the smoke of battle. Control was to be exercised by voice command and through the loud rhythms that were beat on snare drums that were issued to each of the ten companies. These drums were supposed to be shrill enough to be heard over the din of battle. This took some skill and consequently the drummers received a premium of one dollar in pay. Each rhythm was associated with a command that the troops in the firing line were supposed to learn by rote. Hardee's manual also required learning thirty different bugle calls (Hardee 1855: I, 217–18).

Hardee had early on come to grips with the significance of a recent innovation in military technology, the conoid bullet or minié ball, which had been invented by a French captain named Claude Étienne Minié. This flanged, oblong ball expanded when the gases in the breech flared it and propelled it into the grooving of the rifled barrel, sending it spinning toward its target. This invention made the musket three to four times more accurate than a smoothbore—up to 600 yards.[4] The potential lethality of this infantry weapon obliged Hardee to modify tactical doctrine by changing the speed and deployment of the regiment. No more halts in maneuvering under fire, because every minute lost meant that many more casualties. Maneuvering had to be continuous, deployment was to be done on the move to cut down the time exposed to enemy fire. Futhermore, Hardee emphasized a two-rank line instead of Napoleon's dense column formations, also to reduce the target density of the regiment. Last, Hardee called for advances at a new, faster pace that he called double-quick time. There were to be no stops while crossing no-man's-land. It was to be like "going over the top" in 1914–18, one mad rush across the killing space to limit casualties. Here elan was essential. Fast maneuvering, the continuous evolutions, and the haltless advance had major implicationss for the quality and training of volunteers. It required more highly skilled infantrymen than ever before. Evolutions were more rapid and more complicated. The formation was still a close-order concentration and had to remain so to ensure control and massing of firepower, but the new maneuvers were more difficult to master (McWhiney and Jamieson 1982: 36, 48, 51–53, 73, 101, 146–49). Alexander Varian, Jr., of the 1st Ohio described the training schedule's heavy emphasis on drill (To Hattie, September 8, 1861).

5:00 Reveille.
5:30 First drill call.
6:30 Recall from drill.
7:00 Breakfast call.
7:30 First call for guard.
8:30 Second drill call.
10:00 Recall from drill.
10:30 Officers' drill.
12:00 Dinner call.
1:30–3:00 Third drill call.
4:00–5:00 Non-commissioned officers' drill.

5:00–6:00 Fourth drill call.
Sundown: Recall.
Taps.[5]

   Thus the average Union recruit spent approximately five hours in drill every day. This is about the same pattern that was used south of the Ohio, for example, at Camp Cheatham near Nashville (*The Republican Banner*, June 5, 1861). However, in looking over the training routine, one quickly notices a glaring gap: there were no provisions for physical training, no mention of calisthenics or field exercises with full packs. Because of the lack of physical training and the perfunctory medical screening, large numbers were unfit and later succumbed to the effects of the elements in the first winter of campaigning.
   Furthermore, there was little opportunity to get the men used to the noise of the battle. Weapons training was often perfunctory and poorly organized. It was frequently a great lark. James Williams was in charge of drilling the men of the 21st Alabama. He described how he "put them through an exercise in skirmishing—firing and loading lying first on the ground and kneeling—and when it was all over [the men were so excited that] they went to their tents cheering and waving their hats" (Diary, December 5, 1861, cited in Folmar: 1981). Second Lieutenant William Vaught, with the elite 5th Company, Washington Artillery, was enthusiastically participating in the training exercises. "We drilled all day in the sleet, but I enjoyed it. . . . I enjoy it all." Chortling, "ain't I a queer fish for enjoyment" (Letter, March 22, 1862). The same enthusiastic confidence emerged from the Northern soldiers' correspondence. A Hoosier infantryman, named L. M. Garrigus, wrote to his local newspaper that "no persons enjoy themselves better than our company" when out drilling as skirmishers (*The Howard Tribune*, September 17, 1861). Using a cheeky pseudonym in his letters to the editor, "Phil I. Buster" declared confidently that the 72nd Ohio had drilled so effectively that "we don't drill any now. . . . It don't take us long to acquire knowledge, especially, military, we are born smart and brave" (*The Fremont Daily Journal*, January 3, 1862).
   Soon the novelty of soldiering wore off and discontent gave way to disruptive behavior, especially when officers were incompetent or brutal. Howell described a "fracas on Regimental parade. . . . The acting adjutant Lieut. Sessions of Cedar Falls struck two Oskaloosa men with his cane. . . . Considerable fuss about it after parade. Nearly a fight. The adjutant was in liquor" (Journal, June 18, 1861). Discipline was lax throughout both Western armies. Because the men saw themselves as citizen volunteers, they refused to be subject to the same harsh discipline as regulars. For example, when Private T.B. Hadley, Company B, 4th Tennessee, was found guilty of striking a superior officer, the court-

martial sitting at Fort Pillow sentenced him to only a "public reprimand" (J.J. Thornton Scrapbook, General Order No. 9, August 15, 1861). Towns cringed even when their own side's troops were passing through. Several companies of Louisiana infantry got drunk at the Percy Hotel in Grand Junction, Tennessee. They rioted and burned the hotel down. Confederate infantry was sent to restore order. They fired a volley into the rioting volunteers and nine were killed on the spot and four more died later. Further south, in Holly Springs, Mississippi, an entire regiment got drunk and seized a train and headed for Virginia preferring to serve in the East (*The Nashville Union and American*, August 7, 1861). Their Northern counterparts were just as defiant. There was Varian's 1st Ohio that clashed with Dayton civil authorities who they suspected of "copperhead" sympathies. The affair involved a very patriotic hospital orderly at Camp Corwin, nicknamed Live Yankee, who had gone to the town fairgrounds to make a pro-Union speech. The Dayton police, however, arrested him, but Varian's Company D marched to his rescue, freed him, and headed back to camp with Live Yankee hoisted on their shoulders. The police tried to intercept them with reinforcements and a "general muss ensued in which the police got very roughly handled and had to flee for their lives" (Varian, to father, September 15, 1861).

The inexperienced officer corps was having no easy time maintaining discipline. Reuben Weisner remembered how his company in the 14th Illinois refused to do guard duty because they had not received any rations. The captain "came charging and said that the first man that refused to go on guard he would shoot him" (Diary, July 31, 1861). In Paducah, Kentucky, "Tom Woolridge of [the 23rd Indiana] . . . was drummed out of camp for running off . . . and when the officers went after him he threatening to kill [them,] they s[h]aved half his hair and whiskers of[f]" (Vanderbilt, to mother, December 2, 1861). Discipline problems and officer brutality became enchained. In Paducah, Vanderbilt witnessed another example of growing animosities between the soldiers and officers. "One of our boys was killed by the provost gaurds[.] he tried to escape the gaurds when the gaurd shot at him killing him instantly[.] the gaurd run a bayonet through him after he had shot him[.] it saired [seared] the boys to highest pitch so that the provost gaurd could not [go into] . . . camp for fear of getting killed[.]" He concluded ominously, "the boys swear vengeance" (To mother, January 30, 1862). The novice officers no doubt contributed to the lack of discipline by inciting disruptive behavior themselves. Weisner described how an officer in the 14th Illinois allowed and even encouraged fighting. The captain in question went so far as to threaten to tie a man to a tree if he did not participate in a fight (Diary, August 20, 1861).

The state of the two armies at the conclusion of their military indoctrination was hardly encouraging. The two essential purposes of the process, improving the physical fitness of the troops and imposing discipline on the new recruits, were far from being attained. On the other hand, the volunteers remained highly motivated by patriotic zeal.

WHY THEY JOINED

The Shiloh volunteers were committed and politically articulate soldiers. More of the soldiers' correspondence was about the issues at stake than about any other motivation-related factor such as equipment, supplies, officers, etc. The correspondence was replete with declarations supporting national unity, independence, or abolition and avowing patriotic duty.[6] When comparing the officers and enlisted men their comments were not significantly different, except when it came to expressing racist attitudes. On this issue, the enlisted men were twice as likely to express racist sentiments as were their officers, but there were, however, only a handful of comments on the racial issue.[7]

Both the officers and men in the Western armies of 1861 were part of a popular political movement that was sweeping the country. There were no divisions between the educated upper class and the rank and file on this question. Contrary to the Vietnam War where commitment to the cause was in inverse ratio to the level of education, in the Civil War, the educated elites were not only in step with the population at large, but they were often even more active in supporting the war (R. Holmes 1986: 82). All classes were prepared to share in the war effort. The educated classes in the Civil War not only led the armies in the field, but they mobilized support at home.

In this effort, homefront efforts were crucial, because a territorially recruited army needed the community and the army to work in tandem. The chief instrument for coordinating this effort was the hometown newspaper. Shiloh's soldiers were generally literate and abreast of the issues. Their keen interest in the news from home and their frequent complaints that the local newspaper was not arriving with regularity testifies to their ongoing interest in the issues behind the war.[8] Recent research suggests that public interest in constitutional issues had been building in the ten years preceding the Civil War. The general public interest in constitutional questions reached a peak between the Supreme Court's decision on the *Dred Scott* case and Lincoln's first inauguration (Kammen 1986: 104). The soldiers were assiduous newspaper readers.

Jesse Young, an underage Illinois volunteer, echoed the patriotic surge when he remembered, "Many of the boys of that time were just as patriotic as the grownup people. They did not know much about the causes that led to the war; they could not see all the dangers that threatened the nation . . . but they loved their flag, and they adored the Union, and they trusted Mr. Lincoln, and they were ready to do their share toward saving the government from destruction" (Young 1894: 15).

Like Young in Illinois, Samuel B. Franklin was also borne along by the same irresistible patriotic urge to share in deciding a great historic issue. Franklin lived in Cumberland County, Pennsylvania, along a railway line whose "every train had soldiers . . . going to the front or returning. This aroused my patriotism," he recalled, "and I could hardly keep from going along. I bore this up until the fall 1861" ("Memoirs"). That fall he could sit home no longer and he enrolled in the 77th Pennsylvania.

Loyalty to country was the most frequently voiced reason given for enlisting; more than two-thirds of the soldiers voiced patriotic themes when they talked about their reasons for joining up. Patriotism was expressed in many ways by Unionists and Confederates. The soldiers of Mr. Lincoln's army championed liberty and democracy, the sanctity of the Constitution, and the integrity of the Union. These themes pervaded the ranks. For example, the sutler with Augustine Vieira's 14th Illinois Infantry sold letter paper that appropriately symbolized these patriotic themes with the image of a tree, each of whose branches sprouted a flag with a state's name. Next to it was a poem titled *Tree of Liberty* with these stirring lines:

> Traitor, spare that tree
> Touch not a single bough
> In youth it sheltered me,
> And I'll protect it now.
> (Vieira, Papers)

Some Union recruits saw the conflict as a fight for freedom and democracy. "I was kneedid to help put down rebellion in our country," wrote R. A. Brenton to his brother while he and the 24th Indiana guarded bridges in Missouri. "I know," he declared, "I love my home as well as any one and love to enjoy the society of my friends and associates but I love freedom the best" (Letter to John, October 10, 1861). For Martin Armstrong, who held a captaincy in the 81st Ohio Volunteer Infantry and was one of the bright young men of Lima, it was a struggle for democracy. Instead of becoming a candidate for prosecuting attorney, he raised a company for three years' service. He called on his fellow citizens to eschew partisan politics and join as in a crusade as "laborers in the temple of Human Rights" (*The Lima Weekly Gazette,* October 23, 1861). He argued that democratic government was at stake and that its failure in America meant its failure in the world (*The Lima Weekly Gazette,* February 19, 1862). The young captain felt that he "would prove one of the most ungrateful sons, were [he] . . . not willing to peril

[his] . . . life to maintain and perpetuate the good form of government, to which [his grandfather] gave seven years of the best of his life, [and] which has made me what I am" (*The Lima Weekly Gazette*, December 4, 1861).

These ideas were echoed by an Ohioan marching with Buell. He wrote from Cave City, Kentucky, that "the strength of the Nation is to be tried here, whether we have a country or not; whether our constitution is a rope of sand, that it may be severed wherever it is smote." Defeat meant "the overthrow of our liberal institutions, and [would] revive the tottering thrones of despots of the old world" (*The Daily Steubenville Herald*, January 8, 1862). Levi Wagner, a comrade with the same regiment, expressed the same deep sense of obligation to his country. Echoing Socrates' *Crito*, he declared his reasons for enlisting. "I was planted, cultivated and nourished in a Democratic soil . . . [and] was strong on preserving the union" (Levi Wagner, Recollections of an Enlistee, 1861–64; see also *The Fremont Daily Journal*, January 3, 1862 and William Kennedy, letter, March 7, 1862).

The threat to democratic institutions came not only from traitors at the front (Barber 1894: 31), but from the ranks of a fifth column at home. John Craft took time out from soldiering with the 57th Indiana to warn his wife to beware of Democrats. "I often think that our Country must have been guilty of some gross and flagrant outrage, for which the Great Ruler of the Universe as a punishment for our national sins ordained that the Democratic party should be permitted to exist, to bring this great calamity upon our Nation." He then admonished his wife and sons with the following warning. "I never want you in any way to be connected with this hypocritcal party. . . . Remember that if anything is so rotten and mean that you cant find any word to express its meaness anywhere else[,] the name Democrat will express every characteristic of its meaness. . . . Boys," he told his sons, "I want you to keep this, and if I should not be permitted to advise you in after years. I want you in public life to be governed by this" (To Eliza and Children, December 29, 1861).

In the South, patriotism was even stronger; Confederates invoking patriotic themes even more frequently than Northerners.[9] Theirs was also the holy cause of "Anglo-Saxon constitutionalism" and liberty (*The Republican Banner*, October 29, 1861). They argued, much as Rufus Catin did in correspondence from the base of the 19th Louisiana, that they were taking up arms because "The Magna Carta of our liberties, the constitution . . . [is] misinterpreted and its aims perverted, [for] the government has fallen entirely into the hands of fanatics who refused to listen to the voice of the South" (Rufus Catin to Cousin Fannie, June 26, 1861). Catin's views were shared by Confederate officers. Colonel M.H. Moore believed the Confederacy was struggling to "maintain inviolate the principles and rights of the Constitution" (*The Memphis Daily Appeal,* January 23, 1862). These views were echoed by an assistant surgeon, Lunsford Yandell, "If the Southern Confederacy is destroyed, Republican government in America is at an end" (To Sally [sister], February 16, 1862). The national consensus on basic constitutional principles had been violated, so that a Mississippi cavalryman named Thornton Bowman saw himself fighting a "sectional President" who no longer represented the national consensus (1904: 20). Lincoln was not their president, he was their invader, "a despot . . . enthroned upon the alter of liberty" (*The Memphis Daily Appeal,* January 23, 1862; see also John Williams Green, Diary, June 1861).

The threat of invasion spurred Southern patriotism. Five of the six states with the highest percentages of patriotic statements happened to be the ones that were being invaded or immediately threatened: Missouri, Alabama, Mississippi, Kentucky, and Tennessee. A Kentuckian with the 6th Kentucky Confederate Infantry, who had to flee his home in Louisville, angrily vowed that "the Usurper's minions shall never plant their unholy feet upon [Kentucky's soil]" (*The Louisville Daily Courier,* December 2, 1861). His sentiments were seconded by an Alabamian with the state's 18th Regiment who vowed that "the Lincoln forces . . . will rue the day upon which they are brought in contact with [Kentucky]" (*The Mobile Advertiser and Register,* October 31, 1861).

Confederate Colonel Moore was the only Western Confederate to confirm Reid Mitchell's (1988: 4) contention that racial control was a significant motivational factor. The Northern invaders were not merely foreign occupants, they were also revolutionary agents bringing abolition and threatening the South's institutions. Moore accused the federal leadership of harboring a secret agenda that included servile insurrection. The blacks would be allies of the Northern armies and would operate as "irregulars" committing "arson, rapine and murder to help them crush" the South (*The Memphis Daily Appeal,* January 23, 1862). Fears of servile insurrection circulated in the Mississippi Delta area with its large numbers of slaves (T.L. Connelly 1967: 21). It did not appear in Kentucky and west Tennessee.

Few Union recruits probably even thought much about slavery before they enlisted. And those who did oppose slavery did not predicate their ideas on its immorality. Instead, they merely judged slave labor to be inefficient. Such views were exemplified by Joseph Ruff, the German immigrant who came from Michigan, a state with a stronger anti-slavery tradition than any other state in the West. Michigan was one of five Northern states where the predecessors of the Republican party—the Liberty party and the Free Soil party—had enough organization and support to field candidates in at least two of the three congressional elections between 1844 and 1848. It later became a radical bastion, and

Ruff was one of its advocates. The first book he read after he mastered English was *The Impending Crisis*. Ruff believed that the book demonstrated that free labor was more productive than slave labor. When election time came, he decided to support the Republican party, proclaiming that "one of the proudest acts of my political life was when I voted for Mr. Lincoln" (Ruff 1943: 275, 271).

Generally, however, the volunteers on both sides expressed little sympathy for the plight of slaves during the initial stage of their service, and racist sentiments abounded in the letters of the troops. Suprisingly, almost all of the pro-slavery and racist statements were made by Northerners rather than Southerners. Captain Martin Armstrong of the 81st Ohio exemplified this attitude when he wrote to the editor of *The Lima Weekly Gazette* (February 19, 1862), "It is not to free this justly hated negro race," that the army fights, for the blacks are "unworthy" of liberation. And on the other side, H.M. Stanley could not imagine white men fighting over blacks. Stanley averred "a secret scorn for people who could kill each other for the sake of African slaves." He could not understand why "a sooty faced nigger from distant land should be an element of disturbance between white brothers" (Laurie 1985: 43). Because of such ingrained racial prejudices, the Northern troops often treated black "contrabands" with contempt. They were objects of barter, commodities, not people. James F. Drish wrote that "we are all supplied with contrabands. I have got a very fine mulatto Fellow and we find him verry useful[.] [T]hey are very good cooks[.] I am bound to have a half dozen if the war lasts much longer," and he promised his wife that "when I come home I am going to Get a Girl to cook for you" (To wife, February 21, 1862). John Hardin, an orderly sergeant with the 23rd Indiana, asked his sister to "tell John Smith [a friend] I will capture a Negro Woman and send it to him" (To Mandy, March 4, 1862, Civil War Letters).[10]

Most felt that the slavery question should not even be broached, because it would hinder the repression of the rebellion. John Steele, a chaplain with the 13th Iowa, argued, "if that Radical Spirit that is in Congress would let the generals do their own work, it will all be done up right soon. But if they continue to throw obstacles in the way, by tacking on emancipation . . . I see no end but destruction—the old ship must founder and all her precious freight be lost" (To Brother Cooper, February 8, 1862). A Hoosier with the 6th Infantry, bivouacked on the Green River in Kentucky, agreed and argued that the South would surrender much sooner when they no longer saw abolition as a Northern war aim. "When [Southerners] . . . find that their peculiar institution is to be respected, and the slaves are not to be emancipated and put upon the level of the white race; when they become entirely satisfied of all this, then will Kentucky, Tennessee, and most of the Southern States down their arms and become loyal" (*The Daily State Sentinel*, December 27, 1861; see also *The Daily Steubenville Herald*, January 18, 1862). Colonel William H. Gibson, commanding the 49th Ohio Infantry, growled that "statesmen had better let the 'nigger' alone at present and address themselves to suppressing this great rebellion." Seeing slavery in Kentucky, Gibson contended that master and slave wanted to maintain the relationship. He testified that "I have witnessed some touching scenes between exiled masters, returning to their homes and their faithful slaves. It is strange how few try to escape or run away. . . . It is my deliberate opinion, that in their present state of ignorance the slave rather fears than desires emancipation. They only regard their appetites and comforts. They appear to want no more." He even maintained that the slaves "love the South and are devoted to their masters" (*The Tiffin Weekly Tribune*, April 4, 1862).

Lucius Barber, with an Illinois outfit, blamed abolitionist and proslavery elements for the war. "Honest men of every political creed," he wrote, "will unite in saying that the institution of slavery and the persistent advocacy of its abolishment by the Abolitionists [was one of] . . . the main causes which brought about the rebellion" (Barber 1894: 1). This sentiment was echoed by Andrew Walker who was soldiering with the 55th Illinois at Camp Douglas near Chicago. The young man complained in a letter to home that "Senator Trumball [Turmbull] has introduced today a Bill confiscating rebel property. . . . I will [as] soon place my property in such condition before I find I have to go into battle" (To father, December 2, 1861). The slavery question would solve itself, according to an Iowan doing garrison duty in Missouri. "Speaking about the nigger," he wrote to his hometown newspaper, "I take it that the 'institution' will give up the ghost after it ceases to pay. Now for a fact. Negroes that could have hired out at $12 and $20 per month, one or two years ago, would not now sell or hier at 6 bits a dozen. If the hated abolitionists can strike any harder blow at slavery than that—let them lay on—but in God's name let the abolitionists have some peace until they can do something to rival the efforts of the devoted friends of the divine institution" (*The Daily Gate City*, February 20, 1862).

Some Northern volunteers saw that economic conditions in the slave states were meaner than in their home states. They began to view slavery as a drag on the South's standard of living, and if left to itself it would atrophy. Seeing the slave society firsthand in Missouri, Martin Armstrong told friends at home, "Let the people know that [slavery is] . . . worse than European Feudalism—American Slavery—[and] is dying even slowly but surely, and that Labor, the expression of a people's progression, is made honorable everywhere in the land—that this cursed incubus, the sole instigator of Treason, shall not poison our lifeblood forever" (*The Lima Weekly Gazette*, February 19, 1862).

Also, the troops' experiences with runaways in Kentucky and Missouri softened their racist sentiments. As the Northern armies penetrated into the South and increasingly came in contact with its black refugees, their letters began to echo some sympathy for the plight of these people. E.B. Bush, an army chaplain, came to oppose returning these blacks to their Kentucky masters. Bush described an incident that reinforced his opposition to returning contrabands. His men had turned a runaway over to the local sheriff. Before long, the owner came to seize his "property" and make an example of him to discourage other slaves from fleeing. "His master headed a mob of fifteen or twenty men," wrote Bush, "who went to the jail and, the master presenting a pistol to the breast of the Sheriff, demanded the keys, which were given up, and the trembling victim was led to slaughter. Taking him to a tree a little out of town, they hung him up before he had time for confession and, while hanging, they fired shots into him. Tell the world these are the fruits of Southern lies," he angrily reported (*The Tiffin Weekly Tribune*, November 15, 1861).

Nor did Order No. 3, the policy requiring the return of escaped slaves, sit well with the Unionist levies. A Hawk-eye soldier argued that it should not be enforced.

I must confess, conservative as I have always thought myself to be, that it was with a pang of regret that I saw the gate of liberty closed against those who were claimed chattels of persons who aided and abetted the unholy rebellion. And the impudent exultation which some of them evinced on claiming the right to search for their chattels, was not calculated to make one feel in a praying mood, by any means. I am not, nor do I think I ever shall be an abolitionist, according to the popular understanding of the word; but I must confess that all of my favorable predilections for the institution, which I entertained at the commencement of the rebellion, have vanished behind the mist of blood shed as a sacrifice to that modern Moloch (*The Daily Gate City*, March 7, 1862).

Regarding other reasons for fighting, such as hatred toward the enemy, the analysis of the letters and diaries did not reveal more than a half dozen showing strong animosity toward the enemy. Among them was the wellborn Kentuckian Lunsford Yandell, who denounced Unionists as "negro stealers," and "fiends incarnate" (To sister Sally, August 10, 1861; to father, November 29, 1861). While on the other side, Tom Honnell, a vengeful Federal training with the 15th Ohio Infantry in Zanesville, poured out his invective against the "traitors and villains," who were tearing asunder his national birthright (To friend Ben Epler, May 21, 1861). But the most hostile letters seemed to come from the men from regiments that were fighting the mini–Civil War in Missouri. Lieutenant Payson Shumway, with the 14th Illinois, was chasing guerrillas from Jefferson City to Springfield. "There is suffering and death. Wrong and outrage brought about by the rebels and traitors who have plundered and the honest farmer until his little ones cry for bread. . . . May God send the day soon . . . when these robbers and murderers shall meet their due reward," he vowed (Diary, March 25, 1862; see also William Richardson to Father and Mother, December 27, 1861). An Iowa cavalryman spoke pitilessly of prisoners rounded up at Sedalia, "With a few exceptions a more ignorant, shabby, degraded, treacherous, lying gang of villains cannot be found even among semi-civilized tribes of the earth. It were a compliment to them to say that they would compare favorably with the scourings of Northern penitentiaries" (*The Daily Gate City*, March 15, 1862).

A small minority went to Shiloh with no real reason for justifying their enlistment, regrettably concluding that people kill and maim each other for no valid reason. Such an acknowledgment must have borne heavily on soldiers such as Julius Power, a bandsman and stretcher-bearer with the 39th Indiana. In a letter to a friend, he admitted that he could see no cause to encourage him in his commitment. "Some say that this war is all for the best. . . . But I am willing to confess their superiority over me in foreseeing any such good. . . . And cannot see where history records any good arising from a war such as ours" (To Mattie, July 14, 1861). In the South, there were similar sentiments expressed. An officer with the 24th Tennessee Regiment believed that the whole war was pointless and that it threatened all the gains heretofore attained. "We have gotten to be a great people for stupendous undertakings and wars are conducted with the same grandeur and magnificence of which we boast in our national character. As a step up this ladder of grandeur we are now attempting to cut one another's throats. . . . After we have wasted our substance of years of honest industry in settling the knotty questions which wire-working politicians have floundered upon, and plunged the country into a commotion & turmmoil. Into a bloody war" (Mott 1946: 237).

The volunteers held powerful patriotic beliefs that were widely shared among nineteenth-century Americans. The men were far more politically motivated than is often assumed (Wiley 1978a, 1978b;[11] Maslowski 1970; Donald 1966: 72–73); the Civil War soldier was an integral part of the community from which he emerged and shared its patriotic values when he took up arms in its name.[12]

STYLES AND TOOLS OF WAR

The Victorian romantic military style characterized by several themes such as purple prose offering self-sacrifice for "the cause," chivalric rituals, generosity to the enemy, optimism in adversity, and above all, the dashing deed valued as an end in itself—the beau geste—appeared here and there in the letters and diaries of the several hundred soldiers in the sample. Lucius Barber's prose, in recounting how his 15th Illinois Regiment spent the night before the battle at Pittsburg Landing, exemplifies this dramatic tradition. "How unconscious are we that the morrow will be ushered in by a blood-red sun and the echoing notes of the deep-toned artillery; and that thousands who are now all unconscious of danger will, ere another sun sets, be sleeping that last long sleep that knows no waking. Thousands of broken home-circles in our land will gather around the family board this day unconscious that their loved ones had laid their lives upon the altar of their country" (1894: 50). The same patriotic heroism was voiced by a volunteer, writing from his training camp near Zanesville, Ohio; Thomas Honnell of the state's 15th Regiment resolutely thundered, "I would rather die in the battle field than to see our liberty taken from us and this country ruled by *traitors and villains*" (To friend, Ben Epler, May 21, 1861). Another Ohioan in camp at Munfordville, Kentucky, gallantly proclaimed, "We are in the right, and for the right I am willing to fight . . . if I fall on the battlefield, I shall probably fall just where my country needs me" (*The Fremont Daily Journal*, January 10, 1862). Inspired by patriotic exaltation, not to mention his recent promotion to orderly of Company E, 3rd Iowa Infantry, Gustavus Cushman renewed his heroic resolve to do well as battle approached. "The next time you hear from me, or of me," he wrote, "I may be cold in death" (To brother, July 8, 1861). Some Southerners also took up the theme of heroic self-sacrifice. There was, for example, George T. Blakemore of the 23rd Tennessee Regiment, whose diary entries are replete with romantic verse. His entry during the last maneuvers leading to Shiloh read, "e'er I again write . . . I may be sleeping in the cold ground, yes, alas! I may before 48 hours fill a soldiers grave, as a battle is daily yes hourly anticipated" (Diary, March 29, 1862).

Another Victorian theme in the soldiers' letters and diaries was a chivalric attitude toward the enemy. The war was supposed to be fought according to a set of rituals. Before armies joined in battle, their generals were supposed to issued knightly challenges. War took on the style of a duel, with all its incumbent ceremonies. This image of the chivalric way of war was described by Iowan George Richardson. He believed warfare required formal challenges inviting opponents to battle. When Fremont was "getting near enough to old Price to make him feel uncomfortable for [he] sent word to the General," according to Richardson," that if he [would] . . . wait 20 days, he [would] . . . fight him" (To mother and father, October 25, 1861). Elsewhere, the twenty-day ultimatum was also de rigueur. John L. Harris, whose 14th Illinois was fighting with Grant's army, shared G. Richardson's knightly image of war. He wrote home that General A. S. Johnston "had sent Generals Grant and Smith word that he would give them 20 days to get out of his boundary, if not gone then we would have to take the consequence"

(To parents, March 21, 1862; see also Samuel Sheperdson to mother, October 13, 1861).

The romantic ethos also proclaimed profound respect for courage for its own sake. There was nothing wrong with admiring a daring enemy who carried out a particularly brave act with grace and elan—the beau geste. One Union soldier remembered an incident during a Confederate charge. "A rebel sergeant," he recalled, "advanced in front of his command and with his own hands planted the rebel flag on a piece of our artillery that they had captured; but this act sealed his doom. . . . I shot at him, but I hope that it was not my bullet that sealed his eyes" (Barber 1894: 53).

Heroism and elan were assumed to be peculiarly Southern traits. Southerner by adoption Henry Morton Stanley believed this to be so— he admired Southern chivalry. "This spirit," he affirmed "consists in being reputed brave, truth telling and [being] reverent towards women" (Laurie 1985: 43). Sam Watkins, a fellow Southerner, shared Stanley's belief that Southerners were more chivalric than Northerners. He explained the difference this way. "We are an agricultural people; they are a manufacturing people. They are descendents of the good old Puritan Plymouth Rock stock, and we of the South from proud and aristocratic stock of Cavaliers" (1962: 21). More recently, Sharon Hannum found that "southerners increasingly, through the 1840's and 1850's rallied to support the cavalier as their vision of perfection, their picture of themselves painted in ideal tones" (Hannum 1965: 2). Sam Watkins and Henry Stanley assumed that the two peoples, and consequently their two armies, were intrinsically different and that by this fact their styles of warfare were also distinct—one being more daring, possessing more elan, and having a "cavalier" tradition and the other being better organized and supplied and championing the "roundhead" culture. This is an old theme and has found proponents as late as 1981–82. These researchers have argued (1) that the Civil War soldiers were imbued with romantic, viz. chivalric, ideals, (2) that it was more pervasive in the South (at least among its officer class), and (3) that the source of this tradition was either quasi-genetic, Celtic racial traits versus Saxon origins (McWhiney and Jamieson 1982), or attributed to cultural factors (Barton 1981).

Barton argued that the Northern troops were more "willfully controlled" whereas Southern soldiers were more romantic and volatile, and thus more spontaneous in their behavior on the battlefield. They were more apt to adopt a chivalric fighting style. He suggested that "in Victorian America there may have been mainly one general theory of moral character but at least two distinct and patterned expressions of character" (1981: 21). He also claimed that Southern officers were more verbose, suggesting they were more tempestuous, admiring the beau geste (1981: 53). McWhiney and Jamieson also ascribed different traits to the two sides. They argued that there were two cultures confronting each other, two different value systems, and thus two different styles of warfare. Yankee culture was English and Saxon whereas the Southern culture was Celtic, i.e., Scotch, Scotch-Irish, Welsh, Irish, or Cornish. Celts, they noted, are romantic, aggressive, and individualistic and the Anglo-Saxons are more disciplined, thorough, and organized. Thus the two ethnic groups had different fighting styles: the Teuton was more apt to fight defensively and the Celt to rely more on elan to carry the day (1982: 172–73). The two authors further argued that these differences led to strategic and tactical mistakes by the South, which squandered its manpower by its frequent attacks during the first three years of the war and exposing the infantry to heavy casualties. These reckless assaults decimated the Confederate armies and ultimately lost them the war (1982: 180). The question of tactics in the battle will be discussed later in this study.

On the other hand, military historian Cunliffe found little evidence of pronounced variances between Northern and Southern soldiers—or at least traits that were important enough to demonstrate a decisive difference in fighting style (1968: 358). After all, the officers who trained and led the troops studied the same tactical doctrine as had been elaborated by Mahan, Hardee, and Jomini.

Edmund Wilson (1984: 650) was closer to the truth when he claimed that neither side had a romantic style associated with an agrarian culture. The Scott Syndrome was already in decline before the Civil War broke out. The North was well into the industrial revolution, which had already affected social values. The South too was in the process of developing a more balanced economy. Patrick J. Hearnden's *Independence and Empire: The South's New Cotton Campaign, 1865–1901* shows that even before the war, the South was encouraging the creation of a textile industry, first in the tidewater areas and then into the heartland, to modernize from an agricultural colonial economy to an industrial one (1982: 4–7). Furthermore, if the South had not been firmly embarked on the path of industrialization, how could it have supplied and equipped an army against a major industrial power for five years. The point is elaborated in Frank E. Vandiver's *Plowshares into Swords: Josiah Gorgas and Confederate Ordnance* (1952) and Charles B. Dew's *Ironmaker to the Confederacy: Joseph R. Anderson and the Tredegar Iron Works* (1987). Science and technology had already transformed communications, industry, and agriculture as well as the concomitant values. Precision, discipline, and realism were the key principles of the ethos of scientism and technology. They were in contradiction to the older, disappearing romantic values of pre-industrial chivalry. Only a handful of the soldiers in our sample used purple prose and knightly imagery.[13] Their style was generally quite straightforward; and rather than gushing with sentiment, their accounts often contained humorous anecdotes and realistic assessments of their situation. In other words, they were not much different from the soldiers of the Second World War.

The style of war is not only a function of psychological and cultural factors, it also depends on material factors—the quantity and quality of the tools of war. An army's cohesion can easily disintegrate and morale can tumble when the rear echelons fail to expedite supplies (R. Holmes 1986: 77, 322). There was a great deal of resentment among Shiloh's soldiers directed against the quartermaster. Supplies and weaponry were not minor elements in the morale equation at Shiloh. This preoccupation with victuals was not merely a matter of taste or whim, it is rooted in body chemistry; malnutrition has an effect on the mind. Furthermore, in dismal conditions, food may be the only thing that a soldier has to look forward to, huddling around a fire cooking up something tasty and savoring a hot cup of coffee at the end of a day's march. The preparation and consumption of food has both physical and social importance for morale (R. Holmes 1986: 125, 128). A Hoosier soldier-poet named Jim Vanderbilt humorously expounded on the importance of supplies in the outcome in this *Soldier's Prayer*.

> Our Father who art in Washington,
> Uncle Abraham be thy name,
> Thy victory won, thy will be done;
> At the south, as at the North;
> Give us this day our daily rations of crackers & pork,
> And forgive us our shortcomings,
> As we forgive our quartermasters,
> For thine is the power, the soldiers, and the negros,
> For the space of three years; Amen
> (Vanderbilt, Letters, 1861)

Stouffer and his team, who studied the GIs' combat morale in World War II, shared Vanderbilt's emphasis on the importance of logistics. Their study noted that the "feeling of participation in group power" was integrally associated with "the degree of confidence the men felt in the supply system and in their arms and equipment" (Stouffer 1949: II, 145).

The matériel had to be distributed to armies scattered throughout the Western seat of war, a region several times larger than the Eastern theater with a sparser railroad network. As the armies moved out to their far-flung posts, supply problems began to crop up. The situation reached a nadir in the winter of 1861–62. Mud, snow, and flooding washed out bridges and made railway and river transport difficult.

The ensuing supply problems soon arose in the men's correspondence. A large portion of the troops' letters and diaries lamented the state of their army's logistics.[14] In comparing the impact of supply problems on the morale in both Western armies, it was found that the proportion of complainants was exactly the same—about two-thirds. The main subject of the grumbling was food.

The bill of particulars against the rations was both graphic and humorous. John Beach of the 77th Ohio disdainfully described the fare as "mouldy crackers and sowbelly with hair on it" (Dairy). Another soldier commented that the crackers would "be excellent to cover our gunboats being proof against water and bullets" (*The Aurora Beacon*, January 23, 1862). A soldier with the 65th Ohio wrote to his hometown newspaper that he and his comrades had been reduced to "three crackers and a cup of coffee per day. . . . [And]," he added humorously, "it takes something less than an hour . . . to demolish . . . 'hard crackers.' The barrels that contain these specimen brix," he continued, "are marked L.O. 12, which . . . means 'left over from the war of 1812' " (*The Daily Commercial Register*, January 28, 1862; see also George Soners to Friend, March 2, 1862). The same soldier later advised any potential recruits "not to enlist . . . but to purchase full sets of dental instruments" because the returning troops will come back with toothaches from the chewing (*The Memphis Daily Appeal*, February 4, 1862). The bacon was also getting a bad press. Lucius Barber recalled that it was so "maggoty that it could almost walk" (1894: 20). Sergeant John Hardin described his first Christmas dinner at the front. "I had *sow belly* and beans and crackers . . . I will tell you what I mean by sow belly . . . it is fat bacon with tits on it as long as your finger . . . the boys have a good time playing with them" (To sister Mandy, Letters, January 14, 1862).

Shortages became acute when the armies changed their bases and uprooted their supply lines. As the Confederates abandoned their depots in Columbus and Bowling Green, Kentucky, and the Unionists penetrated deeper into the South, the situation grew grim. During the three months before Shiloh, penuries were increasingly mentioned in the soldiers' correspondence. Letters home and to the editors of the local papers soon reported the shortages, and a lively debate exploded in the press over supply problems. Others tried to allay homefront concerns. One of the quartermaster's defenders, a soldier with the 39th Indiana Regiment, assured his hometown newspaper that Company D was provided with "2 pounds of nourishing food to the man per day," and he added that, "no army in the world was so well provided for as ours" (*The Howard Tribune*, February 4, 1862). An Ohioan wrote from the wilds of what is now West Virginia that he and his comrades were "like horses fed on buckin feed, . . . our hair is slick and we have stiff tails and high heads." Morale was good, he wrote and added that the only thing they hungered for were some "buckeye girls . . . so that we can tame ourselves down" (W.S. Word to brother, November 13, 1861). Colonel W.H. Gibson, commanding the 49th Ohio, was outraged by the stories reaching home about privations in the army. Perhaps also seeing it as an implicit indictment of his administration of the regiment, the angry colonel called any man who wrote such things "*a liar . . .* a croaker and [a] *coward,*" and he vouched that the regiment had a surplus having accumulated "$500 worth of saved rations" (*The Seneca Advertiser*, December 13, 1861).

The main tool of the new soldier's trade, and a key factor in morale, was his firearm. A prayer circulating in the 39th Indiana's camp at Nolin, Kentucky, made the same point.

> To us the promise fulfill,
> we the soldiers and sons of
> Abraham, unto us is joy,
> come unto us a rifle's given,
> and his name it shall be called
> wonderful Enfield,
> and with'em we'll go spread the
> gospel of republicanism to Southern
> Gentiles.
> (*The Howard Tribune*, November 19, 1861)

The arms that filtered into both armies in the Western theater were a mixed assortment. For example, Union armies during the war fought with eighty-one types of musket, with an immense variety of firing mechanisms and loading systems, not to mention the plethora of calibers with median ranging from 0.45 to 0.75 (Mahon 1977: 254). A.F. Davis, in Company B, 15th Indiana Infantry, arrived late for the battle of Shiloh, following in the wake of the two armies to catch up with the fighting. He found the trail marked by an immense variety of arms cast off during the fighting. The weapons ranged from "the best Enfield to the single barrel shot guns," as well as "excellent double barrel fowling pieces . . . and [there were also] Arkansas tooth picks weighing from 4 to 6 lbs each," and even "a great many pikes and spears" (to F.D. [brother], April 21, 1862; see also O.E. Cunningham 1966: 138). That some Southerners at Shiloh had pikes is lent some credence by John Williams Green, who was probably with the 6th Kentucky in Trabue's brigade, and wrote that on the march to battle he saw a blacksmith at Monterey "turning out old fashioned pikes to arm some of our troops who had no guns" (Diary, April 4, 1862). However, no account was found about a unit actually going into combat at Shiloh carrying pikes.[15]

Comments were almost evenly divided on the quality of the recruits' weapons. Among those who believed themselves poorly armed, the weapon that was most disliked was the Austrian musket, because it was heavy to carry and inaccurate (Ruff 1943: 280). Worse yet, it was undependable. A German recruit with the 6th Iowa averred that "aw man might be killed more as twelve times de tam ding would shoot off" (*The Daily Gate City*, October 19, 1861). Belgian muskets also had a bad reputation because of uneven bores and bent barrels (Wiley 1978b: 290–91; William J. Kennedy to wife, December 27, 1861). John Beach wrote in his diary that the Belgian muskets that his unit had drawn in Paducah "were about as much danger behind as a rebel was in front" (Memoirs). Furthermore, the British "Brown Bess" was just too big and cumbersome (T. Johnson, "Experiences"). Another imported musket that was criticized was the French one, which Alexander Varian, an officer of the 1st Ohio, claimed often burst and was finally condemned and withdrawn (To father, October 30, 1861). Some states had reputations for arming their troops better than others. Texans and Hoosiers were reputed to be better equipped (John Ellis to sister, March 16, 1862; see also *The Howard Tribune*, October 15, 1861).

The weapons that got most favorable mention were the British Enfield and the Springfield rifle. The former was favored because of its accuracy and its robustness, it was lighter and shorter and easier to carry than the Springfield. Both rifles were well made and beautifully finished. Many of the European-made weapons were as robust and accurate, but they were crudely finished, leading many of the men who received those guns to compare them unfavorably to the British and American models. W.R. Phillips, a Hoosier lieutenant who met his Maker on the first day at Shiloh, wrote to his brother (the editor of *The Howard Tribune*) of the delight experienced by his company when they were issued Enfields instead of European smoothbores. "You can't imagine how good it made us all feel. All felt happier than a nigger at a camp meeting, or a Dutchman at a lager beer saloon. Bully for old [governor] Morton and the rest of mankind," he wrote ecstatically (*The Howard-Tribune*, November 19, 1861).

With mixed feelings about their arms and equipment, the recruits undertook the obligations, discomforts, and hazards that since time immemorial have been associated with army life.

NOTES

1. This perhaps distinguished the volunteers of Shiloh from their compatriots who served in the infantry in World War II. Weigley (1981: 39) pointed out that the American army habitually filled the ranks of its combat infantry with its least promising, least educated, and least skilled recruits.

2. Sixty-eight of the men indicated their hometown.

3. See *The New Orleans Daily Crescent*, January 11, 1862. The costs of equipping a regiment were considerable; a three-month regiment cost $40,000—just for the pay for 700 men (*The Lima Weekly Gazette*, August 7, 1861).

4. The rifled musket was accurate at 200 yards when used by a good marksman. Beyond that, a soldier could hit a target six feet by six feet at 500 yards and a target eighty feet square, such as a dense formation, about half the time at 1,000 yards. Even at this extreme distance, the standard 500-grain bullet,

driven by 60 grains of black powder, would penetrate four inches of soft pine (Peterson 1962: 152).

5. Taps were beaten on the snare drum, according to Anglo-Dutch military tradition going back to the seventeenth century. The bugle came into use later.

6. Eighty-nine of the soldiers commented on their reasons for joining. Their responses were checked to find out whether they were saying one thing in public, in letters to a newspaper and published reminiscences, and something else in their diaries and letters to intimates. A cross-tabulation comparing their comments according to whether they were destined for public or private reading, however, yielded no significant difference.

7. Given the fact that officers were usually better educated and thus more politically articulate, one could assume that their response rate would be proportionally higher. But this did not turn out to be the case. Officers responded at the same rate as the enlisted men.

8. See Kellett's excellent discussion of soldiers' patriotism (1982: 327).

9. Seventy-five percent of the Confederates voiced patriotic themes, compared to 64 percent of the Union soldiers.

10. There was a strong racist tradition in states such as Indiana and Illinois. There groups agitated in favor of slavery in the 1820s. When these efforts yielded no results, these states enacted legislation excluding both free and slave blacks from entering the states (Berwanger 1966: 197).

11. Wiley's findings about the Confederates were different. He found that the "dominant urge" of many of the volunteers was the "desire for adventure," seeing new places, making new friends, and the excitement of battle and glory (1978b: 17). This impression does not, however, come across in the Shiloh sample, especially after the troops moved out into Missouri and Kentucky.

12. The reader is directed to the following authors: Kohn (1981: 554–55), Hicken (1969: 20), and T. Harry Williams (1962: 44).

13. Twenty-three out of the 381 men (6 percent).

14. Among the sixty-six men who discussed supplies, rations were the target of over half of the complainants (54 percent), with the rest of the complaints almost equally divided between shoddy uniforms and inadequate shelter.

15. Cunningham wrote that the Confederates were so poorly armed that Corinth blacksmiths were churning out pikes (1966: 138).

2

"The Tented Field"

ARMY LIFE

The soldiers began campaigning in autumn 1861. Some of the troops went to what is now West Virginia, others to Kentucky, and still others to Missouri. The recruits that are the focus of this study saw little fighting in the early operations while they were becoming acquainted with life in the field, where they had to cope with inclement weather, learned field crafts, and endured life without any privacy. They also came in contact with the new camp mores when young men are turned loose on their own for the first time. And above all they became acquainted with the monotonous routine of army life.

Most of the new recruits took it in stride. Two-thirds of the men were happy in the army and were adapting quite well to their new life.[1] Amid the mud and flooding at Paducah, one the dreariest military "hell holes" on the Western front, Thaddeus Capron waxed enthusiastic about life with the 55th Illinois. "I am enjoying myself well," he wrote in his diary, "and have worked just hard enough to keep me out of mischief" (1919: 339). William Robinson was camping and marching with the 34th Illinois. After being organized at Camp Butler in September, the regiment moved into Kentucky, reaching Lexington and then Louisville. It had all been great fun marching and camping in new places. "I am almost beginning to feel that this 'war business' is nothing but one grand Fourth of July, got up for the especial gratification of vanity of a few favored ones, and some recreation for 'the boys,' " he wrote cheerily to a friend back home (To Charlie [Abbot], November 7, 1861).

But the dreariness of winter camp life soon set in. There were men in huge masses living in one confined area, walking in it, marching in it, digging in it, ripping out its wood for fires, and relieving themselves in every corner. After absorbing the imprint of thousands upon thousands of men, the area was soaked with rain and wet snow. Adding to the desolation, it was overlaid with the smoke from thousands of cooking fires that were kindled with wet and green wood. This temporary slum was the typical military city of an army in the field that Colonel Tom Harrison and the 39th Indiana came to know after they left Kokomo. The colonel described the most omnipresent aspect of campaigning in winter. "The mud," he wrote, "is 6 or 8 inches deep, reminding one of a well worked mortar-bed. . . . [It] has a peculiarity of its own, it is as slippery as if it had been well oiled. . . . 40,000 human feet . . . are constantly moving, mixing and working [it]." And he admitted "in such cases war loses some of its pomp and circumstances" (*The Howard Tribune*, January 28, 1861). Jim Drish had had enough by March 1862. For what seemed an eternity, he had braved the winter mud at Bird's Point evading the flooding waters at the confluence of the Mississippi and Ohio rivers. The weather had been miserable, alternating between rain and snow, making bottomlands along the rivers an endless quagmire. Drish dejectedly wrote, "I hope it will be over soon . . . I dont care how soon. . . . For the next time I go home I want to stay that is quit Soldiering. . . . there aint much fun in it" (To wife, March 24, 1862).[2] While half the Confederates were disgruntled with army life at this point in the campaign, less than a third of the Union soldiers were complaining. The difference could be attributed to the strategic situation of the two armies during the fall and winter of 1861–62. The North was on the move. Its soldiers were securing Missouri. They were invading Kentucky and threatening Tennessee at forts Donelson and Henry. They had conducted a very successful campaign in what is now West Virginia, forcing the Confederates to flee into the Shenandoah Valley. Conversely, defeat and retreat seemed to dog every step of the Southern soldiers. The tables had turned. Gone were the halcyon days of spring and summer when the South had been on the march threatening the border states and successively defeating the North at Manassas and Wilson's Creek. The bad winter weather also affected troops from the deep South more than others, compounding the morale problem. Then there were the officers to cope with.

OFFICERS

"Bob, you ought to be here [Mobile, Alabama] to see all the regiments drill," Elihu Squiggs wrote to his friend. "The officers in particular with their cocked hats and swords . . . they do cavort around beautiful. And there is so many of them as every officer has to have six assistants and seven clerks. How the Confederacy will ever manage to pay them, and such awful big salaries, too, beats my grammar. It'll take sights of money" (*The Natchez Daily Courier*, February 4, 1862). Numerous they were, perhaps expensive, but essential nevertheless, for as long as men conduct war in groups, leadership is critical (Gabriel 1978: 54). Field-grade officers had a vital role in the melding of green recruits into effective units. Furthermore, command and control in Civil War tactics required dense formations operating in sight of the commander. This was one of the reasons leaders were mounted or marching—leading from the front by example. They could exercise command and control more effectively, and above all, they could sustain the unit's morale (Baynes 1967: 110). The basic unit led by field-grade officers was the regiment. During the Civil War, the next unit down was the company, commanded by a captain or a company-grade officer.[3] The colonels were important for combat effectiveness at Shiloh for two reasons: first, because of the rapid and complete breakup of any unit larger than a brigade during the fighting at Shiloh and second, the field-grade officers were also key elements in developing combat skills, because they were charged with teaching their commands small-unit tactics. Contrary to later wars when troops were drilled at central depots, in the Civil War the recruits went through their training with their own regiment. Thus, their officers not only led them in battle, but they also supervised their basic training.

The new officers were usually selected from within the same communities as the men they were to command. They and their men were bound together by ties of friendship, kinship, similar backgrounds, and shared values. In effect, officers and men were militarized civilians. They still chose their leaders as they had done in private life—they elected them (Rudolph 1984: 10). The civilian soldiers were determined to choose their leaders democratically and they clung to those principles. When Colonel Cam of the 14th Illinois opposed the notion, a confrontation with his men and officers ensued, with the recalcitrant colonel losing out. Cam's officers and men banded together and petitioned the brigadier to force an election. Cam lost in a humiliating defeat to a man named Hall by 303 to 2 (Backus, Diary, January 14, 1862). Yet, although this system did not guarantee competence, it nevertheless provided something equally important: a source of cohesion during the early stages of the war when the troops were untrained.[4] The community base provided an underlying network of communal loyalties binding officers and men through the first year of the war.

The democratic system of choosing officers that was transposed from civilian life to the army probably strengthened the units' homogeneity. It provided officers who came from the same communities, men who were more easily accepted by the rank and file. Consequently, the rank and file had a positive attitude toward their officers.[5] The most appreciated traits were social ones associated with the officer's demeanor and his empathy for the men. Attributes such as "thoughtful," "upstanding," "popular," and "gentlemanly" most often appeared in the men's correspondence. At this stage of their military experience, personality seemed more important than tactical competence. The men did not mention leadership traits that would be crucial in combat, such as "brave" or "competent," nearly as often. Later, the order of priorities of valued officers' traits will be re-examined in the light of the men's combat experience to see if these priorities had changed.

In comparing the soldiers by nationality, the Confederates were somewhat more critical of their officers than the Unionist troops. One out of two Southern soldiers at Shiloh were unhappy with their leaders whereas only slightly more than a third of the Unionists were critical. Two reasons come to mind for explaining why the Confederate rank and file were more critical of their officers. The first, and most obvious, reason for the difference between Northerners and Southerners is that the Southern armies in Kentucky and Tennessee were constantly in retreat between February and April 1862. Much of the blame was directed at the chain of command. Second, the brigade, division, and corps commanders in the Confederate army were more likely to be professionals and therefore more likely to call for a higher level of discipline from their regimental commanders. This may have caused more resentment among the citizen-soldiers.

Janowitz has argued that the ideal military leader is not a technician, but the commander or fighter. The leader is not motivated by money or personal gain, but by "national patriotism" (1959: 20). Gabriel and Savage (1987) pointed out that a technician's managerial style reduced military effectiveness during the Vietnam War. This holds true for the volunteer army of the Civil War. The new volunteers expected officers to inspire them with the same high patriotism. With true revolutionary rhetoric, an Alabamian lauded the patriotic devotion of the officers of the state's 18th Regiment by writing that "the field officers, feeling the great responsibility which rests upon them as the defenders of the best cause that ever enkindled the pure fires of patriotism in manly breasts . . . leave no stone unturned in the pursuit of theoretical and practical knowledge of their profession" (*The Mobile Advertiser and Register*, October 26, 1861).

To some extent, leadership and authority are also a question of appearance (R. Holmes 1986: 68–69). Lacking any knowledge of the reality of war, the early Civil War officers had to rely on the image provided in the press. The press' vision of combat was romantic and heroic, and the officers modeled their behavior to conform to it. They assumed the proper martial poses, with the sight of a determined-looking regimental commander riding majestically in front of the ranks inspiring ardent admiration among the men. Colonel William H. Gibson, commanding the 49th Ohio, was apparently such an officer. One of his men wrote home to the newspaper that the "men will fight for Bill until there is nothing left to fight for," adding that the colonel was "endowed with Roman firmness" (*The Fremont Daily Journal*, November 22, 1861).

Modern military historians, such as Lord Charles Moran, minimize the role of personal magnetism and appearance in military leadership (1966: 192). This may be so in combat, but in the garrison, the officers' appearance and comportment were often noted. Proper bearing and appearance drew many comments from the recruits in the new armies. When appearance did not match expectations, the officers' hold was even more tenuous. For example, William S. Bradford with the 57th Indiana complained that his colonel did not impress him much, because he looked "too small" (To Lucie [wife], March 20, 1862). On the other hand, a recruit from the 34th Illinois named Edwin Payne held his commander in high esteem, because of his "quiet, dignified" manner (1902: 11–12). William T. Sherman also had favorable reviews from his men— even though the press had accused him of mental instability. He was lauded as a "high toned" and "gallant" figure (*The Tiffin Weekly Tribune*, October 18, 1861).

In the territorially recruited regiments, the highest praise for a proper military bearing was associated with the officers' local origins. An Ohioan named William Culbertson Robinson wrote home that "[We] have the best Captain in the Regiment. He is a splendid fellow and perfect gentlemen. . . . I believe there is not one but would die for him. He is a native Buck-eye, which probably accounts for most of his good qualities" (To Charlie [Abbot], September 20, 1861).

These communal ties strengthened and shaped the relations between officers and men. The egalitarian personal bonds that had held the men together as neighbors never entirely dissipated in the army, so that affection, respect, friendship, and compassion remained essential attributes that the recruits sought in their officers. The new recruits wanted their leader to display a personal interest in his men. He had to show affection for them by being concerned with their physical and psychological well-being. Ideally, the officer should share the same hardships as his men (Janowitz 1959: 72). He was expected to stay in camp with his men, partake of the same fare, mingle with the men whenever possible, and show concern for their situation and feelings. On the march, he should be considerate when passing the column on horseback, leaving the road to the men to ease their burden as they slogged along. He was expected to exchange pleasantries with the rank and file and not behave "high and mighty." Such small gestures built a bond of affection that would provide a reserve of cohesion when authority alone would not suffice.

A Hawk-eye recruit named I.W. Carr mentioned these traits in his diary. He was serving with Company F, 11th Iowa Infantry, whose Colonel A.M. Hare had taken a detachment of the regiment including Carr's company from Booneville, Missouri, to Fulton to chase away marauding Confederate bands. It was Christmas, not a time to be out on the march, and to make matters worse, it turned out to be yet another wild-goose chase. However, Carr commented appreciatively that the colonel was "a very just and humane man allways looking to the welfare of his men and never exacting more of them than was necessary for the welfare of the country" (Diary, December 27, 1861). Some officers went above and beyond the call of duty in seeing to their men's welfare by dipping into their own pockets to provide for their men. Leander Stillwell's 61st Illinois Infantry was blessed with officers who were both generous and attentive. His regiment had been rushed into service without its full complement of men or provisions. While on the march, the regiment ran out of food. The men were going hungry, and there were no army commissary stores available. Stillwell gratefully recalled how the officers pooled their own money to buy food for their men (1920: 25). Civilian soldiers also expected to be treated with the dignity due them as volunteers and neighbors. They were not recalcitrant conscripts, but patriotic enlistees coming to the aid of their country in an emergency, and they assumed that their leaders would bear this in mind. Lieutenant Colonel Addison Sanders of the 16th Iowa was another especially esteemed officer. The regiment had been waiting in Davenport to fill out its roster, and it was taking a long time. The men had waited all through December and on into January to board steamers to be conveyed to the front. Cold weather set in, sick lists grew, and morale skidded downward. Sanders rose to the occasion, to the everlasting appreciation of his men. A private reported home to Dubuque that the lieutenant colonel "attends personally to the comfort of his men. He is in the hospital every day, and sees the sick lack nothing, while he seems to conduct private foraging expeditions down town to procure the patients luxuries they cannot obtain in camp" (*The Dubuque Daily Times*, January 24, 1862). Jim Dugan, of the 14th Illinois, liked his lieutenant for treating his men "as human beings, and not as machines made expressly to obey a set of military officers and to further their private interests" (1863: 29).

The weeding out process of inept officers began with the first stresses of campaigning. The volunteers were especially hostile toward arrogant and supercilious officers. J.H. Wiley was acting commissary of the 22nd Alabama as it marched to Corinth, Mississippi. Wiley's position at headquarters gave him a unique opportunity to see the regimental leadership at closer vantage than the rest of the enlisted men. He found officers so arrogant that they would not bother to "speak to the enlisted men except to give an order" (To Josie, April 4, 1862). These superior types refused to share the men's hardships, demanding special accommodations for bivouacks or on the railways. Saul Howell with the 3rd Iowa recalled an incident illustrating such arrogant behavior; it happened near Chillicothe, Missouri, as the unit was boarding "the cars." "There were two [railroad cars], one passenger and the other a cattle car. There was plenty of room for all in one car. The Adjutant, Major, Ass't. Surgeon, Lieutenant and Captain only a dozen rode in the decent car. But the adjutant ordered us 'mud sills' to get into the cattle car. It provoked me. The simple act of riding a few miles in a hog car is nothing, but the attempt to show great distinction between privates and officers" was inconsiderate (Journal, July 28, 1861).

Such conduct was in complete contradiction to the citizen-soldiers' egalitarian traditions. It was a constant source of resentment that embittered the relations between the officers and their men. "Garrigus" with Buell's army encamped near Nolin, Kentucky, took advantage of the lull to write a bitter indictment to his hometown newspaper, in which he denounced the way some of his fellow townsmen had taken to behaving ever since they donned sash and sword. "What a vast difference it makes in a man to put a 'brass buttons and blue coats' on him. It puffs him up with 'divine inflatuo,' stiffens his neck, and makes him as proud as the jackass with the lyon's skin upon him," and he added, "some high officers don't know a common man in the company that was and is yet their equal at home. . . . Of course dress a man up, feed him big, and let him boss and have an easy time, and ride and strut around. . . . But put a musket and his budget of 50 to 60 pounds on him, let him be put through on 'double quick' and live like sheep like the soldier does, with the same dress, privileges and pay, and you would soon test their manhood and patriotism" (*The Howard Tribune*, November 26, 1861).

The armies thus embarked on first campaign with untried officers, most of whom had no military experience. The officers were trying as best they could to learn enough about drill to keep one step ahead of their recruits. The quality of the officers was spotty, to say the least, and this hampered the development of their combat skills. As the campaign proceeded, their faults were pushed up like stones after a frost. George Russell's assessment of some of the young officers of the 55th Illinois Infantry was probably equally valid for the whole army at this stage of the war when he wrote, "Our Lieutenants has Bought each of them a new sword and when They get their rig on they look savage enough. But they are not at all dangerous" (To Betty, November 13, 1861). Yet these units had something more fundamental going for them that compensated for the inexperience and heterogeneity of their officers; they shared the same background having come from the same communities. This provided the cement that held the regiments and companies together through the trials and tribulations associated with learning to be soldiers. Such an army needed to maintain strong ties to the homefront to sustain morale.

THE HOMEFRONT

Marshal Bugeaud, veteran of Napoleon's campaigns, maintained that strong attachments to home would keep a recruit from ever becoming a real soldier. His civilian identity and dependence on contact with the homefront had to be submerged by his new life in the army. The ties with home are never, however, totally severed, nor is such a break with home always conducive to morale (Richard Holmes 1986: 80). Bugeaud underestimated the importance of home ties for combat morale in a mass army. The community plays an important role in reinforcing morale by providing legitimacy to the cause for which the men enlisted. The community's recognition of the importance of the cause and of the efforts of its soldiers is extremely important for sustaining combat motivation as is attested by the problem of the United States' effort in Vietnam. Close contacts with home were an especially important influence on morale of regionally recruited armies such as those in the Civil War. There was a tacit contract between the citizen-soldiers and their people at home. Being a member of a regionally recruited regiment was concomitment to being part of its parent community. The men believed they were the military emanation of their town, county, and state.

Cohesion was strengthened because Shiloh's volunteers realized that when they eventually returned to the bosom of their friends and family, they would be held accountable for any lapses at the front. The Civil War soldier came from small close-knit communities, which exerted powerful social pressures to hold the volunteers to their duty. A torrent of letters flowed between the recruits and the homefront. This exchange defined their reciprocal obligations. In its broadest terms, the tacit agreement provided that in return for doing their patriotic duty, the troops could expect the homefront to wholeheartedly support "the cause" and to provide for their families in their absence. The local newspaper was an important means for voicing these mutual expectations, by publishing personal letters turned in by friends and relatives of soldiers and by printing the soldiers' letters to the editor. Thus, both soldiers and civilians used its pages as a conduit for providing community oversight of their boys at the front, while simultaneously conveying the needs of the soldiers to the folks back home. The enlistees also exercised social control over their own comrades by informing on those who they deemed guilty of disreputable conduct at the front. Prior to going into battle, a soldier-correspondent promised the people back home "i will send you a list of all the names of the men and officers of Co. G, 49th O.V.I. and what they are doing and who has deserted . . . exposing them to the public" (James M. Cole from William McCutchen, Cole Papers, March 9, 1862).

The press was the political and strategic sounding board of the soldiers and their communities. With high literacy rates in both armies (B.I. Wiley 1978b: 336–37; 1978a: 305–6), the soldiers were able to read discussions of strategy and tactics. Moreover, there was no censorship. And with access to press reports from the other side, the local press carried information of the enemy's movements and intentions as well, which heightened the interest of the rank and file (*The Republican Banner*, June 6, 1861). The hometown press regularly made its way to the soldiers at the front and exhorted them to do their duty. Its editorials and published personal letters kept up a patriotic drumbeat calling on the town's sons to do their duty and do honor to their community and state. An epistle, in *The Louisville Daily Courier*, from a Confederate soldier's wife exhorted her husband to harken to "the clanking of the chains by which the traitor tyrant of the North would bind us to his triumphal car," and went on to incite him to "come boldly forth, armed for the conflict . . . [to] drive back the ruthless hordes of blood hounds" (July 3, 1861). The message was there: better to die for the sacred cause than return home a shirker, because there was no home to return to for the soldier who failed in his duty. A rebel grandmother fiercely admonished her grandson "never turn traitor, and do not come back until the war is over" (Cunningham 1966: 373). The torrent of bellicosity and patriotism that poured from home fires to camp fires inundated the volunteers. Captain William S. Bradford of Company J, 57th Indiana Infantry, who died soon after Shiloh, was spurred on by his wife and his father with histrionic exhortations. His wife, Lucy, wrote after the fall of forts Henry and Donelson, "I pity you for there seems to be no chance for you to be in a fight any way soon." She went on to add that "I thought your father would go crazy he so rejoiced" at the news of the victories. "He went into town [Marion, Indiana] and it was ten o'clock before he came home" (From wife, February 21, 1862). For their part, the men expected to be treated fairly in the press. They resented slights or favoritism when the local paper recounted the adventures of the regiment. A Hoosier soldier complained that the local editor was slanting the news about the officers in the regiment to favor his own son. Such coverage was intended to ensure his son "the future he is after," grumbled the NCO (J.J. Hardin to J.A. Cravens, Cravens Collection, September 15, 1861).

The soldiers had their own expectations of the people at home. In exchange for fighting for constitution and country, the volunteers expected firm backing and patriotic loyalty from their community. "We are willing to do anything and suffer anything," pledged Bill McCutchen of the 49th Ohio, "if only our friends at home will support us and not desert us and turn traiters to . . . the best government that ever was" (To Jim Cole, Cole Papers, March 9, 1862). Supportive letters were the staple of the soldiers' morale. One new recruit from Indiana explained their importance by observing that "the boys think that half the charms of soldiers life is taken from them, when they cease to receive encouragement from home" (*The Howard Tribune,* October 29, 1861).

The World War I adage, when a soldier is at war his heart should be at peace, holds true for America's Civil War volunteers (Moran 1966: 201). For the heart to be at peace, the enlistees needed to feel assured that they had the support of their friends and families. The people at home manifested their backing for the boys in the army in many ways. The first of these were the enthusiastic send-offs that the communities gave to their company or regiment when it left for the front. Typical of such shows of community support was the adieu that Nashville gave its lst Tennessee. The regiment paraded through the city preceded by Horn's Silver Band and a "large concourse of . . . citizens" who bade the "noble band of Tennessee patriot soldiers" farewell. Silk colors were presented by the "female academy," followed by a stentorian patriotic speech by the headmaster, C.D. Elliot. In reply, Colonel Maney, the regiment's commanding officer, vowed that "a thousand brave hearts before you are throbbing an appreciation of your deed beyond the power of the tongue to speak" (*The Nashville Union and American,* June 4, 1861).

Female academies did their part, providing a bevy of belles to inspire and "comfort" the volunteer's manhood in the name of home and flag. Buntings and beauties held vividly in Leander Stillwell's memory of the war, despite the four intervening years of boredom and horror that could have blotted them out. He remembered how the 61st Illinois rolled through Illinois past the Monticello Female Seminary, "The girls . . . were all out by the side of the road, a hundred or more with red, white and blue ribbons in their hair," he fondly recalled. "They waved white handkerchiefs and little flags at us, and looked their sweetest. And didn't we cheer them. . . . We always treasured this incident as a bright, precious link in the chain of memories" (Stillwell 1920: 25). The cheering throngs along the line of march to the front had a euphoric effect on the enthusiastic youth, who were bound for great events. A private in the Crescent Louisiana Regiment, which was hastily organized and rushed north to block Grant's invasion, remembered the train ride between a phalanx of cheering crowds. The young private was taken aback at first and then exhilarated by the enthusiasm of the crowds that lined the tracks. "I imagined much interest was taken in the movements of volunteers, but when you see every woman and child . . . and every man and nigger wave you on with handkerchief or cap . . . you are bound to be elated, moved to do your duty" (*The New Orleans Daily Crescent,* April 7, 1862).

The adulation, however, was not left behind after entraining for the front. Patriotic delegations of civilians and local notables followed the recruits to their camps. Jim Vanderbilt's 23rd Indiana was visited by John L. Davis, a former congressman from Floyd County. Mr. Davis "made a short speech to the soldier boys[.] He spoke to us with tears in his eyes that made us feel bad[.]" Young Vanderbilt also recalled how Davis swore that "before he would have one of his boys come back dishonored . . . he would hear of them both being killed[.] After his speech the boys gave three cheers for him and three for the . . . regiment" (To Aunt, September 5, 1861).

The young recruits appreciated the politicians' visits even more if they were accompanied by young ladies and plenty of food. One such delegation included all three when it arrived at the camp of the 6th Indiana on Thanksgiving day. William Doll and the rest of Company C were delighted when the Loyal Ladies of Louisville's 6th Ward alighted, formed up, and then marched up the hill from the siding.

The Colonel received the delegation and dispatched some soldiers to unload a great number of boxes and baskets. . . . This was a bountiful thanksgiving which they brought us, it is needless to say it was heartily relished by us and that we did it ample justice. . . . The Colonel was requested to form the Regiment in close order, this being done, the Hon James Guthrie then called the silver tongued orator of Ky. mounted the box and made a most inspiring speech to the men concluding by presenting the regiment from the Ladies a beautiful regulation Silk flag. . . . The flag was received by Col. Crittenden [pledging] . . . the Regiment's honor for their loyalty to the flag (Reminiscences, 46–47).

Oratory and flags were fine for morale, food was even better, but the best thing for livening up camp was the visit of "young ladies [who] resolved that regardless of all consequences, [they] would give some tangible and manifest evidence of [their] devotion and adherence to the Union." The men of the 6th Iowa were ever grateful for being favored by such visits to improve their "morale" (*The Daily Gate City*, March 7, 1862).

Eventually the visits petered out as the regiments moved farther afield until their only contact with home came through the mail. There was never enough news from home. "I cant get any news as I steal it by listening at the shoulder strap gentlemen talk," complained J.L. Harris from the camp of the 14th Illinois at Pittsburg Landing (To father and mother, March 21, 1862). Another wrote a letter to the editor of his hometown newspaper to scold his townsmen, "you folks at home must write very often, as the boys who do not get letters when the mail comes look and feel so badly" (*The Howard Tribune*, October 15, 1861). Another recruit confided to his diary the cheering effect of a letter from home.

"I feel very much revived I wish I could hear from home every day[.] It would do me so much good" (W. Ward, September 2, 1861).

The men who filled the ranks of the volunteer armies were literate and evinced a lively interest in politics. To keep abreast of local and national events, they avidly read newspapers, especially the ones from home. A soldier at Pittsburg Landing wrote to the editor calling on the folks at home to make sure that the flow of news be uninterrupted. "Send me your newspapers promptly," he urged. "The only news we can get must be through friends at home. Let them send the soldiers papers, even old ones." To make his point he added, "I was strolling along the river bank [when] my attention was called by a man running at the top of his speed . . . in pursuit of a newsboy." He went on to conclude, "the miser covets not his gold as we our poor souls covet a newspaper" (*The Fremont Daily Journal*, April 11, 1862).

The people at home and the soldiers maintained a mutual surveillance over each other's devotion to the common effort and their patriotism. The volunteers directed their strongest revilement against those people back home who were not holding up their side of the contract by not providing for the volunteers' families while they were at the front. It was hard enough to suffer the hardships of life in the field, but to do so while being concerned for the welfare of their loved ones was almost too much to bear. The soldiers went to war under the assumptions that the community would provide aid and succor to their wives and children and that the neighbors would help plow, harvest, and tend the livestock in their absence. When this help from neighbors was not forthcoming, the men in the army felt betrayed and morale suffered. After all, they saw themselves as the militarized arm of their state and county and when their fellow townsmen failed to fulfill their civilian obligations to the men at the front, they were breaking faith. Compared to profiteers and shirkers, those who failed in their undertaking to care for the men's families were the most reprehensible characters and the worst betrayers of the cause.

In a particularly vivid letter to the newspaper editor in Kokomo, Indiana, Lieutenant W.R. Philips related news from several soldiers whose families had been left in the lurch by their neighbors. He indignantly thundered against those at home who had abandoned his men's families: "O! shame! shame! shame! this morning I was shown a letter by . . . Mr. Julow, from his wife, that made my very flesh creep with feelings of anger and contempt against the neighbors by whom she is surrounded. Mrs. Julow says," continued Philips, "that she has had to carry every stick of wood she has burned—that lately her children have been sick, and that she could not leave them long enough to get her wood." The lieutenant went on to relate how she "had to take her children and leave her home, and go to a neighbor's to keep them warm. [Mr. Julow] . . .

tells us that before he left home, a Mr. John T.," in answer to a remark of his that his family was the only thing that kept him from volunteering, "said that the time had come for every man to put his shoulder to the work, and that if [Julow] . . . would go, he would see that his wife would be provided for." Lieutenant Philips concluded facetiously, "we expect that Mr. T.'s shoulder pains him very much from the large amount of work it has done." The young Hoosier officer then took up the case of another of his men in his indictment of the community. "We are also informed that Harvey Carr of Jerome, got a similar letter from his wife, after being promised by another Mr. T. and others, in a manner similar to the promises of the first named. For God's sake how long is this thing to last? Are the feelings of our brave volunteers to be lacerated by such accounts from home? We do not intend to be mealy-mouthed in this matter, but shall 'plump' right out hereafter the names of those who neglect the trust reposed in them." He concluded his denunciation of his neighbors with a threat on behalf of the men at the front,

we sometimes wish that the band of robbers [the Confederates], that the boys of Howard [County] are helping to keep back, could visit for a few days the homes of certain men scattered here and there all over the state of Indiana. We mean by that, those who have abundance and give not—those who are tories at heart and dare not utter their vile sentiments—those who were in favor of the war and no compromise and who will not go themselves nor let their friends go. We think a little house-burning, horse-stealing, murder and starvation would awaken them to the duties they owe their country and their God (*The Howard Tribune*, November 5, 1861).

The county commissioners often promised that the volunteers' families would never know want (*The Howard Tribune*, November 12, 1861). Sums ranging from one dollar per week per family were appropriated out of county budgets (*The Daily Steubenville Herald*, November 26, 1861). The married men who went off to war assumed that their wives and children would be able to rely on the local authorities to keep them from need, but once they were at the front many began to get letters from their loved ones complaining of penury. The "volunteer funds" that the communities were supposed to set up were either not appropriated or were so inadequate that the families of the soldiers found themselves in want as winter approached. Letters of distress from the soldiers' wives gnawed at their spirits as the men plodded through the dull military routine in their muddy smoky camps. For example, there was George M. Elliott who was serving with Company H, 1st Ohio Volunteers in Harlin County, Kentucky, when he received news that the county had not appropriated enough money to care for the wives and children of the men. "[S]ome of the women," he complained to the newspaper editor in Steubenville, Ohio, "are barely allowed one dollar a week to provide for themselves and four children. Where is the patriotism of our county Commissioners and other stay at home patriots. . . . Our public servants in Jefferson County must remember that . . . [we] will return . . . and consign such political hypocrisy to its dishonored grave." His complaints, alas, were to no avail. His wife continued to report her privations as the winter wore on. Elliott wrote again demanding an explanation and action, "who is to blame? Is it our County Commissioners? Is it the People? Do the tax payers of Jefferson County enter their solemn protest against [support payments for veterans' families], because it would increase their taxes a little?" He concluded by denouncing the venal spirit exhibited by many people back home. "It is a settled matter, beyond contraventions, that there are plenty of people in the loyal States, that don't care whether our Government goes up or down. Their only motto is to still worship the 'Almighty Dollar' " (*The Daily Steubenville Herald*, November 26, 1861, January 26, 1862).

Such people were breaking faith with the soldiers who had gone to fight on their behalf. The volunteers expected that in exchange for risking their lives, the people at home would see to their families. When this trust was betrayed, the men at the front promised retribution. Lieutenant Philips ominously warned his newspaper editor back home that "we . . . repeat that anyone who promised to take care of the families and has not done it, is worse than a perjured villain, and we believe the time coming when vengeance [will be] visited upon the offending by the offended" (*The Howard Tribune*, November 26, 1861).

On the other side of the lines, the same problem existed as well. Among the men under General Gideon J. Pillow, who were manning the fortifications above Memphis, morale was so bad over this issue that the general warned the people back home that he would furlough the men for the winter so that they could provide for their families, because the homefront had apparently abandoned the recruits' kin to their fate (*The Natchez Daily Courier*, October 23, 1861). General Pillow was expressing a widely held assumption among the men of the volunteer armies, that when the tacit commitment was broken, the soldiers had every right to return to their homes.

The bond that tied the homefront to the territorially recruited army was tight and it was supposed to be mutually supporting. It was anchored in the tacit understanding between the recruits and the communities that had sent them in response to the national call. The communities had exercised considerable pressure on their youth to volunteer and they maintained their influence through their letters and the local newspaper. The unspoken "contract" was based on the undertaking that the soldiers would defend their country and their homes, and in exchange their loved ones and neighbors would show the same selfless devotion to their men. Only a handful of the troops were complaining about inadequate homefront support. Those that did denounced civilians back home for harboring traitors and profiteers and for failing to provide for their families while they were at the front. Later in the war, particularly in the South, the states began to realize how important this was to the morale of the men at the front, and an extensive support system began to be put into place to provide help for families of the ordinary soldier.

The volunteers eagerly waited for letters and newspapers with news from home. The post served to keep up morale on both fronts—at home and on the lines—as soldiers often bore the additional burden of bolstering their loved ones' spirits as well as their own. Finally, this citizen army of neighbors and friends was yet able to persevere as long as their loved ones remained faithful and above all remembered them. This they expected, and for the most part, this they received. For contrary to a professional army used to long absence, a citizens' volunteer army relies far more on close supportive ties to the homefront to maintain morale. But this alone was not enough to bear the burdens of war. Morale also depended on the men's stamina to withstand the hardships of combat, and their competence as fighting men to win victories.

TACTICAL COMPETENCE AND HEALTH

"I am well, fat, [and] saucy as a hog," Jim Vanderbilt told his mother in high summer of 1861. His outfit, the 23rd Indiana, had just disembarked in St. Louis and felt fit for whatever rigors the coming campaign would entail (To mother, August 1861). Uniforms had been issued and muskets distributed; the men were improving their tactical proficiency and their officers were starting to gain pride in their units' military skills. Captain James Lawrence boasted, "I have the best drilled and best disciplined company in the Ridgement [61st Illinois]" (To wife, October 15, 1861). Vanderbilt and Lawrence were alluding to two important elements that affected the fighting morale of the green recruits at the Battle of Shiloh: the health and the maneuver competence of the new regiments.

Unit pride was clearly evident among the 120 soldiers who commented about their outfits, two-thirds expressing pride in their unit's tactical competence. Shiloh's green volunteers marched to battle confident that they would be able to outfight their enemy. There was no appreciable difference between the Federals and the Confederates regarding their own and their unit's fighting skills; only one percentage point separated the two sides' troops. When we compared the attitudes of Buell's, Grant's, and Johnston's armies about their military competence, we found, not surprisingly given Buell's reputation for drill and discipline, that Buell's troops tended to be somewhat more confident in their military capabilities than the men in Grant's or A.S. Johnston's armies. Next came the Confederates who had one of the best training officers in either army—Braxton Bragg, commander of the 2nd Corps. Finally, there were the green units in Grant's command, most of whom had only recently reached the front, often almost directly from their depots. These were the newly organized 5th and 6th divisions.

Hyperbole and humor colored much of the boasting about the men's military capability. In Buell's formation, a Hoosier with a penchant for pornographic poetry, Eli Clampitt, chortled confidently to the folks back home, "I think we will trompel their heels for them [so] thare eyes stickes out fer enofe to be snared by a grape vine." Clampitt concluded his eulogy to his comrades' skills crowing a poem to the effect that they were "all good fellows that was not born in the thicket to be scard at a cricket or anything that boasts at night and hides when light" (To brother, October 14, 1861; to friends, November 2, 1861). In Grant's army, Captain Jim Lawrence felt just as sure of the fighting ability of the men of the 61st Illinois Infantry. Having heard rumors that the Confederacy was resorting to the draft to stem the invasion, he concluded they must be desperate, going on to swagger "we can cut our way through there lines Just as we ar a mind to" (To wife, March 1862). And from another Illinois regiment, Lucius Barber boasted that "no prouder regiment stepped to the time of martial music than the 15th" (Barber 1894: 52). The same sentiments were voiced by many of the Confederates. A recent recruit in the 18th Alabama trumpeted to the people of Mobile, "in the all important matter of drill . . . the regiment is surprisingly proficient considering that [it was] two months since probably not fifty of the thousand of the men here present knew a squad from a 'corp d'armee.' In fact," he proudly bragged, "I have not seen a regiment at all equal to it" (The Mobile Register and Advertiser, October 31, 1861). A fellow soldier from Tennessee expressed the same high degree of regimental pride in a letter to his unit's hometown newspaper. "We [the 1st Tennessee from Nashville] have now reached such perfection in drill, especially in the battalion drill that I would be willing to stake my 'pile' on the success of our regiment" (The Republican Banner, July 2, 1861). And as the Southern army coiled itself for its counteroffensive against Grant, John A. Cato of the 7th Mississippi vowed, "if we do not whip the Feds this time I shall always think we ought" (To Martha [wife], March 20, 1862).

In comparison to their high level of confidence in their military skills, the green troops at Shiloh were far less satisfied with their physical fitness. Overall, the soldiers were almost evenly divided between those who felt fit and those whose comments tended to reflect a pessimistic assessment of their physical condition.[6] When the troops were divided by nationality, the Union troops had a somewhat higher level of confidence (one out of two) in their stamina and general health than their enemies—two out of five of the Confederates felt fit. This is not surprising because death rates were higher in the Confederate army.[7]

Disease and death rampaged through the ranks. Unit after unit fell further below strength as the winter campaign wore on. The 31st Indiana left a trail of bodies to ship home as it trudged south; twenty-seven cadavers were left in Evansville. When they crossed into Kentucky, they left forty-five more for shipment north (J.B. Connelley, Diary, December 30, 1861). The 31st was still able to send the bodies home "in style," having a supply of tin coffins available as far as Calhoun, Kentucky, but as it progressed farther south, the stock gave out (J.F. Fee to brother, December 21, 1861).

Campaigning in winter was a hard test for raw recruits, not yet enured to living out-of-doors. Henry Backus' Company D, 14th Illinois Infantry, was down to 61 men out of its original complement of 101 by January 1862 (Diary, January 1, 1862). John Hardin's 23rd Indiana reported that "the *regi*[ments] . . . average 500 and not more," adding that "ours is the largest and we have only 650 for duty" out of 1,000 (To J.A. Cravens, Cravens Collection, March 25, 1862). Peter Bailey's company "lost seven men in the last five days, and several more are not expected to survive." His regiment, the 30th Indiana had 73 men in the hospital at Camp Nevin, Kentucky, after the cold weather set in in late November (To Mrs. McCulloch, November 29, 1861). Seeing comrades die one after the other, Jim Vanderbilt of the 23rd Indiana at Paducah lamented, "it seems like weare bound to have a funeral every sundy" (To mother, September 22, 1861). Winter persisted into March dousing Grant's army with cold rains as "men died by the score like rotten sheep," wrote Leander Stillwell with the 61st Illinois (Stillwell 1920: 37). A.S. Johnston's men were in poor condition too, when they fell back from Bowling Green to Nashville. Things had already been bad in Bowling Green, where 4,000 of his effectives were sick. By the time the army staggered into Nashville, an estimated one-third needed some sort of medical care (Baird 1978: 46). Jim Crozier was among them, noting that his 3rd Kentucky Volunteers (C.S.A.) was already down to 66 percent of strength and still declining (Diary, December 2, 1861). So that as the men campaigned, their physical stamina in no way matched their high confidence in their soldierly abilities.

NOTES

1. Thirty-four of the soldiers discussed army life in their diaries and letters. Of these a large majority had generally positive comments with the rest expressing mostly negative reactions and often suggesting that they would like to be out of it if an honorable way could be found.

2. The 32nd Illinois was part of the "Ten-regiment call." It arrived at Bird's

Point on January 20 to relieve the 8th Illinois. It had one company, Company A, actively engaged in the fighting at Fort Donelson. That detachment only guarded a battery and sustained only "slight" casualties. For these reasons, it has been included among the green units at Shiloh.

3. State militia regiments were not subdivided into battalions during the war. Sometimes several companies would be split off for tactical purposes, but this would be strictly a temporary arrangement.

4. Van Creveld (1982: 75) pointed out this was a factor in the superiority of the German army over American units in World War II. The United States army no longer relied on territorial recruiting for its regular forces. This was in contrast to German policy.

5. Sixty-seven of the recruits commented to some extent on their officers. A respectable majority were satisfied with the leadership, despite the officers' inexperience.

6. Seventy-four men wrote about the health of the army in their letters and diaries.

7. The death rate in the Confederate army during the first year of the war was 3.81 percent, whereas it was only 2.01 percent in the Union army (G.W. Adams 1952: 14).

3

Campaigning

ENTERING THE WAR ZONE

The Western armies at last shook themselves into motion and headed toward the front. We will look through the eyes of the soldiers to see how they reacted to the people and places of the war zone and to see how this affected their morale. "All things look like marching," wrote a soldier to Howard County, Indiana, as the regiment's baggage was lightened, the men were issued their forty rounds of ammunition, and they embarked on steamers (*The Howard Tribune*, November 12, 1861). The army of volunteers were at last en route to the war zone.

No one would have thought there was a war on as the convoys headed to the front. The country along the rivers looked peaceful enough, at least until the first sign of hostilities emerged starkly from the surroundings gliding by. For Levi Minkler and the 18th Wisconsin, steaming up the Tennessee River, the first sign of hostility was "a dead man floating" past, bobbing on the wash of their steamboat (Diary, n.d.). Union troops encountered their first hostile reception in the war zone as they steamed along the south shore of the Ohio. Passing Concordia, Kentucky, a volunteer with the 15th Indiana saw "a secesh tatter demalion" appear along the riverbank; "the boys . . . hollowed to him to take off his hat and hurrah the Union. Where upon he commenced cursing . . . and hurrahed Jeff. Davis, when one of the boys turned his Colt in that direction and fired" (*The Princeton Clarion*, February 15, 1862). Shooting at hostile civilians was not an isolated incident. Jesse Connelley's men in Company I, 31st Indiana killed a Kentuckian near Ashneysburg, Kentucky; he had shouted insults at the Union convoys. The civilians retaliated by hiding along the banks and sniping at the passing steamers. In reprisal, Connelley's men turned a six pounder on the snipers (Diary, September 23, 1861).[1]

Both Confederate and federal recruits described the people of the border region disparagingly. The mode of dress was a target for Lieutenant Frank Doyle. "Every man . . . wears jeans—every boy wears jeans—every nigger wears jeans, and some women—wear jeans," he reported home to Iowa (*The Dubuque Daily Times*, April 26, 1862).[2] An Alabamian serving in Tennessee shared the Hawk-eye soldier's curiosity about the people in the area. He found the "women are large, healthy, strong, ugly and stupid. . . . [And] the men are entirely worthy of the women" (*The Mobile Advertiser and Register*, September 1, 1861). Elihu Squiggs, another Alabamian, wrote to a pal that the Kentucky women were not like those back home in Mobile, "it is true they have the same number of legs, but they've lived in the swamps so long they look like alligators" (*The Natchez Daily Courier*, February 4, 1862). The ladies of Missouri also got a bad press from the Iowa troops. Alexander Downing remembered attending a dance with some of his friends from Company E of the 11th Iowa. The girls "either smoked or chewed tobacco." Worse yet, their affection for tobacco impeded their dancing. "They dance a while, then rest and smoke, but those that chewed did not care to stop" even during the dancing, he complained (Downing 1916: 28).

The border region of Kentucky, Tennessee, and Missouri was a land of complex loyalties, an area where both armies had enemies among the civilian population. They sensed they were not welcome. The troops felt enveloped in cold hostility. Landing at Henderson, Kentucky, J. Connelley noted ominously in his diary, "we are now among the rebels and expect stirring times" (September 23, 1861; see also H. E. Backus, Diary, July 5, 1861). A Buck-eye infantryman voiced his own sense of foreboding as his unit moved deeper into hostile territory. "The further we get . . . the larger the *elephant* gets" (*The Lima Weekly Gazette*, October 9, 1861).

An army fighting among its own people has a decided morale advantage over the invader. Their reasons for fighting are more clear-cut and immediate. But in the border region, neither army felt that the population was totally committed to their side. The Southern troops, especially from the Gulf states, accused the population of tendering only marginal support and of panicking in the face of the Union advance, while the Northern troops were embittered by guerrilla attacks, bridge burning, and other forms of sabotage.

For all these reasons, the reactions to the people and places of the war zone were generally negative. Four out of five soldiers voiced unfavorable impressions. They wrote of the devastation, the hostility of the civilians, the poverty, the inequality that was associated with the slave economy, and the sniping and sabotage in the war zone. This was just as true of the Confederates as of the Unionists.[3] The Confederates also surprisingly evinced hostile comments about the people of the border region they were supposed to be defending from invasion. Like their adversary, they felt that the population was disloyal to the Confederate cause.[4] Campaigning in such a hostile environment could only have a corrosive effect on morale.

The mixed loyalties of the northwestern arc of the Confederacy, encompassing Missouri, western Tennessee, and Kentucky, was typified by the very county where the Battle of Shiloh was fought. Hardin County, Tennessee, was known for its pro-North sentiments (*The New Orleans Daily Crescent*, April 7, 1862). And further west in Memphis, there were elements among the business class who were decidedly unhappy with the economic decline that followed the Union blockade of the Mississippi, which was strangling the city's traditional links with the rest of the Mississippi Valley. Assistant Surgeon Lunsford Yandell of the 4th Tennessee, manning the fortifications at Columbus, recalled that "[t]he citizens are decidedly leary" of a battle to defend Memphis. "Capital," he astutely remarked, "is always timid, and property holders naturally dread the approach of the enemy" (To daughter, November 20, 1861). What was the point of sacrificing one's life for places such as Memphis, if their citizenry was not as committed to the cause as the soldiers who were there defending them?

As the guerrilla war became more nasty and brutish, it hardened the troops. War was becoming personalized, it was turning into a mean business against a cruel and treacherous enemy. The change was reflected in the letters of William Richardson, a native Missourian who had moved north to Half Breed Tract, Iowa, and had joined the 6th Iowa Infantry. Richardson believed that "the only way to get the country rid of these sneaking devils . . . is to play their own game. Just shoot them down where ever we find them" (To father and mother, December 1, 1861). Others were hardening their attitude toward the Southern sympathizers and they too were calling for a more brutal war policy. Believing that Southern collaborators were even poisoning the men's food, Sergeant John J. Hardin, Company E, 23rd Indiana, declared, "I always had some sympathy for them til now but the time has come that I could burn every one of them" (To father, Cravens Collection, August 8, 1861). Edwin Sackett, with the same regiment, believed that only such a brutal policy would put an end to the guerrilla movement. "I don't know any other way to subdue them [except] . . . to shoot them or hang them up and confiscate their property" (To family and friends, December 27, 1861). A Wisconsin soldier reflected this transformation when he affirmed, "I honestly believe every man of them who owns a slave is a rebel at heart. Many of them are loud mouthed in their union professions while union troops are in force in their neighborhood; but as we get further south I expect (so bitter are they) that assassinations, picket shooting, etc., will be frequent. I am inclined to think that extermination only will ever fetch back a union sentiment in the hearts of our 'southern brethren' " (C. R. Johnson in Quiner, Reel No. 2, Vol. 5, p. 139).

The Northern recruits were also struck by the poverty and backwardness of western Kentucky and southwestern Tennessee. A soldier from Wisconsin estimated that "from general appearances of things[,] I should judge that the people of the western part of Tennessee are 175 years behind the people of Jackson County in agriculture" (C. R. Johnson in Quiner, Reel No. 2, Vol. 5, p. 139). A Hoosier noted the rarity of mowing machines and revolving hay rakes on Southern farms (*The Daily State Sentinel*, August 8, 1861).

Some Federals came to believe that slavery itself was a major contributing factor to the backwardness of the region, by relegating all labor to the black population and allowing the rise of an indolent and arrogant class of whites, who used their leisure to foment treason. Sergeant F. J. Beck sent home his first report from the Confederacy immediately after his regiment, the 30th Indiana, had marched through Nashville. "We have at least come into a part of the country in which all the benefit that can be derived from the institution of slavery is enjoyed by the citizens." Beck went on to observe that "very little labor is performed except by slaves who are much more ignorant and degraded than in Kentucky" (*The Indiana True Republican*, March 20, 1862). While white men apparently lounged about, the economy of the South was built on the exploitation of black servile labor—male or female, child or adult. This outraged William Ward. He was indignant over the sight of a "Negro woman plowing in the field. It looks Strong to me," he maintained, "to See a woman with a team and plow doing the work of a *lazy white man*" (Diary, March 12, 1862).

Here they were, at last, in the land of magnolias and mint juleps, crowned by luxurious manor houses and supposedly peopled by a fine landed gentry. But these preconceptions of the South quickly dissipated in the reality of war. The Union volunteers found, instead, a poor region where "[the] people owning . . . slaves live no better off than many a logging shanty up in the pine woods of Wisconsin," observed C. R. Johnson as he marched through the region with a Wisconsin regiment (Quiner, Reel No. 2, Vol. 5, p. 139). This theme was echoed in other regiments serving in the area. E. E. Thornton, with the 39th Indiana, commented, "The soil is poor as well as the people—they have worn out the soil by careless slave cultivation" (*The Howard Tribune*, October 15, 1861). George Elliott of the 1st Ohio reported home, "If it were not for the sale of their surplus negroes, they would starve to death" (*The

Daily Steubenville Herald, November 26, 1861; see also J. F. Drish to wife, March 20, 1862).

These unflattering impressions of the border region were shared by Confederate troops from the Gulf states, an area that had been settled longer than the area of southwestern Tennessee.[5] A Confederate gunner with the Washington Artillery, William S. Vaught of the battalion's 5th Company, thought Grand Junction, Tennessee, was the "meanest place it has ever been my lot to be stuck [in]" (To Albert [brother], March 22, 1862). Another Gulf state recruit from the Mobile area felt the same way, declaring that Tennessee was "the poorest, meanest country I ever stopped in, and the people are poorer and meaner than the country" (*The Mobile Advertiser and Register,* September 1, 1861). Neither Union soldiers, nor the Confederates from other areas of the south, realized they were moving into an area that had been passed over in the first wave of westward expansion. The band of land on each side of the Tennessee river had been settled for less than forty years. Capital was just building up and farmers were investing in land and equipment, not houses and clothes. Comments about the older, more settled areas that the armies had marched through were more favorable (T. Harrison to wife, March 5, 1862).[6]

There were Northern volunteers who were coming to the conclusion that slavery was the root cause of the area's underdevelopment and was also the cause of the Civil War. It was an evil that was dragging the rest of the country down just as it had already done in the South. A young trooper with the 3rd Battalion, 4th Illinois Cavalry articulated this view. "With . . . [its abundant recourses] this region ought to be in the forefront of trade and overflowing with prosperity and high life. Yet . . . a curse has paralyzed enterprise, checked commercial activity, deadened everything. Nature and Providence have done all that it is possible to do for any land in offering it such ample resources and opportunities. But all these advantages are wasted, clean thrown away, just as long as slavery is revered and worshipped as the sacred institution" (Young 1894: 53).

By the time the Union troops had finally completed their campaigns in Missouri and Kentucky and had reached southwestern Tennessee, they were convinced of the superiority of their political and economic system and were confident that they could, with flame and sword, extend its "benefits" to the benighted South. The area around Shiloh Meeting House, where the battle was to be decided, ironically exemplified the backwardness of the entire country. The land was hardly worth "$3 per acre," according to a soldier with the 72nd Ohio in Sherman's division (*The Fremont Daily Journal,* April 11, 1862). The 72nd regiment was at the forefront of the battle and would pay dearly in other coin for the miserable piece of real estate. It was a place "it may do to fight and die for but it was too backward to earn a living on," according to Sam Sheperdson of the 30th Indiana Infantry (To sister, May 13, 1862).

Marching on muddy roads, delayed by wrecked bridges, and camping under the leaden skies of winter must have taken its emotional toll on the men in both armies. By then the war had already become drab, toilsome, and bitter. Gone were the bunting and banners that had brightened the warm hues of the previous summer. All around them was desolation. All was gray, black, and brown, and everything stank; dead livestock, charred buildings and bridges, rotting carrion, and polluted water characterized the war zone (A. Varian to father, February 19, 1862).[7] In Missouri, George Hamman recalled how the 14th Illinois eagerly quenched their thirst at a water tank only to find a corpse bobbing in it. Needless to say it "caused considerable heaving and vomiting" among the hapless infantrymen (Diary, n.d.).

The retreat from Bowling Green eroded Southern morale. In reprisal, the retreating Confederates implemented a scorched-earth policy. A soldier with the 6th Indiana described the hell-like appearance of the war zone as the troops advanced deeper into Kentucky. Ahead "parties of rebel cavalry were seen ... about three-quarters of a mile distant. ... Their fires were distinctly seen in the distance, which proved to be barns, outhouses, grain and hay stacks, and straw piles set on fire. ... Stock of various kinds have been killed by them and thrown in the ponds along the route to decompose and render the water unfit for use. This is very cowardly, and shows their hopelesness" (*The Daily State Sentinel,* January 18, 1862). After Bowling Green, the sights were even more depressing. Captain William S. Bradford commanded Company J of the 57th Indiana on the road from Bowling Green to Nashville and described how "the destruction to the country is beyond anything you can conceive. Some places for miles in extent there is not a rail to be seen[,] the fences all having been burned by the soldiers ... not even yard fences of no kind have escaped, and in some instances some pretty good houses been torn down and used for fuel. It makes one feel sad even though it is rebel country to see large nice farms in such dilapidated condition" (To Lucie [wife], March 6, 1862).

The nadir of the Confederate retreat happened on the bridge over the Cumberland River to Nashville. The Cumberland was open to Union gunboats now that Fort Donelson had fallen; the soldiers and civilians feared that they would be cut off at any moment on the north side of the river. Panic ensued on the city's two bridges when A. S. Johnston's men heard rumors that Buell was six miles north of them and the gunboats were approaching to close the trap. There was jostling on one of the bridges, while others scrambled away from the riverbank apprehensive that they would be caught in the gunboats' line of fire. On the other side, in Nashville, "the grand depot of wholesale speculation and swindling" was dying. It was being abandoned—"a death blow to the valor of Tennesseans," according to W. H. Mott, a staff officer with the 24th Tennessee Volunteer Infantry. For Mott, the sight that day of the destruction and abandoment of Nashville was the saddest sight he saw before his death at Murfreesboro. "Of all gloomy pictures that I have witnessed, the one presented on that morning wore the palm, the streets and the walk were a complete jam of citizens and soldiers with down cast looks and muddy clothes. Stores . . . closed, people were vacating houses . . . government stores were being distributed to the people . . . wholesale plundering of the government property" was in progress (Mott 1946: 239–40). The city was in panic; the mobs bent on plundering the government stores were impeding Colonel Nathan Bedford Forrest's efforts to carry off whatever equipment and food could still be evacuated. The scene turned ugly when civilians clashed with soldiers over the spoils. The cavalrymen had to deploy and beat the crowd off with the flat of their sabers; fire hoses soaked the crowd with muddy river water (Foote 1958: I, 216).

Destruction, not glory, was left in the wake of the army on the march. It was a sad and miserable sight to behold. "God spare our State from the horrors of Civil war, its famine, its murders and all its accursed evils," lamented Lieutenant W. R. Philips in a letter from the 6th Indiana Regiment (*The Howard Tribune*, July 2, 1861). A Confederate concurred warning that "the advent of an army is . . . to be dreaded by any people . . . for wholesale destruction is sure to follow in its wake." He estimated that "the mere passing of an army renders a country almost worthless for at least one or two years" (Mott 1946: 244).

The war zone had a sobering impact on the volunteers. The destruction, the hostility of the populace, and the frustrations and discomforts inherent in campaigning hardened the recruits of both sides. For many Confederates, the civilians of Kentucky and Tennessee were at best half-hearted supporters of the cause of Southern independence. For the federal troops, they were either neutral or enemy sympathizers, who did not deserve the army's protection. The conduct of the war was quickly becoming harsher. It was already becoming an implacable conflict—a total war!

PERCEPTIONS OF THE OBJECTIVES AND CONDUCT OF THE CAMPAIGN

"Old Jollycoffer [General Felix Zollicoffer, C.S.A.] . . . has been whipped and what is better been *killed* [at the Battle of Logan's Cross Roads]. Is not this glorious news by his defeat and death," rejoiced Ross Ingerson when the 15th Indiana got the news of the first Union victory of the new year. "Johnson [Johnston] and Buckner's right-flank is left exposed," Ingerson explained to a friend, but the amateur strategist vented his impatience at the pace of the campaign by noting that "this should . . . be improved by our Generals, but I suppose that *the* time for our advance has not yet arrived, and I begin to think it never will" (James M. Cole from Ingerson, Cole Papers, January 28, 1862). Ingerson's comment points to an important element in the combination of factors that affect the morale of an army. It suggests the importance of a shared perception among all ranks of the army's mission. This is especially true of a citizens' army whose recruits had volunteered for a great cause. Such soldiers fight best when there is a consensus on the political issues at stake, when they understand the strategic and tactical objectives, and when they believe that the campaign is being led competently.

Frequently, it appears that the common soldier is indifferent and ignorant about the strategic and tactical implications of his army's movements; that his view of the campaign is confined to parochial concerns such as safety, shelter, and food; and that he has no interest in or even the capability of measuring the effectiveness of political and military high command. In this light, the enlisted man is only a cog in the military machine. His morale is only a function of proper training, logistical support, and command.

To the contrary, it is argued, along with Kellett (1982: 251) and Marshall (1947: 105), that soldiers assess the strategic significance of their army's actions, and this in turn has an important bearing on their morale. The better a soldier knows what is going on, the more effectively he can cooperate in working toward the goals at hand. This was especially true in the volunteer armies of 1861–62, whose recruits were not as amenable as professionals to organizational constraints and blind obedience.

The volunteers who went to fight at Shiloh had a fairly clear idea of the general outline of the campaign, and their awareness of the "big picture" fostered morale by integrating the men into the aims of their respective armies. Yet, the men were impatient with their generals for the slow pace of the operations and the generals' perceived reluctance to come to grips with the enemy and administer a decisive blow. The recruits had no patience for a limited war over the disposition of this or that boundary or fortress. It was a total war fought by "nations in arms," for unconditional terms. A young Illinois soldier in Company A, 32nd Infantry, encapsulated this vision of the war when he wrote to his friend, "I have no desire to see the thing ended until it can be thoroughly ended, and honorable too. If ruin comes to the South[,] She can not reproach us for it, for she has willfully brought it upon herself" (J. P. Snell to John G. Copley, June 2, 1861). While the nations' military and political leadership hoped for a limited war and a quick peace and—at least in the North—were closing recruitment offices. The rank and file saw it as a life or death struggle. For a young Kentuckian, "The success of one party is the annihilation of the other; for no matter which side is victorious, the vanquished people are abolished as a nation." Total war must be fought to the finish, because "neither party can afford to give up" (Lunsford Yandell to sister [Sally], February 26, 1862).

The volunteers viewed the conflict in dramatic terms even at this early stage of the campaign. Their perception proved more accurate than their leaders. It is appropriate, however, to point out that the purpose of this work is not to evaluate the tactical and strategic theories of the armies' high command, but rather the perceptions that the average soldier had of what the generals were up to during the campaign. And in this regard, the men firmly believed that the generals were not prosecuting the war aggressively. The generals appeared to be predicating their strategy on a classic war of maneuver, a limited war of an earlier age.[8] Along this line, T. Harry Williams contends that they were still inspired by the ideas of Jomini, Mahan, and other theorists of the classic age in Europe (1962: 40).[9]

For their part, the soldiers sought a fight to the finish, preferably in one big battle where the issues would be put to the test by the soldiers of the two sides. Their strategic objective was not geographic, it was the destruction of the enemy. Maneuvers were significant only to the extent that they brought the soldiers to the killing field. For the average soldier, war was a straightforward affair of killing so many of the enemy that they would have to capitulate or be wiped out. Geographic objectives such as railroad junctions, navigable rivers, or industrial centers were really secondary to the actual killing of the enemy. One of A. S. Johnston's Tennessee volunteers reported disdainfully that the Confederate army and the Union forces were merely "having a very interesting dance" (*The Republican Banner*, October 11, 1861).

The vast majority of the volunteers believed the generals were not pursuing the war with enough vigor.[10] As the winter approached, their impatience grew. How was it that after all these months, after the mobilization of such enormous armies of volunteers, they had not yet been used? Was this great army to be squandered in an indecisive campaign that would prolong the war? A soldier with the 49th Ohio Volunteer Infantry, fretted at the delay. "Our army is large enough for an advance, but it looks as if this was a peaceful war against the rebels." He chided the leadership "for such dilatory action," and he demanded, "let the war be prosecuted with vigor" (*The Fremont Daily Journal*, November 22, 1861).

This sentiment was especially strong among Buell's troops as they slowly progressed up the Louisville and Nashville railway. A Buck-eye volunteer in Buell's army vented this reaction to his hometown newspaper. "Winter is upon us, and yet no battle has been fought; no victory tells of the bravery of our men, and no trophies tell of the daring exploits"

(*The Fremont Daily Journal*, November 22, 1861). Later, after Grant fought the Battle of Belmont, the despairing Ohioan lamented that in comparison to Grant, Buell's army "are like Old Maids. . . . Ready but not wanted" (*The Fremont Daily Journal*, December 13, 1861). Buell's "wall flowers" did not even get invited to the reception when Grant captured forts Henry and Donelson, and later Grant even sent a detachment up the Cumberland to get to Nashville in the Army of the Ohio's zone of operation. Dr. George R. Weeks, the surgeon of the 24th Ohio Volunteers with Buell, grumbled, "I am tired of the system of warfare, known and characterized as 'masterly inactivity.' I don't believe in the doctrine, and it is not my mode of doing business." Weeks characterized the rank and file's belief in total war writing, "I have some where, the text, that, 'Whatever thy hand findeth to do, do it with all thy might' " (*The Tiffin Weekly Tribune*, February 21, 1862; see also *The Fremont Daily Journal*, February 14, 1862).

Grant was also chided when the offensive seemed to have come to a halt short of Corinth, Mississippi. Captain Harley Wayne, commanding Company D, 15th Illinois Infantry, criticized Grant for yielding the initiative to A. S. Johnston. How was it that after the daring February moves, the army now lay quiescent? Was Grant under orders to halt according to some Eastern "scheme to assist Genl McClellan and to enable him to face wooden guns in Virginia?" he asked in a letter to his wife (To wife [Ellen], April 4, 1862).[11] Wayne foretold his own death, which occurred two days later at Shiloh, when he warned that A.S. Johnston "may concentrate and get strong enough to attack and overwhelm us" (To wife [Ellen], April 4, 1862). Along with Colonel Everett Peabody, who commanded the 1st Brigade of the 6th Division and who sent out the patrol that met the advancing Confederate force on the morning of April 6, men such as Wayne proved more astute in assessing the enemy's intentions that Sunday morning than many of the upper echelon.

Among the Confederates, the fall of Fort Donelson and Fort Henry made many "down spirited" (J. E. Magee, Diary, February 1862). A "wild hour is upon us," Lunsford Yandell wrote; the assistant surgeon realized that withdrawal was imminent. Nashville, he feared, must now fall too, and his home state, Kentucky, would have to be abandoned to the enemy. "But," he vowed, "still there will remain a small band of patriots, who will oppose the Usurper." It was going to be a war to the finish, "because to end the war and allow us to leave [their homes] would be their destruction. [Thus] . . . our only hope of avoiding destruction and utter ruin is to fight our way through our troubles and conquer our independence" (To sister [Sally], February 26, 1862). The perusal of their diaries and correspondence suggests that the ordinary soldiers were adequately informed to measure the progress of the campaign and were able to deduce the goals of their commander. The main reason is that the soldiers had access to local and national newspapers. The newspapers came by steamboat, which was only twenty-four hours from St. Louis. The steamboat captains—private contractors ever out to make each trip pay well—could easily load up with newspapers to sell in the camps. Mess mates shared the newspapers and passed them on to other soldiers. They read them avidly throughout the campaign. Because censorship was non-existent, the press freely reported the location, estimated the numbers, and the expected intentions of the protagonists. For example, the local newspapers even printed lists of all the state's regiments and gave their locations each month (*The Daily State Sentinel*, December 29, 1861). Also, the front lines in the Civil War were porous allowing a relatively unimpeded flow of news between the North and the South. Thus, newspapers carried the reports of both sides. For example, *The Republican Banner*, in Nashville, carried reports from *The New York Herald* (June 6, 1861). The recruits frequently commented on strategic questions in their letters to the editor of their hometown newspaper. Their observations were generally quite accurate regarding the broad strategic objectives of the campaign. On the other hand, when it came to estimating the size of their forces or those of the enemy, they were often wide of the mark. But here the men were not alone. Most of the commanding generals consistently overestimated the enemy strength as well.

It would be useful to travel with the Northern soldiers to find out how they perceived the conduct of the campaign as it progressed. Operations began with Grant's riverine operation in western Kentucky. No one knew for sure where he would go, although there were three likely avenues of invasion: via (1) the Mississippi River and the fort at Columbus, Kentucky, (2) the Tennessee River and Fort Henry and Fort Heiman, and (3) the Cumberland River defended by Fort Donelson. After reviewing these possibilities, Corporal William Ross of the 40th Illinois guessed that it would be Columbus. His calculations were sound, because ultimately the Mississippi was the most important objective of the Western theater of operations (To father, January 2, 1862). Jesse B. Connelley's reasoning proved more accurate as he pondered the objective of his regiment, the 31st Indiana. "From the best information I can get, we are going either up the Cumberland or the Tennessee River. If up the Tennessee," he astutely surmised, "our destination will be Fort Henry, if up the Cumberland, Fort Donelson" (Diary, February 10, 1862). Thaddeus Capron was with the 55th Illinois waiting to embark from Paducah to join in the offensive against Fort Henry. He knew enough geography to accurately locate Fort Henry. Capron situated it "about fifty miles on the Tennessee River," but he totally underestimated its strategic significance, brushing it off as "a point of little importance" (1919: 339).

After Fort Donelson fell, Francis Bruce and his comrades of the 14th Illinois tried to determine what the next move would be. Being on the Cumberland, the next operation had to be against Nashville (To mother, February 1862). He was right, but the 14th was once again not involved in the action; instead it was sent up the Tennessee to Pittsburg Landing. Now that the Cumberland and the Tennessee had been opened, the men and Grant would move against Corinth.

George Elliott's 1st Ohio Volunteers were waiting impatiently for the bridge over the Green River to be completed. He understood the strategic implications of the fall of Fort Donelson and accurately predicted that Grant's gunboats could seize Nashville. Elliott also showed a keen interest in the political consequences of Tennessee's capital. "Whenever our army approaches Nashville the spirit of Parson Brownlow [a Union sympathizer] will again roam over the mountains of East Tennessee. The persecuted martyrs who have lost their all by their tried devotion to the cause of their country, will fly to the sabre and bayonet" (*The Daily Steubenville Herald,* January 20, 1862). After the Tennessee and Cumberland rivers were opened up and Nashville fell, Grant's men believed that there would be an ascent of the Tennessee to Decatur or Florence, Alabama (*The Aurora Beacon,* March 20, 1862). As J. J. Hardin's 23rd Indiana stood at Fort Heiman, Kentucky, waiting to embark on the next invasion flotilla, he guessed the next objective would be Florence, because it would put the army into the deep South. From there they could cut the rebel supply lines through northern Alabama and eventually even move on Mobile (J. J. Hardin to Mandi [sister], Hardin Letters, March 4, 1862; see also J. Vanderbilt to mother, March 4, 1862; A. Varian to Hettie [sister], March 28, 1862).

However, when the shoals above Eastport, Mississippi, prevented riverboats from reaching Florence, the next Union objective became the rail junction at Corinth, Mississippi. The concentration point became Pittsburg Landing. As the troops assembled there, frequent skirmishes signalled the proximity of the Confederates, who were also marshaling their forces at Corinth twenty miles away (J. Connelley, Diary, March 30, 1862). The soldiers' letters and diaries often referred to a big battle in the offing. It would be the big one; rumor had it that "General Sherman thinks the Waterloo of the war will be fought between this place and the Miss[issippi] River in the course of two weeks," wrote Colonel Cassius Fairchild (To Sarah [sister], March 21, 1862; see also G. W. Levally to father and mother, March 30, 1862). But George Hamman, with the 14th Illinois, correctly judged that Grant would wait "until Buels Army arrive from the northeast" (Diary, March 20, 1862).

The Union ranks' estimates of the size of the opposing armies were not as accurate as their understanding of the objectives of the campaign. They tended to guess that the opposing armies were twice as large as they really were. Letters and diary entries between March 21 and 29 estimated that Grant had 100,000 men at Pittsburg Landing and Buell's army had 50,000; while the Confederates were thought to have between 70,000 and 125,000 men massing at Corinth to decide the war (J. Lawrence to aunt, March 30, 1862; C. Fairchild to Sarah [sister], March 21, 1862; T. Capron 1919: 343; E. C. Sackett to family, March 21, 1862; J. F. Drish to wife, March 23 and 29, 1862).[12]

Meanwhile on the Confederate side, they too felt the next battle would be the biggest and most decisive engagement. A member of the 16th Louisiana explained the strategy to his sister from Corinth in the middle of March. "We could have attacked them and driven them to their boats long since, but the idea is to get them some distance from their gunboats and then we will show them a trick" (J. Ellis to sister, March 18, 1862).

The coming encounter would be the ultimate paroxysm. And such a decisive struggle had, perforce, to involve the largest dramatic cast; numbers had to be commensurate with the battle's significance for the cause. John L. Harris, an infantryman with the 14th Illinois, assumed that the rebels were concentrating all their forces in the west to fight the battle that would decide the war. "Since the evacuation of Manasses, Richmon & Collumbus without opposition . . . it seems like they thought some other place would suit their convenience better. And this [Pittsburg Landing] may be the place. If they make a stand here . . . [i]t will be with the combined force of Manases[,] Richmond[,] Collumbus and those tha[t] Floid and Pillow stole away from Donelson. . . . I suppose if we have a fight . . . it will be the hardest battle of the war and the last one. If we don't fight I don't believe we will have anymore of it" (To father and mother, March 21, 1862). The question in the Union soldiers' minds was how would the Confederates go about making their last stand. Most of the correspondence assumed that the Confederates were not going to carry the battle to the Unionists, but instead would try to draw the Yankees into attacking them in their improved positions around Corinth. Cassius Fairchild wrote, "It is thought that the Rebels will not make much of a stand at Purdy [southwest of Pittsburg Landing], but will fall back to Corinth as we advance. The latter place is said to be strongly fortified" (To Sarah [sister], March 21, 1862; see also Leroy Guthrie to family, April 4, 1862; W. C. Robinson to brother, March 29, 1862). But it was this assumption that worried Colonel Thomas J. Harrison. "The war is progressing very fast, but the enemy may concentrate their forces at some point and in despair may make a formidable resistance which . . . will greatly prolong the struggle, *Our Army is becoming too easy going and less careful*" [emphasis added] (To wife [Louisa], March 5, 1862).

Harrison turned out to be right. The Southern troops had been driven to grim desperation after their long retreat. Mirroring this attitude, Augustus Mecklin wrote from the ranks of the 15th Mississippi that "our men are anxious to see the matter decided and if a battle must be fought, let it be fought now" (Diary, March 20, 1862; see also *The Opelousas Courrier/Le Courier des Opelousas,* March 15, 1862). Watching the arrival of regiment after regiment, James O. Knighton of the 4th Louisiana Infantry was also sure that "the big battle will come off at Corinth in a few days" (To family, April 1, 1862). There were several rumors "afloat as to the strength and purposes of the Federals," wrote Captain John W. Caldwell, a Confederate Kentuckian. "We are going to attack the enemy on the Tenn River and [General Earl] Van Dorn and [General Sterling] Price have crossed the Mississippi to reinforce Genrl Johnson's [sic] Army" (Diary, April 3, 1862). The rumor that Captain Caldwell referred to was generally accurate; the trans-Mississippi army was hastening to join A. S. Johnston, before Grant's force had a chance to link up with Buell. Meanwhile, Grant was of the opinion that nothing would happen at Pittsburg Landing. He too expected the next battle to be at Corinth, Mississippi, and he believed that he would win it and the Civil War would be over in the West. He was basing all of his plans on what he expected the enemy would do, not what the enemy could do.

The soldiers on both sides realized that the climax was at hand, and they believed that this great engagement would be so big and bloody that it would decide the outcome of the war. This dramatic conception emanated from the fact that it was a people's war that could only end in total victory and the slaughter of the enemy. It was not a classic war of maneuver with strategic geographic objectives. Shiloh turned out to conform to what the troops expected, not to what Buell or Grant or certainly not Halleck wanted. The recruits took a keen interest in the strategy of the campaign. They followed the reports of their movements in the press and made their own observations. They became impatient with their generals' conduct of the war. They believed that their leaders were delaying the decision, because the great battle had, heretofore, been deferred in Kentucky and Tennessee. When, however, the armies finally came to a stop at Corinth, Mississippi, and Pittsburg Landing, the rank and file accurately perceived that the great moment was at hand. They sought battle so that they could get it over with one fell swoop. Then having at last decided the issue, the soldiers would return home heroes. They had enlisted for a great cause; they wanted to be direct principals in deciding its outcome. They wanted the most dramatic moment of their entire life to coincide with the most decisive moment in the life of their country. Only a great battle was appropriate for such great commitments and such a great issue.

ASSUMPTIONS ABOUT ENEMY EFFECTIVENESS

News of victory buoyed Union morale. The conviction that the Confederates were ineffective fighters came across emphatically in the Northerners' correspondence (Saul Howell, Diary, February 7 and 13, 1862; Josephus Cunningham to unidentified recipient, March 26, 1862; J. Kirkpatrick to John Walters, January 30, 1862; W. J. Kennedy to wife, February 17, 1862; *The Howard Tribune*, February 11, 1862; Boyd 1953: 19). In Buell's command, Colonel William H. Gibson of the 49th Ohio Volunteers blithely assured his wife to "fear not as to fighting," because "the rebels," he believed, "are 'gone up' " (*The Tiffin Weekly Tribune*, February 28, 1862).

The Union troops assumed that their adversary was incapable of putting up an effective resistance. Colonel D. C. Loudon of the 70th Ohio was encamped at Shiloh Meeting House awaiting an end to the war. The colonel was convinced that the "two great armies not confronting ours in the East and the West are broken up by disastrous defeat" (To Hannah [wife], March 23, 1862). The same assumptions prevailed among the men in other areas of the Western theater. From Jefferson City, Missouri, Able Griffith boasted, "We are giving them fits on all sides and as sure as the sun shines it will be over in two or three months at furthest" (To friend, February 13, 1862; see also George Hurlbut, Diary, March 24, 1862). Another soldier, this one with Buell's forces, crowed, "Bowling Green, Forts Henry and Donelson, Winchester, Port Royal, Fernandia, Brunswick, Centerville and Manassas ours! and Price and McCullough [sic] whipped like thunder in the west; Our dreaded Gunboats after them on the Mississippi and we with Nashville for headquarters, are luxuriating with our acres of white tents [while the rebels flee].... Glory Hallelujah!" (*The Howard Tribune*, April 1, 1862).

The Confederates did not have their hearts in the rebellion. Sam Sheperdson of the 30th Indiana with Buell's army had come to believe that "if the Rebels had had any rights or honor at steak [sic], we would have had a terrible battle, at Bowlinggreen" (To sister, March 10, 1862). A similar sentiment was echoed among Grant's men after they saw forts Donelson and Henry fall so easily. Jim Drish of the 32nd Illinois declared contemptuously that "they all run like cowards" (To wife, February 11, 1862; see also J. Connelley, Diary, February 18, 1862). Captain Wayne, 15th Illinois, was impressed with the defensive installations and wondered why the rebels had not defended them more effectively. "They had a fortification that was almost impregnable," inclining the captain to judge that they did not have "any necessity of Surrender ... [and] must have been Scared into it [by their leader]." He was convinced that if those forts had been held by 10,000 men from Illinois, they "could [have held] . . . this position against all Secession" (To wife [Ellen], February 18, 1862; see also Payson Shumway to wife [Hattie], March 2, 1862; H. E. Backus, Diary, February 18, 1862; *The Aurora Beacon,* March 6, 1862.

The Southern army was no match for Grant's and Buell's irresistible hosts. Peter Pinder's 52nd Illinois was on duty at Camp Douglas in Chicago guarding Confederate prisoners as he compared the quality of the levies from the various Southern states. "Some are quite intelligent," he conceded, "but many are lamentably ignorant. . . . The Tennesseans," he observed, were "a right smart lot of chaps." But Pinder attributed this to political factors, noting that "a strong Union sentiment prevails among them—that is among the more intelligent of them" (*The Aurora Beacon,* March 6, 1862; see also *The Daily State Sentinel,* July 27, 1861).

Union soldiers were convinced that the enemy was ready to give up. In Missouri, Payson Shumway found that the Confederates were turning themselves in and were "all nearly sick of the war" (Diary, November 24, 1861). In what is now West Virginia, a Buck-eye infantryman, firing at some Confederate skirmishers near Beverly was surprised to see how easily they surrendered, while "swearing they were pressed into the rebellious ranks." According to the Ohioan, the Confederates were so demoralized that they only went through the motions of fighting, adding that "a large number of the rebel troops shoot blank cartridges" (*The Lima Weekly Gazette,* October, 9, 1861). These beliefs were reinforced when Zollicoffer's defeated remnants capitulated in late January. "There was very little enthusiasm among them," reported a guard from the 65th Ohio. "They seemed possessed of a cool indifference as if they won or lost." And he noted that the rebels "had no confidence in their leaders and consequently did not accomplish much." He, too, claimed that the Confederates had been firing blank cartridges during the battle at Logan's Crossroads (*The Daily Commercial Register,* February 4, 1862). The same reports of enemy despondency circulated among the troops that took charge of prisoners in western Kentucky. Captain Wayne's Company D, 15th Illinois Infantry, guarded men of the 49th Tennessee, who had surrendered at Fort Donelson. The captain "found but one sentiment among the soldiers and but little else among the officers—and that is that—they were forced by public opinion to take up arms" (To wife [Ellen], February 18, 1862). Two days before A. S. Johnston's men crashed into his camp, Leroy Guthrie was erroneously reporting that large numbers of prisoners "are leaving the Rebbles and coming to the U.S. Army." He and his comrades in the 18th Missouri Infantry heard that "the greatest dissatisfaction prevails in the Rebble camp" (To family, April 4, 1862).

Bloated with self-assurance, William Robertson of the 34th Illinois boasted, "We can whip the rebels anytime and when we whip them twice more then I am going home" (To brother, February 10, 1862). He feared that he would not have a chance to see the elephant before the war ended. "We have not had ary a fight yet and dont expect one during this service," lamented Hoosier Jim Vanderbilt of the 23rd Infantry, "peace will be made in a shart time" (To mother, March 1, 1862). With the victories of February, "the hissing serpent of rebellion is now dying in horrible convulsions," wrote Lieutenant W. R. Philips from the camp of the 6th Indiana at Bell's Tavern, Kentucky (*The Howard Tribune*, February 22, 1862). The Confederacy was collapsing and nothing short of English and French intervention could save the South now, opined Thaddeus Capron, and he ruefully concluded "that this war will be closed in less than six months from this time" (1919: 340–41). The vast majority of the soldiers in Grant's and Buell's armies held the same view.[13] It was just a question of finishing them off. The rebels had lost heart and would only fight behind massive defensive works such as Fort Donelson or Corinth. Sergeant Gustavus Cushman of Company E, 3rd Iowa, called them "the greatest cowards in the world." He boasted confidently that in a skirmish at Carlton, Missouri, it took only thirteen men to disperse sixty of the Southerners. He disdainfully rejected rebel trumpeting "about one southern man being good for 2 northern men" (To brother, July 23, 1861).

During the first months of the war, the Confederate volunteers who trooped to the colors were equally convinced that their enemies were no match for them. The Southern military tradition would prove decisive against the Yankees. They marched off to war confident in the certitude that the Northern troops would soon be defeated. "I have given the U.S. government 60 days from the convening of Congress, to proclaim peace," a Mississippi officer prophesied (W. Thornton to brother, July 3, 1861). The Northerners, it was assumed, were a commercial, urban people with no taste or talent for military life (B. I. Wiley 1978b: 123). Furthermore, federal armies included immigrants, such as Germans, in their ranks, and these "Hessians" had no stake in the war and would bolt at the first sight of the Southern ranks (*The New Orleans Commercial Bulletin*, March 28, 1862; see also *The New Orleans Daily Crescent*, June 5, 1861). The disdain for Northern military prowess was confirmed by the victory at Bull Run. Sam Watkins of the 1st Tennessee Regiment recalled after Bull Run that the men felt "that the war was over, and we would have to return home without even seeing a Yankee soldier" (1962: 24).

But as fall turned to winter, the volunteers in A. S. Johnston's army began to have second thoughts about the military effectiveness of their enemies (G. W. Johnson to Ann [wife], February 15, 1862). Gloom began to set in as the army abandoned its main defensive line. The fall of forts

Henry and Donelson tried the men's souls. W. H. Mott, staff officer of the 24th Tennessee Regiment, was disheartened. "It is a gloomy picture which the future presents . . . and a still more gloomy one to look back upon the brilliant past, laden with so much of promise" (C. R. Mott 1946: 237). Lieutenant J. M. Foxworth of Company D, 7th Mississippi admitted to his diary that "we have been fearfully underating the strength and number of our foe" (Diary, February 12, 1862).

Despite the February debacle, the Southern volunteers did not think that the issue was already decided, but they came to realize that it would be much more costly than they had anticipated. "I can not believe that the South will be subjugated, but I see the future red with blood," wrote Lunsford Yandell from Columbus, Kentucky. This was to be a very brutal war, one none had heretofore imagined. "Much of our beloved country is destined to be devastated by the enemy—our homes destroyed, children made orphans and thousands of now happy families, reduced to penury and want." He gloomily warned his sister to steel herself for tragedies. "It is vain to expect that all your brothers will live through the war. All of us, and Pa too may lose our lives in the fierce struggle which has just commenced" (To Sally [sister], February 16, 1862). Yet all eagerly sought battle.

ANTICIPATING BATTLE

"We are all wating in suspense for the ball to open," wrote William Warren of the 13th Iowa to his wife (April 4, 1862). There was at most one more fight to go before the war would be decided in 1862, and the recruits on both sides were overwhelmingly impatient to be in the coming battle.[14]

Henry Backus of the 14th Illinois recalled the nonstop revelry aboard the *Continental* as they headed deeper into the South. The shenanigans were still going on the second day. "The Boys are still on their spree making a perfect pandemonium of the Cabin. It looks like a lot of Hogs were on board." Day three, and the revelry was still continuing, although he now believed that "the Whiskey will give out by morning" (Diary, February 13, 14, and 15, 1862).

The youths sailed into the war borne on high confidence and optimism. "We are all right[,] sound as a cus," chortled Eli Clampitt as his Hoosier regiment set up camp in Kentucky. "Here is the place to see the elephant," he wrote. And told his brother Mark that he was missing a glorious spectacle. "You ort to be here to here the guns roar" (To friends, October 30, 1861). It was all "high glee" and adventure, when Clampitt's 29th Indiana could see the enemy camp fires in the distance and expect a daring attack against their camp. He wondered what the Southerners were having for dinner and gaily declared that he would have liked to have charged hell-bent into the enemy bivouac "to see if they have anything good to eat" (To brother, December, 26, 1861). Meanwhile, on the Gulf, James Williams was also looking forward to the prospect of action. The 21st Alabama was garrisoning one of the forts protecting Mobile. Now and then a federal ship hovering off the coast would engage in a brief exchange of fire with the shore batteries. "Oh! it is glorious music to hear the heavy throb-throb of a vigorous cannonade!" he wrote to his wife, Lizzie (Folmar 1981: 39).

The question arises whether Southerners were more eager fighters than the Northerners. They were supposed to be the ones with a strong military ethos and should have been more eager to engage the enemy (W. L. Hauser 1980: 187). Maslowski found that 56 percent of the Southern soldiers were "willing and eager for combat," while only 40 percent of the Northerners avidly sought battle (1970: 124). Our findings, comparing the Confederates and Unionist recruits during the first year of the Western campaign, yielded no significant differences between Confederates and Unionists, although the Unionists were only slightly more zealous than A. S. Johnston's army—hardly surprising in view of his long retreat.[15] A comparison of the three armies showed that Grant's had a slight edge over Buell's and A. J. Johnston's.[16]

Their eagerness to see action came through in many ways in the new enlistees' correspondence. Initially there was, of course, the excitement of military rituals. No other profession has such a colorful repertoire of displays (Holmes 1986: 273). Marching on the rebel base at Bowling Green, one young infantryman was probably typical of the enthusiastic new volunteer when he signed "GLORY ROAD!" into the register at Mammoth Caverns under the heading "destination" (*The Mahoning Sentinel*, July 15, 1861). Leaving for the front on March 19, Joseph Ruff, a German immigrant, watched with pride as his 12th Michigan marched off to embark on their journey to Shiloh. "The sun broke through the clouds at times presenting an inspiring sight—a sea of flashing bayonets, the colors flying and bands playing" (1943:282). As Jim Drish's men in the 32nd Illinois reembarked at Fort Henry, he marveled at the "thirty or forty Steamers . . . loading and loaded" making a "Splendid Sight" (To wife, March 5, 1862; see also William Kennedy to wife, March 7, 1862).

A second theme reflecting the men's eagerness was their enthusiastic confidence in their unit and the prospect of testing its mettle against the foe. John Ellis, a Louisianian, exemplified the confidence and determination of his Southern comrades when he proclaimed "we are all in high spirits, the troops are pouring in [at Corinth]. . . . When the great battle does come off," he boasted to his father, "expect to hear that Buells best is cut to pieces and scattered like chaff" (February 21, 1862).

A third theme reflecting zealousness was their declarations of patriotic resolve to stand firm. The issue of Southern independence was at stake. There was no more retreating now. Their backs were against the wall and the fate of their new country was about to be decided. Rufus Catin of the 19th Louisiana pledged "to sacrifice my life if necessary in the cause of our independence" (To Cousin Fanny, September 20, 1861). At Pittsburg Landing, Colonel Cassius Fairchild struck a Thermoplyaen pose when he vowed to risk all for the Union. "If I am sent to battle in command of the 16th [Wisconsin] Regt[,] I intend to make them stand right to the work until every man in the regiment is killed" (To Sarah [sister], March 21, 1862).

The proximity of battle heightened the excitement, and letters and diaries remained optimistic and confident. Lucius Barber, whose 15th Illinois landed at Fort Donelson immediately after the surrender on the morning of February 16, was enthralled by the sight. "We rounded a curve in the river and the high battlements and frowning batteries of Ft. Donelson, with the Stars and Stripes floating on the ramparts, met our visions. It was a scene well calculated to thrill the minds of the beholders with enthusiasm" (1894: 43). However, others such as Henry Watts of the 24th Indiana, tempered their attitude toward combat after they had a closer look at the place. He had to admit, after surveying the wreckage, "We . . . was glad it was not us that was laying there cold and stiff" (Reminiscences: 32). Although somewhat chilled by the sight of Fort Donelson and Fort Henry, their ardor, nevertheless, remained undiminished. As the 14th Illinois' steamer resumed its progress into enemy country, James Dugan was amazed at the behavior of his comrades. "It may appear strange, and even incredible," he wrote, "that men situated as these would be cheerful. Far away from home, in an enemy's country, and continually exposed to danger and death, it would seem that they would be dejected and cast down. But it was not so on board these boats. Never did any craft . . . bear men of lighter hearts and more cheerful spirits" (1863: 98). Meanwhile, preparing to march north to ambush one of the Union steamers headed up the Tennessee (perhaps Dugan's own transport), John Ellis of the 16th Louisiana wrote to his father that "our regiment is now ready to march to the Tennessee River distant 22 miles. . . . We have 5 days rations cooked, cartridges and guns all ready and are waiting only for word— The Regiment is enthusiastic, the sick of yesterday are well today and the weary are fresh and eager to meet the enemy" (February 21, 1862). As the soldiers of the Army of the Ohio approached on April 6, they could hear the battle. At least one group saw a boat full of wounded from Pittsburg Landing. "Their groans and lamentations were encouraging music to untried soldiers," he claimed, "all felt all the more anxious to pitt our mettle against that of the foe" (L. Wagner, Recollections). Jacob Ammen, commander of Buell's lead brigade, asked his men if they could march faster. They eagerly complied, declaring, "we want to see him [the elephant] once anyhow" (J. Ammen, Diary (Copy), April 6, 1862).

NOTES

1. Peter Pinder reported that in some cases Confederate sympathizers tried to waylay passing steamers to ground them or set them afire. He described how his steamer, the *Florence,* studiously avoided all requests to stop along the shore to pick up men claiming to be Unionists for this very reason (*The Aurora Beacon,* March 27, 1862).

2. Doyle had the misfortune to be with a regiment that was neither fully trained nor armed. His 16th Iowa marched off the steamer and directly into the battle. He was killed within hours of disembarking.

3. Forty-eight soldiers commented on the topic, with the 81 percent of the Unionists and 83 percent of the Confederates expressing distrust or disdain for the people of western Tennessee and Kentucky.

4. Sixty percent of the Unionists and 50 percent of the Confederates believed that the people of the border region were disloyal.

5. The section of Tennessee that is discussed in this work was settled between 1828 and 1845. It was Indian land until 1828. Missouri was settled between 1780 and 1810 and the Gulf Coast, prior to the American Revolution.

6. Oddly enough, while both sides' troops had uncomplimentary remarks to make about living conditions in Kentucky and Tennessee, the authors did not come across any remarks about poverty and backwardness in Missouri, even though the guerrilla war that raged there was far more ferocious than in Kentucky. Part of the reason may have been that Missouri had been settled longer than the western areas of Kentucky and Tennessee.

7. Alexander Varian, Jr., saw more than his share of war. The son of an Episcopalian minister in Cleveland, he joined the 1st Ohio Volunteers in September and served on the medical staff, where he inventoried all the mutilations that musketry and cannon can cause. He was himself a victim at Reseca, Georgia, where he died on June 2, 1864.

8. T. Harry Williams explained the difference in conceptions about the nature of the war when he wrote, "The Civil War was a war of ideas and inasmuch as neither side could compromise its political purposes, it was a war of unlimited objectives. Such a war was bound to be a rough, no-holds-barred affair, a bloody and brutal struggle. Yet Lincoln's generals proposed to conduct it in accordance with standards and strategy of an earlier and easier military age. They hoped to accomplish their objectives by maneuver rather than fighting" (1962: 44).

9. Grant was indeed an aggressive strategist, but his Western campaign was essentially oriented toward seizing geographic objectives. This was perhaps his genius, for he demonstrated a better understanding of the significance of railroads and rivers than many of his contemporaries. Buell was also a classic strategist, although perhaps an excessively prudent one, who seemed at times to believe he could win his objectives without a major battle, by maneuver alone (J. H. Williams 1962: 44, 50). A. S. Johnston, for his part, made some strategic mistakes, for example, in not acting rapidly to relieve Fort Donelson and in leaving Nashville without adequate defensive works, but when he finally determined to act decisively and attack Grant at Pittsburg Landing, he was acting according to correct strategic principles. Johnston concentrated his forces against

an army that was not expecting an attack and was hemmed in with no place to run. At that moment the Confederacy would have proximate parity in numbers (Marshall 1947: 207).

10. Of the thirty-one soldiers who commented on their generals' objectives, all but three believed that their leaders were proceeding too cautiously.

11. The commander of the Army of the Potomac had been the subject of some ridicule, because when McClellan had finally moved against Manassas he found, to his embarrassment, that the fieldworks were unmanned and the armaments were only "quaker guns." General McClellan came in for considerable chafing among the Western troops, some of whom had campaigned with him in what is now West Virginia as three-month volunteers. Captain J. M. Coleman of the 15th Indiana was one of them, and his esteem for the "Little Napoleon" had not increased since McClellan's promotion to overall command. The westerners thought the "Little Napoleon" inactive in comparison to their progress. "McClellan," Coleman opined, "is in rather poor repute from keeping [the Confederates] . . . so long 'quiet on the Potomac' [a soldiers ballad]" (Coleman to Amanda [sister], March 2, 1862).

12. The highest estimate of Confederate strength at Corinth was made by John L. Harris, of the 14th Illinois, who believed that there were "200,000 men under command of general Johnson [sic]" (To father, March 21, 1862). The lowest figure for Confederate strength was from an Ohioan who put the enemy numbers at 30,000 (*The Fremont Daily Journal*, April 11, 1862, but the letter to the editor was dated April 4).

13. Forty-eight soldiers discussed this in their letters and diaries. Only one among them expressed doubt that the war would last beyond the end of the year.

14. The green volunteers were virtually unanimous in voicing their zealousness for combat: 95 percent of the seventy-seven soldiers who mentioned anticipating combat appeared eager to see the elephant. We controlled for the audience to whom they expressed this attitude by comparing their personal correspondence with their public comments in letters to the editor and in the published reminiscences. There was no significant difference between the two sources.

15. Ninety-eight percent of the Northerners looked forward to the moment of truth, and 81 percent of the Southerners eagerly sought to get into the fray. This lower score could probably be ascribed to the corrosive effect of the Confederates' early defeats and the ensuing retreat in February and March. Our cross-tabulation yielded one of the few significant chi-square scores of this study, 4.46 with a probability of chance of only 4 percent, with one degree of freedom.

16. Grant's troops scored 100 percent; Buell's, 94 percent, and Johnston's, 81 percent. Here too, the cross-tabulation was significant, giving a chi-square value of 8.33 with a probability of chance of only 2 percent, with two degrees of freedom.

"Battle of Pittsburg Landing—Engagement on the Left Wing, General Hurlbut's Division, April 6th, 1362—Charge and Repulse of the Confederates at the Peach Orcha-d." *Frank Leslie's Illustrated History of the Civil War.*

"Battle of Pittsburg Landing—Retreat of Dresser's Battery, Captain Timony, Centre of Federal Position, Sunday Morning, April 6th, 1862." *Frank Leslie's Illustrated History of the Civil War.*

"Battle of Pittsburg Landing—Recapture of Artillery by the First Ohio and Other Regiments, Under General Rousseau, April 7th, 1862." *Frank Leslie's Illustrated History of the Civil War.*

"Battle of Shiloh, or Pittsburg Landing—Left Wing—The Woods on Fire during the Engagement of Sunday, April 6th, 1862—Forty-Fourth Indiana Volunteers Engaged." *Frank Leslie's Illustrated History of the Civil War.*

"Confederate Charge upon Prentiss's Camp on Sunday Morning." *Battles and Leaders of the Civil War, Vol. 1, From Sumter to Shiloh.*

"Checking the Confederate Advance on the Evening of the First Day."
Battles and Leaders of the Civil War, Vol. 1, From Sumter to Shiloh.

"Wounded and Stragglers on the Way to the Landing, and Ammunition-Wagons Going to the Front." *Battles and Leaders of the Civil War, Vol. 1. From Sumter to Shiloh.*

"The 'Hornets' Nest'—Prentiss's Troops and Hickenlooper's Battery Repulsing Hardee's Troops." *Battles and Leaders of the Civil War; Vol. 1, From Sumter to Shiloh.*

"Gibson's Brigade Charging Hurlbut's Troops in the 'Hornets' Nest.'"
Battles and Leaders of the Civil War, Vol. 1. From Sumter to Shiloh.

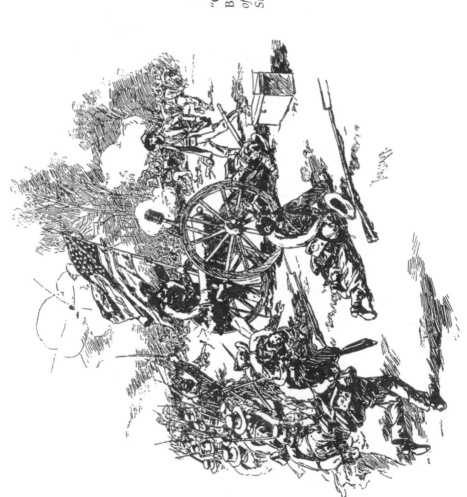

"Capture of a Confederate Battery." *Battles and Leaders of the Civil War, Vol. 1, From Sumter to Shiloh.*

4

"Seeing the Elephant"

TACTICS AND DYNAMICS OF THE BATTLE

"The left of our regt [the 70th Ohio] rests on a log church called Chilo Chapel," wrote Colonel D. C. Loudon to his wife. He described it as "a hard looking structure[.] From its appearance, I judge it to belong to the Baptists of the Hard shell persuasion" (To Hannah, March 23, 1862). By mischance, Loudon and his men were camped at the very vortex of the coming storm, the place where one of the bloodiest engagements of the Civil War took place. More were killed and wounded in the two days at Shiloh, than were lost in the entire Revolutionary War, the War of 1812, and the Mexican War combined.[1]

The interplay of geographic and doctrinal factors engendered the ferocious dynamic of the battle. Armed with hindsight, it is easy for armchair strategists to second guess the commanders in the field. A. S. Johnston should have attacked by column, Grant should have ordered improved positions, Buell should have moved more expeditiously, *ad infinitum*. But all these second guesses obscure one central fact about this battle: that is that the generals lost control of operations and the battle took on a dynamic of its own. The generals got their troops there and launched the assault. But once the combat reached its critical mass, they were reduced to shoveling in reinforcements, no longer controlling the tempo of the fighting through rapid maneuvers against flanks in true Jominian style. As A. S. Johnston and Beauregard could not agree clearly on objectives (and because Johnston was killed on the first day), the army was never able to carry out coherent maneuvers. As a result, there was only frontal attack and counterattack, and the pluck of the volunteer to decide the issue. The battle was basically a front-to-front melee (J. H. Williams 1962: 34). The struggle turned on the sheer power of one opponent to overwhelm the other, rather than a battle of movement and tactical agility to gain leverage over the enemy and drive him from his position by a flanking maneuver.

The impossibility for either side to use maneuver to gain victory relates to the most fundamental structural determinant of the battle. The geographic matrix of the fight was very restrictive. The Union encampment at Pittsburg Landing was shaped like an uneven triangle or funnel bounded on the east by the Tennessee River, on the northwest by Snake Creek and Owl Creek, and on the south by Lick Creek. The funnel conveniently opened toward the roads leading from Corinth, which A. S. Johnston and Beauregard used to pour their forces into its mouth. The whole area was no more than three miles by three miles meaning that the frontage was extremely narrow at any point of the battle. It narrowed even more as the lines fell back to Pittsburg Landing, where Snake Creek flowed ever closer to the river before it emptied into the Tennessee. Thus, as the Southerners advanced, the battle line narrowed and the fighting intensified. Assuming that at any one time each army had 20,000 effectives in the firing line, it would mean about four or five men per yard. However, at the base of the funnel the distance was halved to only about 2,000 yards! Such manpower density meant that the battle line had a much higher volume of small-arms fire, not to mention the shelling by batteries that were posted every few hundred yards.

Besides the restricted size of the battlefield, the nature of the terrain at Shiloh impeded a battle of maneuver. The battlefield consisted of broken terrain cut with deep gullies on its boundaries and it was heavily wooded. The present battlefield is, however, probably more densely overgrown than it actually was in 1862, because the farmers who lived in the area at that time fenced in their fields and allowed their livestock to graze the woods; thus, some of the undergrowth may have been reduced. Also, when the Union troops moved in, they cut down some of the growth for firewood and cleared much of the brush for their camps. Nevertheless, the undulating ground and the broadleaf forests made maneuver by column or by a large formation extremely difficult. It was even harder to deploy artillery in such an environment. A. G. Blakewell, a gunner with the Washington Artillery, blamed the terrain more than the enemy for the loss of the battery's guns when the Confederates were retiring under fire on the second day. The guns, he recounted, became "entangled in the underbrush and trees, and so buried in the soft soil by recoil, that with our reduced strength, we could not extricate them" (Reminiscences). Hence, because of the nature and size of the terrain, the battle turned into a series of frontal assaults with high density fire causing heavy casualties.

In additon to the effect of geographic parameters on the intensity of the fighting, there was also a gap between the prevailing tactical doctrine and weapons technology that added to the carnage at Shiloh (J. H. Williams 1862: 40). Major developments in military technology had occurred in the 1850s, but their implications had not been integrated into military doctrine. New artillery fuses, rifled iron tubes, and oblong artillery shells with new varieties of charges were among the improvements of artillery weapons. The guns were also far more reliable. But the most significant technological innovation was the increase in the accurate range of shoulder-held firearms.

The orthodox tactics of the day were ill-suited for the new types of arm. In contrast to the industrial technology of the mid–1850s, military doctrine was still pre-industrial. It provided for a tactical doctrine that directly contradicted the new technological changes. Frontal assaults were still supposed to be preceded by only one or two companies deployed as skirmishers, while the rest of the regiment moved forward as a compact mass in order to ensure greater fire density for the inaccurate muzzleloaders and allow sight and sound command and control by field-grade officers. These tactics proved to be very costly. In the Civil War, the rifled muskets were far more accurate and dense formations were easy targets at longer distances. However, this effect should not be exaggerated. Woods often provided cover and lessened the open distances to cross in assaults, thus reducing the range advantage of troops with rifled muskets.[5] Actually, most fields were small enough to be covered by smoothbores. For this reason, most defensive positions were set up along the wood line on the edge of a field, thereby requiring the attacker to cross an open field. Losses also were increased because virtually all firearms used by the infantry were muzzleloaders, obliging the soldiers to stand up to pour the powder down the barrel and ram home the ball and thus exposing them more.[2] Although, theoretically, loading could be done from a prone position, it took skill and training that the green volunteers did not possess, and besides, training manuals only provided for loading and firing from a standing position (Mahon 1977: 253). However, there may have been some soldiers who did manage to load their weapons while lying on their backs. This method was mentioned by one volunteer (W. J. Kennedy to wife, April 1862). Field-grade officers still led their units in close-line formations across open ground and even stopped them to stand, load, and fire in an exposed position and making them easier targets for the enemy.

Nevertheless, tight-line formations had certain advantages, especially when the commanders were leading green troops. The line formation was more effective because it reinforced the recruit's sense of security by fighting in compact formation and the supportive effect of having comrades in view at all times. In a dispersed situation, a feeling of isolation yields more easily to panic and disorientation and the sensation of being entombed in the roar of battle (Marshall 1947: 141). Furthermore, as was mentioned above, compact formations intensified a unit's fire-power and facilitated command and control.

In fairness to the mid-nineteenth-century officers, they were aware that the minié ball would have an effect on the tactics of the day. But given the problems they had with controlling men moving to the attack by using voice and drum, the only course they could see was to use the flanking attack as much as possible. However, this approach was impossible at Shiloh. Individual initiative and judgment came to weigh more heavily in the equation. In that situation, the soldier had to be more autonomous and comprehend on his own the strategic and tactical situation (Marshall 1947: 22). The Civil War volunteer nourished these individualistic traits in civilian life and proved he was capable of showing the same initiative in the new situation as the war progressed. Although little is available on the actual mechanics of the fighting at Shiloh, it seems likely that as the battle progressed, troops learned to go to ground as quickly as possible, make shorter charges, and avoid standing in the open to load and fire. They probably also began to move in clusters, instead of the prescribed orderly files. Furthermore, they learned to use terrain advantages wherever possible in order to reduce their exposure to enemy fire. Thus, infantrymen increasingly took the initiative and instinctively spread out, advanced at a crouch, and used cover wherever terrain or the commander permitted these tactics. In effect, despite doctrine, entire regiments were soon deploying as skirmishers, reducing their vulnerability to enemy fire.

An army of green volunteers wedged in the confluence of several streams and unprepared for attack was taken by surprise by A. S. Johnston's Confederates.[3] Their training was inappropriate for the weapons used. These factors caused high casualties, but other factors favored the maintenance of cohesion despite the ferocity of the fighting. First, the troops were highly motivated as was noted in a preceding chapter, which showed a high proportion of the soldiers expressing eagerness and determination to join with the enemy. Actually, only the 53rd Ohio, the 72nd Ohio, and Myer's battery broke for no military reason, such as enfilading fire. Even in these isolated cases, elements of these commands remained operational; for example, about 250 men of the 53rd, nevertheless, continued to fight as independent companies even though their colonel, Jesse Appler, and the rest of the regiment had fled. Even some of Myer's gunners fought on because the battery continued to sustain casualties in the battle. Furthermore, being surrounded on all sides by unfordable streams, the Union troops had nowhere to run, and many of those who fled to the riverbank probably rejoined their units for the second day's fight. Finally, the disorganized nature of the fighting forced field-grade officers and brigadiers to take full responsibility for their sectors and improvise as best they could. This they showed they could do, because they were as yet unencumbered by ossified hierarchical military principles. But the operation of the dynamics of the fighting at Shiloh may better be understood by descending to ground level to see the battle through the volunteer's eyes and works, which is the purpose of the following section.

SIGHTS AND SOUNDS OF COMBAT

The battle was characterized, above all, by its unremitting intensity. "There was no hour during day," wrote General Grant, "when there was not heavy firing and generally hard fighting at some point in the line" (1982: 177). The matrix of the battle of Shiloh was small for the size of the forces engaged, so that in this narrow space "the horrors of a battle was here demonstrated in its fullest sense," recalled Captain Andrew Davis (To F. D., Papers, April 21, 1862). "The scene," wrote a young Illinois cavalryman, "was like a sojourn in the abodes of the lost in hell" (Young 1894: 120). It was an overwhelming concentrated horror. George Hurlbut helped serve the 14th Ohio Battery's guns as they shot hundreds of pounds of metal into masses of people, often so close that he could distinctly see the gore his guns were inflicting. It was "too sickening for the pen to describe" (April 8, 1862; see also T. Blaisdell to sisters and brother, April 12, 1862). Some avoided reliving the horror by summing it up in a succinct exclamation, for example, "The carnage was offel" (A. F. Davis, to brother, April 21, 1862). Thomas Armes simply described the role of Company A, 24th Indiana and left behind the cursory notation and weather report, "Walises Brigad [sic] opend fire at day light . . . driv the Rebils 6 miles . . . seases firing at dark . . . Heavy & Cool rain all nite" (Diary, April 1862).

The first thought of many survivors was to let loved ones know they had not perished and to report who from the community had been killed or wounded. Some sense also had to be made out of the "ordered confusion" of battle for the people back home (Woolridge 1968: 6, 8–9)—no easy task for raw recruits for whom battle easily "insult[ed] the senses" (Prescott 1965: 38–42). John Beach, whose 77th Ohio was in Sherman's division and had been in the thick of it, fell back on a well-worn but accurate cliche, describing battle as "the crash of musketry and the boom of canon" (Memoirs). T. C. Buck, on the other side with Stanford's Mississippi Battery, also resorted to trite metaphors: "The missiles of death . . . flew and flew around was as thick and heavy as a hail storm" (To sister, April 13, 1862).

Others such as Reverend D. Sullins of the 19th Tennessee depicted it in the melodramatic idiom of one of his hellfire sermons. "A thousand East Tennesseans sprang to their feet and swept down the hill an unbridled cyclone. But look! look!," he exclaimed, "the smoke from the battery is clearing; those horrid guns have ceased their work of death. See, they fly! they fly!" (1910: 223). It must at times indeed have been a spectacular sight. Alexander Varian told his father, "I cant describe to you the *awful grandeur* of a raging battle. I could compare it to nothing else but *Thunder & Lightening*" (April 10, 1862). But grandiloquent portraits of battle could not cover over its bloodcurdling visions, and neither the soldiers nor the press tried to hide the gore from the homefront. Even in this early euphoric stage of the war, the newspapers provided realistic descriptions of what war was like. *The Republican Banner* explained to Nashvillians the reality behind the term "broken line" or the phrase "the line gave way." It could best be described as resembling "the scene of a frightful railway accident. . . . There will be the full compliment of backs broken in two, of arms twisted wholly off; of men impaled upon their own bayonets; of legs smashed up like bits of firewood; of heads sliced open like apples, of other heads crunched into jelly by iron hoofs of horses," that is "what is behind a 'splendid charge' " (November 30, 1861).

But accuracy and realism were blurred by the constraints of the soldier's own view of the battlefield. Not only was his environment a frightening kaleidoscope of noise and smoke that paralyzed his senses, but his range of vision was thwarted by the need for concealment from the enemy's fire (Keegan 1976: 47). S. L. A. Marshall stated, "The first effect of fire is to dissolve all appearance of order" challenging perception (1947: 90). It was very hard for the soldier in the firing line to have a clear view of the big picture. He tended to see only cameos of seemingly disconnected events (R. Holmes 1986: 154). Extreme stress and preoccupation with their safety also reduced the soldiers' ability to comprehend the situation and to assess the risks in the rapidly changing battlefield environment. Tunnel vision generated rumors, misjudgment, and panic, which threatened cohesion.

Private Leander Stillwell of the 61st Illinois exemplified the tunnel-visioned effect, admitting that "the generals . . . are sweeping the field with their glasses. . . . [But] the extent of a battle seen by the common soldier is that only which comes within range of the raised sights of his musket" (1920: 38). Captain Parkhurst Martin, who led Company B of the 14th Illinois, was able to see little more than Stillwell, reporting that "I only saw what transpired in my immediate front and vicinity" (Speech to Fellow Veterans of the Kennesaw Post, February 25, 1884, Martin Collection). For this reason, soldiers often tended to describe battle anecdotally, bringing out of their consciousness incidents, ironic details, and vivid cameos of their combat experience (Fussell 1975: 31). Yet this disparate aggregate of sights and sounds was probably a more eloquent description of battle than the space-time matrix of professional reports.

Nevertheless, the volunteers tried hard to write down their observations as accurately as they could for their friends, their relatives, and posterity. When pieced together in very loose form following the stages of the fighting, they provide a graphic image of battle. It began with the approach to the jump-off point. A. S. Johnston's men had a long arduous march to the battlefield. They had been three days on rural roads, were soaked to the bone by spring rains, and nearly exhausted. Many were plagued by intestinal illness from polluted water in the Corinth area. Rations had not kept up, and worst yet, rain gear was virtually nonexistent (Cunningham 1966: 147, 180). An exhausted soldier jotted down a few notes before he collapsed in sleep, "More heavy rain! Hard going, had to abandon light baggage. Again marched more than 12 hrs" (Unknown diarist, April 5, 1862, Walton-Ghenny papers). Ominous portents of that fearful second night's march to battle were long remembered. "The night was very dark and we were alternately blinded and lighted by vivid lightening." The roll and claps of thunder were followed by flashes illuminating struggling men as they tried to pry wagons and caissons from the grips of the mud. Steaming from the exertion, drenched by the unceasing rain, the marchers hobbled north as the "gates of heaven seemed open with flood," recounted a Crescent Regiment infantryman (*The New Orleans Daily Crescent*, April 7, 1862).

The last of the columns to arrive at Mickey's, where the army was to reassemble for the attack, was Brigadier General John C. Breckinridge's Reserve Corps. They hardly had the time to rest a few hours. Mercifully, the rain had finally ceased on the night before the attack so the men were able to sleep with some comfort. The morning sky was also propitious: mild and sunny. The smell of firewood and brewing coffee wafted through the camps as the men bestirred themselves. In Colonel Robert T. Trabue's Brigade of the Reserve Corps, John William Green and his comrades were starting the early ritual of brewing up coffee when "Genl Breckenridge galloped along the line and said 'boys fall in you have better work for you than eating' " (Diary, April 6, 1862). Just then, Green heard the sharp crackle merging into a tearing sound of musket fire as it grew in intensity. "The ball had opened." Green's Kentuckians lined up, the officers surveyed their ranks, and then they began to walk forward toward the sound of the shooting. After covering some distance, "we were halted and told to unsling knapsacks[.] we were ordered to pile them & detail a guard to watch them—volunteers were called for but not a man wanted to miss the fight," he noted with regimental pride (April 6, 1862). Green's sergeant had to order someone to guard the company's equipment. "One of the boys who was detailed to stay behind . . . offered to give three biscuit[s] & then increased the offer to his entire supply to any boy who would exchange with him." But no one would trade places and miss the battle. The fellow to be left behind then told the sergeant that one of his comrades, a fellow named Tom Porter, was too sick to fight, "but Tom would not swap. . . . Poor Tom," wrote the diarist, "was killed before ten o'clock that morning" (Diary, April 6, 1862).

The officers gave final instructions to their commands. The soldiers were told to wait until they were close enough, to shoot deliberately, to aim at the biggest part of the enemy, and to try to kill officers. Furthermore, they were to shoot artillery horses to immobilize the guns, and when advancing, they were not to stop, but to keep going; they had less chance of getting hit if they were on the move. Stopping to help comrades was forbidden; others had been assigned to that task. Nor should the soldiers be frightened by artillery, because, they were told, its noise was worse than its effectivenes (B.I. Wiley 1978b: 69–70). So to duty, all was in order; the command was given to advance; and the attack began.

A mile away from Green and his approaching comrades, the Northern troops were emerging from their tents and sampling the weather. Some patrols from the 5th and 6th divisions were already out checking the roads toward Corinth. The low-intensity patrolling engagements blooded the new soldiers and got them used to facing enemy fire. Chester A. Buckland reported that his regiment, the 72nd Ohio, camped along the Purdy Road on the outer fringes of the Union right, had run into Confederates on April 5 and had sustained several casualties in a forty-five minute skirmish (*The Fremont Daily Journal*, April 25, 1862). So patrols on the day of the battle were exercising extra caution. Colonel Everett Peabody, who command a brigade in Brigadier General Benjamin M. Prentiss' division, ordered out one of the patrols. Joseph Ruff of the 12th Michigan was in the detachment. They had been out about forty-five minutes when the first streaks of sunlight broke over the woods and fields. They may have heard rustling leaves, crunching twigs, and clanging accoutrements; then off in the distance in the far corner of Fraley's field a horseman appeared. The men tensed up and formed up, and then Ruff was greeted by whizzing bullets followed by smoke rising from the woods on the other side of the field. He and his comrades made a stand. Then, overwhelmed by the fire, they ran helter-skelter to their camp to warn their comrades. There would be no chance for breakfast this day, he remembered thinking as he ran into his tent, grabbed his equipment, and got ready to face the oncoming enemy (1943: 297). Ruff's patrol had actually done very well. Their stand probably bought the Union army forty-five minutes to an hour's warning. The woods were alive with marching men, whose advance shook out rabbits and other small game that fled before them into the Union camps (Young 1894: 97). As A. S. Johnston's lines swept into the Union camps, Captain John Caldwell, a Kentucky Confederate with the Reserve Corps followed the debris left in its wake. Most pitiful of his first sights of battle were the Union wounded who asked him not to let his men trample them. "I felt sorry for them," Caldwell recalled, "and cautioned my men not to say anything insulting to them" (Diary, April 6, 1862).

R. H. Jones was a gunner with Captain Andrew Hickenlooper's 5th Battery, Ohio Light Artillery, which was posted just off the Eastern Corinth Road behind Prentiss' division. "We never dreamed of an attack," he reported to the editor of his hometown newspaper (*The Jackson Standard*, May 2, 1862). But there they were coming on, a moving whirl of smoke, glimpses of shapes holding guns, and all swallowed in noise, making a "rushing sound like a train moving by" (B. Grebe, Diary, April 1862). As resistance stiffened and larger numbers of muskets and field-pieces opened fire, the advancing vortex of noise and smoke reached a continuous pitch along the outer rim of the camps of the 5th and 6th divisions. Farther back, nearer the landing in Brigadier General Stephen A. Hurlbut's camps, Warren Olney was out walking in the woods some distance away from his 3rd Iowa's tents. He faintly heard the first sounds of the engagement, but assumed that it was caused by pickets returning from a patrol firing off their muskets before cleaning them. But "a sense of apprehension took possession of" him when he heard the artillery join in. He turned to return to camp, his heart tightening with every step (Olney 1885: 582). Two miles back, Charles Wright in the 81st Ohio heard the sound waft back too. Someone remarked, "I guess it's the cars in Corinth?" But as they approached the distant grumble, the "rattling, rumbling noise became more distinct. We halted listened again, and just at that time the boom of a piece of artillery burst on our ears, and our commander said, 'Boys, that's not the cars; they're fighting!' " (C. Wright 1887: 32–33).

Time for the "long roll"! The rattle of the snare drums sent shivers of trepidation up many a spine, but for the most part, the raw recruits were eager to face the test that awaited them. Charlie Brant, though ill, dragged himself from his cot and staggered after his comrades vowing, "I came to fight and I am going as far as I can." Charlie was hit by a ball just above the left kneecap that ranged upward into the groin. He spent the night lying in agony on the battlefield (J. L. Brant, Manuscript). Robert Fleming's 77th Ohio was right up front in Sherman's division when Brigadier General Bushrod R. Johnson's and Colonel Robert M. Russell's brigades came crashing into their camps after putting several companies and the colonel of the 53rd Ohio to flight. Attached to Colonel Jesse Hildebrand's headquarters, Fleming was in the middle of doing the morning report. It was hard to concentrate on the lists, while the battle raged a few hundred yards away. Every now and then he leaped from his desk and ran out to the line to have a look. "The impression was on my mind that the regiment was going to get into a skirmish, and the boys would be writing home that they were all in it except 'Little Bob' " (1908: 139).

While Fleming agonized, others were rushing into their tents and collecting their equipment. Musket, canteen, maybe a bedroll and pack, and the standard forty-round issue of ammunition. Outside the tent all was commotion: trumpets screeching, drums rattling, officers screaming commands, companies forming files, and battery horses jostling each other with excitement as harnesses were thrown over them. And beyond— where the line was—it was possible now and then to hear shouts and screams emerge from the noise and smoke where the fighting was taking place. Battery E, 1st Illinois Light Artillery commanded by Captain Allen C. Waterhouse swung out in a trot to support Fleming's 77th Ohio. Wheeling artillery was indeed a spectacular sight, bugle blaring, hitches snapping as the six-horse teams strained to yank the tubes into motion (George R. Lee, Reminiscences). The infantry also had its dramatic ritual before going into action. It was usually an officer's harangue to raise morale and remind the men of their duty. Even in Prentiss' division, which was the first to be hit, the ritual was not waived. Old Lieutenant Colonel Jacob Fry lined up the 61st Illinois for a speech. Being a Douglas Democrat and untried in military matters, he referred to them as "gentlemen" not soldiers and spoke in the name of the "state" not the nation. Mobilizing all his earnestness he solemnly proclaimed, " 'Gentlemen . . . remember your State, and do your duty like brave men,' " and then led them toward the noise and smoke (Stillwell 1920: 44).

The long rolls and bugle cries cascaded from camp to camp as the *rip-rattle* of musket volleys punctuated by artillery *poums* drifted closer and closer to the landing. The companies, regiments, and brigades of the army were shaking themselves into action. Belt and straps adjusted and rifle at ready, the men formed up, listened to their commander, and moved out. The march toward the fight was a sobering experience. Moving up, Warren Olney and the 3rd Iowa of Hurlbut's division began to see the wounded heading in the other direction. "It did not particularly add to the cheerfulness to reflect that our Division was the reserve of the army, and should not be called into action, ordinarily, until the close of the battle" (Olney 1885: 583). As the columns advanced they dissolved into confusion. "The field officers were mounted on horses." Cyrus Boyd and his comrades in the 15th Iowa "tried to keep up with them . . . we had to run and then the front [of the column] . . . would halt and the rear would telescope into them." All the while, they were passing soldiers headed in the opposite direction. "Most were hatless and had nothing but clothes they wore. Some were wounded and covered with blood from head to foot." They yelled across to Boyd, " 'Don't go out there' 'we are all cut to pieces' " (Boyd 1953: 29). Sensing the men's thoughts, as a wagon load of wounded lurched by, Lieutenant Colonel Ansel Tupper of the 41st Illinois warned that "if any man left the ranks on pretense of caring for the wounded, he would be shot on the spot" (Olney 1885: 583).

Suddenly there were no more men going the other way, they had reached the line. "We saw right in front of us, but about three . . . or four hundred yards off, a dense line of Confederate infantry, quietly standing in ranks," recalled a Hawk-eye volunteer. "In our excitement, and without word of command, we turned loose . . . with our smooth-bore muskets. . . . [But] after three or four rounds, the absurdity of firing at the enemy at that distance dawned on us, and we stopped. As the smoke cleared up we saw the enemy still there, not having budged or fired a shot in return. But though our action was absurd, it was a relief to us to do something, and we were rapidly toned up to the point of steady endurance" (Olney 1885: 583). It was worst for those who had to wait in frightened anticipation for up to two hours for the battle to come to them (J. N. Cunningham to brother, April 13, 1862; *Lima Weekly Gazette*, April 23, 1862).

Ten miles away, the men of Buell's army were trudging into Savannah on the other side of the Tennessee River. When Chaplain Todd Oliphant of the 78th Ohio heard the cannonade, it went through his column "like an electric shock" (Diary, April 7, 1862). Ambrose Bierce described how "the breeze bore to our ears the long deep sighing of iron lungs. The division as if it had received the sharp word of command, sprang to its feet, and stood in groups at 'attention.' I am not sure," he continued, "but the ground was trembling then." The far-off sound of the battle pulsated with "regular throbbings." Tension grew and was somehow sensed by the unit flags that began to flap nervously in the wind (Bierce 1966: I, 236). The cannonade had a "wonderful effect" on Levi Wagner's 1st Ohio Volunteers. The distant *booms* elicited "such cheering as could be heard for miles, while the walking speed increased to such a rate as to cause the short legged boys to trot lively" (Papers).

Rumors began to make their way back to the men across the river. J. K. Newton of the 14th Wisconsin heard that they had been "completely whipped out & that they were running in every direction" (To father and mother, April 12, 1862). Was there any point in crossing over if it only meant capture? But Buell's lead columns forged ahead. Colonel Jacob Ammen's brigade led the hard march through the swamps that bordered the river on the east side. When the division commander, Brigadier General William Nelson, ordered Ammen and his men forward, "all the men [were] . . . eager to comply." The men asked the colonel if he thought it might not be all over once they got there. Ammen replied, he hoped so, to assuage the men's fears, but was surprised when the answer seemed to disappoint them. The volunteers did not want to miss the fight calling to him that " 'you have seen the Elephant often, we want to see him once anyhow' " (Ammen Diary, April 6, 1862; see also W. Ward, Diary, April 6, 1862).

At last, the lead columns of Buell's army reached the bank opposite Pittsburg Landing and clambered aboard the steamer to be ferried over. Patriotism inspired William Ward and the men of the 39th Indiana. "The Brass band commenced playing 'Stars Spangled Banner.' Never did I listen to a tune which cheered me more," he affirmed (Diary, April 7, 1862). The opposite shore drew nearer, engines ceased pounding, the boat nudged the bank, and the planks dropped. Jacob Ammen remembered that his men appeared cool and marched at a goodly rate despite the mud and the confusion. They still seemed "anxious to meet the foe" (Diary, April 6, 1862). But Ward looked down the line of his comrades wondering, "Who of our Number will be called upon to give up his life in defense of his country" (Diary, April 7, 1862). Then "forward march" and on they went, elbowing their way past stragglers and slipping and sliding up the muddy bank trying to get beyond earshot of their dire warnings: "·'For God's Sake, don't go out there or you will be killed' " (L. Wagner, Papers). And then on top of the embankment, they tried not to look too long at the operating theaters busily processing the maimed unfortunates (*The Indiana True Republican*, May 1, 1862). The gloom and terror closed in on them with each step inland. The soldiers found solace in the proximity of their comrades' swaying back as the column swung into the darkness enshrouding them. During the march, Ward and several pals in Company D of the 39th Indiana formed a pact. "We promised each other that in case either of us should get wounded or killed we would see that they were assisted off the field if wounded and if dead to inform the family of the circumstances of death" (Diary, April 7, 1862; see also W.S. Covill to sister [Arvilla], April 12, 1862; M. Williams, Diary, April 6, 1862).

Once on the line, fighting involved maneuver under fire, resisting assaults, and seeking cover from rifle and artillery fire as well as firing, loading, and provisioning with ammunition. It also meant keeping weapons functioning and securing water, which was as important for men and their weapons as ammunition itself. "When the swish of canister and the droning of musket balls began to give us a new experience . . . we began to realize that we were earning our thirteen dollars a month," said Sergeant Edwin Payne, Company A of the 34th Illinois, as Colonel Edward N. Kirk's brigade of Brigadier General Alexander McCook's division moved to engage the enemy, in a series of frontal charges (Payne 1902: 29).

The standard bearer was central to the regimental ritual. The honor of carrying the flag into battle was eagerly sought, despite the high odds against surviving. The man carrying the flag was in the vortex of the fighting and the most conspicuous target, yet there was never a problem of replacing one who fell (B. I. Wiley 1978b: 81). The flag was the rallying point of the regiment; all eyes followed the flag across the "field of glory." But the military ritual of the frontal assault was not merely heroic posturing. Close-formation attacks concentrated musketry and, more important, the close formations provided mutual encouragement to the men (R. Holmes 1986: 236). Ideally, an effective attack maintained unit formations as it moved across the killing ground, but attacks at Shiloh never matched the heroic perfection and precise display of orderly aggression in the lithographs printed in *Frank Leslie's* or *Harper's*. Infantry might only get in one or two synchronized volleys before smoke and noise overwhelmed the officers' command control, and the line dissolved into a loose formation of individual riflemen loading and shooting at their own rhythm. When the fighting got hot, formations and doctrinal ritual went by the boards. Skirmish lines were dispensed with. Nor did the men move forward at Hardee's prescribed double-quick, instead they "plunged forward holus-bolus" across the open ground.

A volunteer of the Orleans Guard Battalion decribed it as a rush with eyes looking ahead and toward the flag bearer and noticing now and then a comrade fall and be left behind. Each few strides passed someone's martyrdom: "Porce down . . . Gallot down . . . Coiron, arm shattered . . . Percy wounded then forty paces . . . a ragged stand up volley at the Unionists and they scramble off" (Unknown diarist, Walton-Ghenny Papers).

Attacks became ragged, never matching the ideal. Captain Sam Houston, Jr., commanding a Texas outfit described an attack. "With us the formality of a skirmish line was waived, and at the command 'forward,' our brigade moved out, its length of line extending only about two thirds across the field, and with neither of its flanks protected. As yet," he recalled, "[we] were too little versed in warfare, to realize our isolated condition, and went blithely on. . . . I do not remember that on our way across the open space, a command was given or a word spoken. 'Where is the enemy?' I kept asking myself?" As the men drew nearer to the "field's eastern boundary . . . the fence before us became transformed into a wall of flame" (1930–31: 333). Others, such as Henry Morton Stanley with the 6th Arkansas, saw only "a blurry line of figures dressed in blue as volley after volley was exchanged . . . in nervous haste" (Laurie 1985: 44). For other Confederates, the enemy remained invisible and contact was never direct. William Candace Thompson's 6th Mississippi did not see the enemy, they just charged in the general direction of the front. They tried at first, to follow the prescribed pace, but soon excitement got the better of them and they were running and yelling, but there was no sight of the enemy until "the bullets started to rain thick and fast." All they saw was "little clouds of smoke," and then they "heard the crackling of timber splintered by bullets" (1964: 21).

The blue defenders watched transfixed as the Confederates coolly deployed with resolute precision. Then suddenly the enemy column was advancing upon them. Despite the 15th Michigan's fire, George McBride marveled how "their lines begin to unfold and develop" and how "these movements are executed with exact step" (1894: 11). But the reality on the other side was quite different. A soldier with the Orleans Guard vividly described what it was like as they waited in reserve while a sister regiment, the 18th Louisiana, went over a crest to attack a Union position. There was sputter of musket fire heard from the other side of the slope and then "the decomposed line tumbled back over the crest in full view again. "Men scarcely could be recognized . . . shirts covered with blood . . . faces disfigured with hideous wounds." And now it was the Orleans Guard's turn, "fix bayonets," a collective "hurrah," and over the crest they went (Unknown diarist, Walton-Ghenny Papers).

In the smoke and noise of this disorderly and overwhelming environment each soldier tried to come to grips with his own situation. He tried to locate the enemy to determine his activities, tangibly represented only by his fire (Kellett 1982: 254). Thus, when describing what they had seen and heard in their first engagement, the most frequent topic was enemy fire, almost half mentioning this aspect of the fighting.[4] Other frequently mentioned sights were the suffering of wounded men and animals, the attitudes of the dead, tactical movements, and other miscellaneous visions. The preoccupation with enemy firepower is hardly a surprising priority, being directly associated with the average soldier's survival.

Most of the killing and maiming was done by musket fire. The green troops were overawed by its intensity (B. F. Wilkinson to Gage, April 16, 1862). Samuel Buford, an aide-de-camp in Buell's army, thought that "the bullets flew about as thick as the shot did when we were hunting quails" back home (To brother [Charlie], April 21, 1862). Reverting to metaphors of nature that conformed to their rural background, the soldiers described the intensity of the musket fire as a "hailstorm" that made the bushes and trees writhe (Barber 1894: 53). The underbrush had "literally been mowed down by bullets" (Wheeler 1976: 102), and the trees were "whiten[ed] by the blast of minnie balls" (John Caldwell, Diary, April 6, 1862).

Along with the terrifying ferocity of the small-arms fire, the troops were also subjected to very heavy artillery fire, especially the men in W. H. L. Wallace's and Prentiss' divisions who were defending the Sunken Road where the Confederates massed field guns (O. E. Cunningham 1966: 397–98). Although the fire was somewhat ineffective, because it overshot the target and crashed into the trees overhead and behind, the impact was nonetheless just as frightening (*The Seneca Ad-*

vertiser, May 30, 1862). The sight of great tree limbs being sheared off and falling on top of the troops unnerved the soldiers (Fleming 1908: 140; Boyd 1953: 32–33). Nonetheless, artillery fire during the war was not as lethal as small-arms fire, even though its effects were more dramatic. This difference in lethality was accurately perceived even by green troops. The vast majority emphasized the impact of the small-arms fire rather than artillery.

The noise and effects of the explosions and bullets constantly threatened to overwhelm the soldiers and drive them into passivity and to seek whatever shelter they could find (Kellett 1982: 321–27). When pinned, any unexpected turn of events could set loose a panic. At that moment, cohesion was vulnerable to sudden enfilading fire, the appearance of the enemy in an unexpected quarter, or a lack of ammunition. Inexperienced officers handling such brittle troops had their hands full keeping the men moving (Belcher 1980: 50). They instinctively went to the ground if they were defending a position. William Kennedy, whose 55th Illinois of Stuart's brigade was anchoring the Union left near Lick Creek, related, "I have often heard of men in battle laying down but never thought they hug the ground as close as they did on the 6th and the 7th" (To wife, April 1862; see also Abernathy 1958: 17; *The Daily Democrat and News*, April 21, 1862).

Cover was at a premium. Formations dissolved quickly as fear tugged the new troops toward whatever protection was available. Sergeant F. J. Beck reported home that the drill manual went by the boards. Once the 30th Indiana took fire for the first time, the whole regiment "treed" itself (*The Indiana True Republican*, May 1, 1862). When the 3rd Iowa suddenly ran into enemy fire at the Hornets' Nest, Warren Olney recalled how he "jumped behind a little sapling not more than six inches in diameter, and instantly about six men ranged themselves behind" him (1885: 586). Cyrus Boyd remembered with some humor that "it was fun to see two or three fellows running for the same tree." Once Boyd noticed that "two other fellows were there too," a fight ensued and one of the two "gave me tremendous but[t] and sent me out of shelter. . . . It was every man for himself," he ruefully admitted (Boyd 1953: 30–31; see also O. E. Cunningham 1966: 361).

Fighting was exhausting work and mastering terror was in itself fatiguing, over and above the actual mechanics of using the nineteenth-century musket. Although loading was supposed to be done according to a nine-count procedure, it became harder and harder to do as the bore got fouled and the barrel grew hot. When the ball was rammed down, the lead swelled and it took some effort to drive it home. This was particularly true with rifles, whose spiraled barrel required a snugger fit for the expanding flange of the conoid bullet. For this reason, smoothbores proved more effective when it came to firing fast at close range. In this type of action, the most effective shoulder arm was the old 0.69 caliber smoothbore. The capacious bore easily held a load of three buckshot on top of a massive 0.69 ball. The infantrymen called these buck and ball. The standard issue of ammunition weighed about three pounds.

Once the attackers managed to get across a field to the woods beyond, they fought Indian-style. "We would lay on the ground and load our guns stand up and fire sometimes behind a tree or running from one tree to the other," wrote William Kennedy of the 55th Illinois, in his description of the desperate fighting in the woods and gullies next to the Tennessee River. It was a game of hide and seek among the trees with the first to spot the other player having the chance to draw a bead and get off a shot. They frantically rushed through the nine-point re-loading procedure, while trying to keep from being exposed. Kennedy told his wife that "the hardes thing to do was to get a sight of a rebel before they move. . . . It seemed to me," he went on, "that they were all deers but they was a good deal worse for while I was looking for them they were firing at me" (To wife, April 1862).

When the fighting got hot, the forty-round issue of balls, powder, and caps did not last long. A soldier could fire up to three rounds per minute. Firing rapidly, a regiment could conceivably run out of am-munition in twenty minutes (O. E. Cunningham 1966: 474).[5] There was, consequently, a persistent need of ammunition. Details were constantly dispatched to find the mother unit's supply wagons and bring up the ammunition. It was hard work, and moreover, it was very frustrating, because there was a large variety of weapons, some brigades needing five types of small-arms munition.

Even if adequate ammunition were available for sustaining a very high volume of fire, the man in the line nevertheless had to stop every half hour to clean out his weapon. Although robust, the rifled musket quickly became fouled by black powder. Sergeant Harold M. White of Company H of the 11th Iowa complained that, "One of our greatest misfortunes was the want of suitable cartridges. The powder used in them was of such poor quality that after firing the first few shots, the guns were so dirty that it was almost impossible to load them, the bullet being forced down with the greatest difficulty.—Why such powder was used can only be explained on the supposition that poor powder costs less than good and by using it somebody's friend, in the shape of an army con-tractor," made some money (Throne 1954: 255). Fighting with Mc-Clernand's division around Shiloh Meeting House, Alexander Downing, Company E, 11th Iowa, described the problem. "My musket became so dirty with cartridge powder, that in loading it the ramrod stuck fast and I could neither get it up or down, so I put a cap on, elevated the gun and fired it off," ramrod and all (Downing 1916: 41). The only way to clean a clogged musket was to pour water down the barrel and wash it out. Hence, for every man sent for munitions, another was running to refill to his comrades' canteens, and when water was not available, urine served the same purpose. Water was also essential to quench the thirst. Firing a musket was not only hot, tiring work, the act of loading itself caused thirst, because the troops had to tear open the cartridges with their teeth. The powder consisted of charcoal, niter, and saltpeter, and tearing the cartridges open had the same effect as sucking on charcoal. Thirst plagued both armies throughout the engagement and it explained the tactical importance of Bloody Pond, located just behind Peach Orchard on the Union left.

Fighting was sporadic with many factors imposing their constraints on the rhythm of combat. Among these were thirst, fatigue, keeping weapons clean as well as the laborious motions of loading and firing. At Duncan Field where the Confederates made eleven charges as they tried to overwhelm the defenders of the Hornets' Nest, the attacks did not continue in a constant manner. Each charge lasted perhaps one half hour, but during the assault there were only about ten minutes of sustained fighting with an interruption of about twenty minutes to bring up and issue ammunition, clean weapons, and gather the wounded. During one assault, the attackers might fire fifteen to twenty rounds by which time their guns would become fouled and the men fatigued from exertion and excitement. At that point, the unit was vulnerable to coun terattack. If reinforcements did not come up, some were tempted to leave the line and to seek water, ammunition, or clean their weapons or else panic when a new attack began. Because of all these needs, soldiers could sustain intense firefights and melees for only about thirty minutes at a stretch. Low on water and ammunition or convinced that they were about to be overwhelmed, many a unit finally broke and ran. Tom Watkins' 18th Illinois, holding the frontage between brigadier generals Sherman's and W. H. L. Wallace's hard-pressed troops, finally broke when they found themselves "nearly Surrounded. . . . We got out," he recalled, "but it was Done by Some of the tallest Running that we Ever Done" (Diary, April 6, 1862).

The infantrymen's resolve was steeled by having their unit anchored by a battery of artillery. Artillery served as the linchpin of the line with infantry regiments consolidating positions on both sides of a battery. The firepower of a battery was awesome. Four properly served napoleons, for example, could cover a frontage of seventy yards. When triple-shotted with canister, a piece could spew out 650 shots per minute with a good crew. This was as intense a fire as that of a machine gun. With such firepower at their disposal, the gun crews had little trouble clearing fields of fire for meeting attacking units. The infantry looked on in wonder as brush disappeared after a few blasts of canister from the battery. Any infantryman who saw a battery set up a field of fire quickly realized that a frontal attack could be a very dangerous business. Even the smallest piece, a six-pounder with its 3.67-inch bore firing one round of canister, had a spread that would riddle everything within a sixteen by sixteen foot space at a range of fifty yards! To charge a battery, the attacking infantry had a chance at only one volley to disable the crew, and there was no question of stopping and reloading in the open. The best way to attack a battery was by the flank. It had to be done quickly, before the crews could swing the tubes around. It usually took one and a half to two minutes to turn the guns around, and it was in that brief interval that the gunners were vulnerable. The infantry attacks had to be very rapid, with no stopping to load or fire until they were upon the gunners. Delay meant heavy losses.

While the infantryman was exhausted by the procedures of loading and firing his piece, the artillerist had the added burden of manhandling his guns in wooded and broken terrain. A four- or six-horse hitch (two extra horses were preferred to replace losses) had a minimum turning radius of forty feet. Swinging the team, the gun, and the limber around to deploy the weapon among trees, over gullies, and through scrub was a herculean task. Once deployed, the guns began to provide reassuring fire for the infantry line. It was heavy work, and the guns were difficult and dangerous to fire. For one thing, the tubes got very hot and a man could be burned by touching them bare-handed. For another, as the bores became fouled, they grew harder to swab out, and the danger of live cinders remaining to prematurely ignite a powder charge as it was being rammed home increased the risks to the gunners. And finally, the guns recoiled wildly; even a six-pounder would bounce up three feet and rear back another six, putting nearby personnel at risk. The batteries were even more dangerous when in retreat. A battery was a peril to everyone in its path as it careered to its next position. Cyrus Boyd remembered the pandemonium caused by terrified artillery horses, with their caissons still attached, as they "ran through the squads of men and striking trees causing the percussion shells to explode blowing up horses and caissons and everything around them" (Boyd 1953: 32). Generally, all the crews on both sides performed very well, except for Myer's Ohio Battery. This battery panicked and fled. Records, however, show that the battery took casualties, suggesting that some of the men joined other units and continued the fight. The gunners often displayed exceptional courage in defending their pieces. Jesse Young, a trooper attached to McClernand's division, recalled how a German artillery officer rode up to Grant in great haste exclaiming, " 'Sheneral—Sheneral . . . de repels dey have took my cannon. Dey captured my batteree!' " The general replied, " 'Why, captain, I'm sorry to hear that. Did you spike the guns before they captured them?' 'Vot, sheneral? Shpike dem new shteel guns? No sir; it vould shpile 'em. Ve did better as dot . . . ve shoost took'em back again' '' (Young 1894: 111–12).

The cavalry had a limited role at Shiloh. They did not fight as regiments. Instead, the cavalry units were broken up into battalion-size detachments to serve as scouting forces for each division. When the fighting broke out they fought in the line as infantry or were used in a provost function. They had their hands full on the Union side as the troops in blue fell back. A soldier remembered that "cavalrymen were riding in all directions with sabers drawn and revolvers threatening to shoot and 'Cut mens heads off' if they did not stop and all make a stand together" (Boyd 1953: 32).

Another aspect of combat perceived by the green troops was the casualties. The minié ball had such kinetic energy that it was reported to have shattered bone in twenty-six places. The soldiers felt that friends and kin should know what it was like, the regiment and the community being bound together. Amos Currier, 8th Iowa Infantry, recalled matter-of-factly the first time he saw a comrade struck. He was shot in the head, the bullet making "a peculiar spat I shall never forget" (Diary, April 17, 1862). Frequently, the soldiers gave detailed accounts of the severity of the wounds and the circumstances surrounding the tragedy for the victim's friends and loved ones back home. An Alabamian in Chalmers' brigade recited a litany of individual and family tragedies as they plunged into enemy fire and advanced toward the Union line behind the Peach Orchard. "Before we got fairly in battle Corporal Anderson was killed almost instantly. The only words he uttered were, 'I've got it.' . . . The next hurt was Richard K. Jones. . . . He was hit somewhere near the knee, the ball ranging up the fleshy part of his thigh. . . . Daniel King was shot under the eye, next the nose, the bullet passing into his mouth" (*The Mobile Advertiser and Register*, April 11, 1862). As the toll increased, the letters read like an inventory of personal disasters. When Henry Morton Stanley's 6th Arkansas executed its first attack, "One man raised his chest as if to yawn, and jostled me. I turned to him, and saw that a bullet had gored his whole face and penetrated his chest. Another ball struck a man a deadly rap on the head, and he turned on his back and showed his ghastly white face to the sky" (Laurie 1985: 44). On the other side of the line, among Sherman's men, John L. Ruckman of the 57th Ohio recounted the frightful toll to friends back home. It was "hard to see a fellow mortal fall pierced by a bullet and one fall here and another there . . . one with a leg shot off . . . another with an arm broke." The Ohioan counted up his list of horrors destined for the people back home, and then added a final gruesome addendum. "I saw one man get the upper part of his head taken off" (To John Kinsel, April 12, 1862). Men were killed in every circumstance. For example, an infantryman serving with the 14th Wisconsin told how he saw a terrified rebel fleeing ingloriously on all fours when "a cannon ball struck him, tearing him in pieces, and scattering his limbs in different directions" (Quiner, Reel No. 2, Vol. 5, p. 140).

The men often expressed amazement at surviving the impact of a minié ball. A Confederate reported to his hometown newspaper how a ball penetrated his friend's face and went into his mouth; he swallowed it. His comrade thought he was lost, but reported home the next day that his friend was nevertheless up and about and boasting how he had managed to digest "two ounces of Yankee lead" (*The Mobile Advertiser and Register,* April 11, 1862). Being struck by shell or ball, without injury, was a close encounter with eternity; James Griffin, a gunner with the 5th Company, Washington Artillery, described how he was miraculously spared. "I received the full force of a minie ball in my right flank . . . which would undoubtedly have perforated me . . . had it not been for the very large knife I carried in my breast pocket" (*The New Orleans Daily Crescent,* April 19, 1862). John Caldwell was amazed at his own luck. The Kentuckian was in Trabue's brigade and was successively struck on the hip and the shoulder by spent balls. Later his shoulder strap was cut by another, and his leggings were torn by yet another bullet. The gods were indeed smiling on him until his regiment finally tumbled into a ravine where the Union troops caught them and poured fire down on Caldwell and his comrades (Diary, April 6, 1862).

The Confederates mentioned the sight of dead and wounded soldiers more often than the Northern troops. Forty-two percent of the nineteen Confederates devoted most of their comments to describing the casualties, while 31 percent of the thirty-four Union soldiers dwelt on this aspect of the battle. The most likely reason was that the Confederate army had been on the field for both days, whereas only four of the Union divisions saw action on both days.[6] Furthermore, the Confederates suffered proportionately higher casualties. Men in units that had higher than average casualties (more than 25 percent) dwelt on this more often than lightly engaged units.[7]

Some of the men described the wounded and dead with detached precision, others tried to shut the sight out of their minds, and yet others were deeply affected. There was Lieutenant William Candace Thompson of the 6th Mississippi who watched friends and relatives drop by the wayside as the regiment advanced. "I began to see men on the ground and soon realized that they were hurt. At first I couldn't see their faces. Maybe I didn't want to see them. The first wounded man I recognized was my Uncle Henry's eldest son, cousin James Magnum. He had been shot in the face. I wanted to help him . . . everyone was moving forward. . . . We just had to get at those Federals who were shooting us." It was hard leaving friends and relatives behind; the last sight Thompson had of his friend Stephen was his "eyes . . . glazing over " (1964: 21).

The overwhelming misfortune of being hit may in some cases have established a brief but tenuous bond of empathy between friend and foe. But just as often, it did not. Liberty Independence Nixon, 26th Alabama, felt no pity for a blue-uniformed fellow shot through the hips. The Northern lad begged "me to do something for him." Instead, "[I] asked him why he ha[d] left his home to come here to destroy people who had never harmed him" (1958: 152).

T. C. Buck, a gunner with Stanford's Mississippi Battery, tried hard to put it all out of his mind during those two days. But when nightfall came, the scenes overwhelmed him and he told his sister that "I could not help but cry and pray for a merciful God to console the suffering and spare the living." He tried to exorcise the sights of combat by confronting them, detailing to his sister how he "passed many of both our men and the enemy who had their heads blown off by cannon balls," then he abruptly ended the letter, overwhelmed by the horror of it all (To Bettie, April 13, 1862). By contrast, Ambrose Bierce relished rubbing the reader's face in the gore. "A Federal sergeant . . . lay face upward, taking in his breath in convulsive, rattling snorts, and blowing it out in sputters of froth which crawled creamily down his cheeks. . . . A bullet had clipped a groove in his skull, above the temple; from this the brain protruded in bosses, dropping off in flakes and strings." Bierce expressed clinical surprise that "one could get on, even in this unsatisfactory fashion, with so little brain." When one of his men asked if he should put a bayonet through the dying man to put him out of his misery, Bierce hypocritically claimed shock "at the cold blooded proposal," but then admitted that "too many were looking" (1966: I, 255).

"We was in the fight five hours and all this time we was marching over dead bodies," Wiliam Innis, Company B, 39th Indiana, wrote after participating in Buell's counterattack on April 7 (To wife, April 16, 1862; see also W. S. Dillon, Diary, April 6, 1862). Marching through an abattoir made death banal. As the men picked their way among the corpses, the dead became objectified. They coolly and discriminately reviewed the piles of flesh, only taking notice of those with ironic attitudes. There was, for example, the Confederate who Robert L. Kimberly, 41st Ohio, Hazen's brigade, saw "kneeling beside a big log, his head and shoulders bent forward over it, and his gun in his hands as he held it in the position of aiming when he met instant death" (1897: 25). Private Elisha Stockwell, 14th Wisconsin, could never forget the dead man "leaning back against a tree as if asleep, but his intestines were all over his legs" (Abernathy 1958: 15–16). Cyrus Boyd's interest was peaked at the sight of a federal corpse "leaning against a tree with a violin tightly grasped in his left hand" (1953: 37). The implacable brutality of war was driven in as they saw how the battle raked back and forth over the dead and wounded even after they were *hors de combat*. There were the bodies churned into the ground by artillery and wagons "till they were shoved down into the mud and one arm or leg sticking out" (S. B. Franklin, Memoirs: 5). There were also the areas where brush fires caused by exploding shells had tortured the wounded and mutilated the dead yet once more. Gustavus Cushman remembered the "bodies blackened, and half consumed lay in heaps in all attitudes, a good many to all appearance had been burnt alive, being wounded and unable to escape" (To brother, April 13, 1862).

The suffering of the thousands of horses was also noted. Perhaps the suffering beasts epitomized the soldiers' own helplessness in the maelstrom. The suffering animals exemplified the implacable destructiveness of war, the crushing of the innocent along with the guilty (R. Holmes 1986: 106). A Union soldier vividly recalled the sad sight of wounded horses standing forlornly in the mud, "their heads drooping, their eyes glassy and gummy, waiting for the slow coming death" (Wheeler 1976: 103). Horror and poignancy surrounded the abandoned batteries near Prentiss' camps, where twenty-six artillery horses had been butchered by counterbattery fire. The horses were good soldiers, too. A Hawk-eye infantryman observed sadly that "the faithful horses have died *in the harness* right by the cannon. Some of them torn to quarters by the bursting shell" (Boyd 1953: 38). The animals' trusting docility opened them to the battle's worst atrocities. "Immediately in the rear of where we were lying," recalled Corporal Charles Wright, Company C, 81st Ohio, "stood an army wagon with four mules attached. Three of them were dead, and had fallen as they were hitched; a living mule, the off-leader stood by the side of his dead comrade kicking vigorously. The wicked minie balls rattled . . . against the wagon, which was standing broadside to the rebels, the mule was still standing when we left." Years later he wondered if that mule had survived the holocaust (1887: 35).

Much of the misery and horror of combat was alternately magnified and hidden, because of the environment of battle; the drama loomed and subsided from among billows of smoke, while the noise rose and fell with the intensity of the fire. "Such a roaring of guns none of you never heard," James Jones of the 57th Ohio Infantry told his parents, "it was almost enough to make a person deef" (To father and mother, April 13, 1862). The noise was even more frightening when the men could not see what was going on. The "cloudes of smoke . . . made the sky seem like night," wrote an Illinois infantryman (Z. P. Shumway to wife [Hattie], April 13, 1862). The smoke of the black powder fire arms was frustrating to the troops, who were reluctant to engage in untargeted fire. Leander Stillwell of the 61st Illinois "preferred to wait for a good opportunity, when I could take deliberate aim at some individual foe," but he complained that "the fronts of both lines were shrouded in smoke. I had my gun at a ready, and was trying to peer under the smoke in order to get a sight of our enemies. Suddenly I heard someone in a highly excited tone calling me ... 'Stillwell! shoot! shoot! ... I looked around and saw ... Bob Wilder, our second lieutenant. He was ... fairly wild and excited, jumping up and down like a hen on a hot griddle. 'Why lieutenant,' said I, 'I can't see anything to shoot at.' 'Shoot, shoot, anyhow,' '' he screamed back (1920: 54).

The smoke and noise also impeded command and control and caused tremendous confusion. Silas Grismore recalled that his 18th Louisiana first took fire from Hardee's advance guard instead of from the enemy (Bergeron 1981: 42). During the initial confusion that ensued after the surprise attack, units were unsure where the enemy was. This situation was particularly unnerving for raw recruits such as George McBride and his comrades of the 15th Michigan who had the misfortune to arrive only the day before the attack and were as yet unfamiliar with the lay of the terrain and where the enemy was coming from. McBride recalled his first encounter with the enemy. "There appeared over the ridge in front a column of men." The Michiganders waited, hesitated, and peered intently at the advancing column to try to discern their identity. Then "they come down the hill ... and [fire] into us. We stand at an order arms and look at them as they shoot. ... No reply on our part—not a man has a cartridge!" (McBride 1894: 8–9).

To add to the confusion, some of the militia regiments did not have regulation-issue color uniforms. Lieutenant Colonel E. C. Dawes watched from the 5th Division camps as a "regiment with full ranks, uniformed in blue, marched by flank to the drum beat. This course was obliquely across the path of the Seventieth [Ohio] Regiment; a few moments would bring them together." Were they really a friendly unit or were they advancing Confederates? Dawes agonized. Hoping he was right, he yelled, "They are rebels. I am going to fire on them!" Just then the "wind lifted the silken folds of their banner. It was the Louisiana State flag" (Duke 1900: 50). Other units hastily changed their garb just before going into action to avoid being shot at by their own side. At Fort Donelson, the Illinois "Grays" had been shot at, so when the long roll sounded at Pittsburg Landing, their commander halted the regiment in a field to wait for proper-color uniforms. "In about a half an hour," one of their number recalled, "there came tearing up the road a mule team and army wagon with drivers, the quartermaster and the commissary sergt. lashing the poor mules to the top of their speed. They swung in front of our Q.M.C. Sergt., knocked the boxes open and threw out the coats to the company officers, who threw each man a coat, which was exchanged for his grey one. There was no time for fits. Small men got big coats, large men small coats." So attired they marched off into battle (J. Nesbitt letter, G. R. Lee Papers).

The confusion bred wild rumors of disaster among the Union troops during the first day. Major Dawes described the problems of distinguishing fact from fiction in the heat of battle. He was at Sherman's headquarters when a man brought news of disaster. " 'Our army has surrendered.' he said—'How do you know?' " Dawes asked. The man replied, " 'I saw them. . . . I saw a regiment of our cavalry drawn up in a line on the river bank, each man standing at his horse's head with arms and accouterments lying at his feet, and a rebel officer going along the line taking down the men's names.' " Dawes used humor and logic to puncture the rumor, declaring that "if the army has surrendered and there is only one officer taking the names of all of them, he will get along to us about six months after our time is out." Dawes was proved right, when a few minutes later came news that the men lining up on the riverbank were actually Buell's arriving reinforcements (quoted by Duke 1900: 53–54).

After the first day's fighting subsided, the night brought new torments. "Oh, what a night of horrors that was!! It will haunt me to the grave," wrote Joseph Dimmit Thompson of the 38th Tennessee (To Mary, April 9, 1862, Thompson Diary and Letters). Although night brought some reprieve from the constant roar of artillery and musketry and although it hid the ghastly clumps of dead in its darkness, it did not bring the men escape through sleep. The bad weather returned with a vengeance, drenching the troops as they sought whatever shelter they could find. It was a sinister night, whose pelting rain was pierced by the wails of the wounded, the claps of thunder seared by lighting, and added to all this a reminder that the guns waited the morrow. The Union command had struck on the cruel plan of ordering the *Lexington* and the *Tyler* to fire into the Confederate lines throughout the night to impede the Confederates' sleep. Every fifteen minutes a dull boom followed shortly by an earth jarring explosion shook the soldiers out of their slumber. It made "a fellow wish he was some other place," wrote Colonel Alvin Hovey of the 24th Indiana in Lew Wallace's division ("History of the 24th Regiment Indiana Infantry," Hovey Collection: 24–25). Added to the tremendous booms, came shrieks and moans from the hostile darkness as well as crazed and wounded horses thrashing about and trampling sleeping men (Boyd 1953: 35).

EMOTIONAL RESPONSES TO COMBAT

"Ress you have no Idea how a person feeles when they go into battle," wrote Sergeant John Hardin of Company E, 24th Indiana Infantry, to his sister Teressa. "The cannon balls flying in all directions the shells bursting over our heads . . . you had better believe we learned to dodge and lay close to the ground . . . it was a time that every moment seemed the last" (To sister, Letters, April 12, 1862). Going into battle, Hardin, like soldiers throughout history, was subjected to an enormous variety of concerns, arising from fear, hunger, thirst, fatigue, and uncertainty (Kellett 1982: 231).

The range of emotions that were engendered by battlefield stresses are as varied as the number of soldiers in any army (B. J. Wiley 1978b: 29–30), but recent studies have concluded that the predominant emotion was fear.[8] Its "symptoms" in combat include a "violent pounding of the heart," "a sinking feeling in the stomach," "cold sweat," "nervousness," "shaking hands," "repeating meaningless acts," "losing control of bowels," and "urinating in pants" (Stouffer 1949: II, 201; see also Woolridge 1968: 9). Fear—along with the enemy—had to be defeated. On the battlefield, the soldier is in a two-front war: on one front, he fights the enemy, and on the other front, he struggles with himself to hold his fear in check. In his psychological struggle, his mood races through a series of wild oscillations in reaction to the changing situation on the battlefield. Through it all, he tries to hold on, to keep control. Moods change from moment to moment in response to the rapid succession of terrifying stimuli. Going through his baptism of fire, Sam Watkins of the 1st Tennessee gave some idea of this flood of emotions, ranging from sadness to dazed awe and then to elation.

Men were lying everywhere in every conceivable position . . . some waving their hats and shouting to go forward. It all seemed to me a dream; I seemed to dream; I seemed to be in a sort of haze, when siz, siz, siz, the minnie balls from the Yankee line began to whistle around our ears. . . . Down would drop just one fellow and then another, either killed or wounded, when we were ordered to charge bayonets. I had been feeling mean all the morning as if I had stolen sheep, but when the order to charge was given, I got happy. I felt happier than a fellow does when he professes religion at a big Methodist camp-meeting (1962: 42).

The same oscillation affected George McBride of the 15th Michigan. He recounted the cycle of moods. First contact with the enemy fire engendered a dazed feeling. Then as the specificity of the danger took form, terror ensued and with it the urge to flee. However, once he assessed the scope of the situation and he mustered himself, McBride managed to participate actively in the fighting (1894: 8–12). Unlike McBride, Lucius Barber, 15th Illinois, was more effective at resisting passivity and panic.

To say that I was perfectly calm and self possessed would be presuming too much, although, as I then tried to analyze my feelings, I was not conscious of a tremor. They seemed more like a deathly calm. I know that I was equal to the task of doing my whole duty without flinching, but to me, as well as to every other soldier just before entering the battle, an involuntary awe and dread crept over me; but if true and brave, these feelings gradually die away in the excitement of the fight until they become almost extinct unless some sudden reverse throws everything in confusion, then all is terror and excitement (1894: 52–53).

Others made a determined effort to block out the sights and sounds of battle by total involvement in the task at hand. T. C. Buck, a gunner in Stanford's Mississippi Battery, kept calm by trying "not to let anything enter my mind to render me unpleasant" (To sister, April 13, 1862).

Beyond self-control, there are, of course, degrees of courage. Based on his experiences as a medical officer in World War I, Lord Charles Moran set up a scale of valor, which is equally applicable to classifying the combat behavior of the Civil War volunteers. Moran's scale of valor had four levels. First, there were those who simply did not feel fear. Second, there were the men who did feel fear, but did not show it. Third, there were soldiers who showed it but did their duty. And finally, there were men who felt fear, showed it, and shirked their duty (1966: 3).

More than two-thirds of the recruits expressed passive-defensive reactions, involving fear, awe, or surprise during their baptism of fire. Their responses to the baptism of fire put them in Moran's second and third categories of courage. This was no different from the reaction of World War II veterans, 65 percent of whom expressed the same type of emotion (R. Holmes 1986: 205).

On the other hand, less than a third of Shiloh's recruits claimed that they felt calm, steadfast, angry, or elated during their first contact with the enemy, fitting into Moran's highest category of courage in battle. This suggests that only one in three of the raw troops turned out to be what Egbert defined as active and effective fighters. This raises questions about Linderman's suggestion that the early volunteers were exceptionally motivated combatants because of a Victorian ethos equating fearlessness and bravery (Linderman 1987: 18). Egbert defined a good fighter not merely as one who managed to fire his weapon (Marshall 1947), but one who also provided leadership during assaults, got men to fire, encouraged them to stay in the firing line, calmed them and increased their confidence, took aggressive action against the enemy by volunteering for hazardous missions, and fired effectively at the enemy. He performed supporting tasks under fire, such as caring for the wounded and bringing up ammunition. The good fighter also led the men by getting them into position. He set the standard for good conduct by taking aggressive action and remaining cool throughout (Egbert 1954: 3, 8). Most of the Shiloh volunteers did not attain this level of fearlessness and effectiveness in battle. Their emotional response to combat was much the same of soldiers in later wars.

The candidness of their responses was controlled by seeing if the distance from the event made a difference. The soldiers' letters, diaries, and reminiscences were divided into those written in 1862–63 and those written much later to see if the veterans' memories may have embellished their reminiscences with the passing of time. The cross-tabulation showed that their later writings were just as candid. Nor did their published reminiscences and letters express a more heroic style than their letters to intimates or their diaries. The men were just as willing to admit to passivity and fright in battle in public as in private.

There was only one honorable escape from the dilemma of fear versus duty and that was being lightly wounded. Elisha Stockwell, 14th Wisconsin, was slightly injured just as the unit took up positions for an assault. He was struck in the arm by a spent cannonball. He showed his wound to his lieutenant, who told him he did not have to participate in the attack and that he was excused to return to Pittsburg Landing. Stockwell admitted he "was as tickled as a boy let out of school," when he learned he was out of it with a "million dollar wound" (Abernathy 1958: 20–21). Few were so lucky.

The decisive moment of the Shiloh volunteers' baptism of fire occurred just as they emerged from their initial daze and began to perceive the effects of the enemy fire. At that moment, they suddenly became conscious of the dangers around them. Panic swept them up, ebbed, and then engendered a paralytic undertow. Many factors instilled a feeling of terror: there were the rumors of encirclement, the detonations of the heavy guns, the close misses, the sight of comrades struck down, and finally, there was the frightening sight of the enemy deploying ominously in their front.

Bracing himself for a Confederate attack from a nearby wood, Jesse Young, 3rd Battalion, 4th Illinois Cavalry, was seized by panic. "It strikes into the heart of a man . . . [and] it can hardly be conquered. It bewilders and unnerves and maddens. It is the only thing that scares people out of their wits," he explained. He could not see anyone, but he could hear the approaching crackle of musketry, the screams of wounded men, and the yelling mass of rebels crashing toward him. The ancient god Pan was again frightening armies in the woods (Young 1894: 106–7). It was just as terrifying to muster one's courage for an attack as it was to face one. As the 29th Indiana attacked a rebel position, Bergun Brown admitted to his parents that "my hair stuck up some under a most telling fire" (To folks at home, April 12, 1862). And among the gunners serving the pieces of Stanford's Mississippi Battery, George W. Jones' emotions paralleled B. Brown's as he and his comrades took counterbattery fire. "Down I go . . . dodging the big ones. . . . I wish that I were a dwarf instead of a six-footer. My hair, good heavens, is standing on end like the quills of a porcupine" (Spradlin 1981: Diary, April 6, 1862).

Most surmounted the urge to flee and stayed in the line to meet the enemy. However, others such as George McBride were overcome by fear. He and the 15th Michigan had the misfortune to bear the brunt of the Confederate attack at the very opening moments of the battle. Even thirty years later he could vividly relive the scene as the Confederate onslaught battered the green troops of the 6th Division. He remembered looking terror-stricken at the shot bouncing along the ground throwing up little clouds of dust and at the sight of men falling all around them. It "impressed me with a desire to get out of there. I recollect," he continued, "that the hair now commenced to rise on the back of my head . . . and I felt sure that a cannon-ball was close behind me, giving me chase as I started for the river. In my mind, it was a race between me and that cannon-ball" (McBride 1894: 9).

Many situations elicited panic. The demoralizing effect of shirkers was often mentioned. Shirkers were resented not for their weakness, but for their corrosive effect on morale. Levi Wagner was with one of the units from Buell's army that had to pass through numerous panicked soldiers at the landing as it moved up. As he and the 1st Ohio disembarked, they were engulfed with dire imprecations but the fate that awaited them if they proceeded farther. " 'For God's Sake, don't go out there or you will all be killed,' " were "cheering words for raw men," he recalled (Papers). Yet no unit broke completely; even after the 53rd Ohio fled, many of its companies continued to function as independent units.

Other situations corroded morale as well: near misses from enemy fire, wounds and pain, seeing comrades fall, and fatigue could cause the volunteers to lose control and withdraw from the fight. There was also the terrifying sight of enemy regiments resolutely deployed for an attack. Even without a shot fired, this sight was a supremely frightening spectacle, leading to the suggestion that the majestic evolutions of compact masses of infantry had as much effect on green troops as the actual shooting. Watching such a display on Prentiss' left, Leander Stillwell conceded, "I am not ashamed to say . . . that I would willingly have given a general quit-claim deed for every jot and title of military glory falling to me . . . if I only could have been miraculously . . . set down . . . a thousand miles away" (1920: 44). Seeing the formidable ranks of enemy battalions preparing to march on the 11th Iowa Infantry, Henry Adams thought it was "an impossibility to stand such a force" (Diary, n.d.).

Even more terrifying was enemy artillery unlimbering in one's front. Seeing the enemy gunners go through their preliminaries, knowing that in a few minutes they would be taking fire was a sobering experience. Young crouched behind what cover was handy and watched in horrified anticipation as an enemy battery wheeled into position on a little hill in front of Shiloh Chapel, just opposite his position. There was a wounded man caught in the no-man's land between the unit and the Confederate gunners. "In agony of alarm, [the helpless soldier] . . . saw the men loading their guns. The cannon seemed to be aimed right in his face. He called out . . . 'Don't shoot me!' And even while he spoke he saw flames belch from the guns" and he disintegrated in the smoke (1894: 102)

A brush with death was another event that could shatter morale and cause panic. A close call could put some of the green soldiers *hors de combat* just as much as an actual wound. Henry Stanley was attacking with his Arkansas regiment, when he was sent sprawling by a Union bullet in the stomach. He thought he was finished and would now die in agony from one of the worst-feared wounds, but he soon regained some composure and discovered that the bullet had only slammed into his belt buckle leaving it bent and cracked, but had not pierced him. However, it was just as effective. Stanley's nerve was as shattered as his belt buckle, and he crawled to cover leaving the rest of the 6th Arkansas to sweep on (Laurie 1985: 44). Warren Olney had a similar experience. He described how "a ball struck me fair on the side just under the arm. I felt it go through my body, I struggled on the ground with the effect of the blow for and in an instant, recovered myself, sprang to my feet . . . felt I was mortally wounded and—took to my heels." Terror-struck, he soon even overtook his own regiment, which was also fleeing from the Sunken Road area. Olney's stamina surprised him as he pounded past his comrades. He "began to suspect a man shot through the body couldn't make such speed, and perhaps [he] . . . was not mortally wounded after all; [he] felt for the hole the ball had made, found it in the blouse and shirt, bad bruise in the ribs, nothing more—spent ball" (1885: 587). A like experience happened to Green of the 6th Kentucky (C.S.A.).

Just as I had loaded and was raising my gun to fire I fell from a bullitt which struck me just over the heart. I felt sure it had gone clear through me and it flashed through my mind that I would live until the arterial blood started back to my heart, when I would drop dead. I was surprised to find that I was alive. I felt my breast to learn the extent of my wound when I found one piece of the bullitt laying against my skin inside my clothes just over my heart. The ball had passed through the stock of my gun, split on the iron ramrod of my gun and burried itself in a little testament in my jacket pocket (April 7, 1862).

Others were less fortunate, for them there was the awful assessment of the extent of their injury as they waited in dread for the pain to begin to well up and the effects of the stress-generated anesthesia [endomorphine] to subside. They were physically immobilized by their injuries or were in such pain that they could no longer function. If ambulatory, they sought shelter nearby or ambled befogged toward succor. Ultimately, where possible, they were gathered up and brought to the captured Union camps where the Confederate surgeons set up makeshift aid stations. On the Union side, they ended up at the landing, and there they sat or lay waiting. The least fortunate ones languished in no-man's-land.

Seeing casualties all around as they headed into action also eroded morale. Men who fought with units that took above average casualties (over 25 percent) evinced aggressive combat attitudes half as often as soldiers from outfits that had suffered light casualties.[9] The results coincide with World War II studies that found a high correlation between low morale and high casualty rates (Hicken 1969: 247). This effect was registered by Sergeant Edwin Payne as his Company A, 34th Illinois passed through Savannah with Colonel Edward Kirk's 5th Brigade of McCook's division. The town was already filled with wounded. "We saw long rows of white cots . . . visible in an empty store building as we . . . marched by raising in the mind many questions as to whether or not their lot was not better than ours who were yet to take the chances of the battle the next day" (1902: 16).

Finally, along with the experiences of watching in fearful anticipation as the enemy deployed, the shattering effect of a brush with death, and the sight of the wounded, combat morale was also eroded by sheer fatigue. A soldier in battle may reach the point where he is emotionally and physically exhausted. He simply cannot take any more. At this moment, men may begin drifting away from the firing line as a response to the stress (R. Holmes 1986: 229). Withdrawal may not be a tumultuous panic, but simply a gradual pullback by men who have reached the limits of their endurance. This began to occur by late afternoon of the first day. Exhausted by the physical exertions and tired from the psychological stress of combat, the volunteers were fought out by late afternoon. Contrary to modern wars, the time that Civil War soldiers spent in the firing line was relatively short, but it was very intense fighting. At the end of the first day's fighting, the troops were so tired that they could not carry out further sustained operations. Unit cohesion had become extremely fragile. Sleep was the only way to restore morale. Even if the opposing forces had any organized forces available, fatigue had nullified what fighting morale remained after fear and wounds had taken their toll. The men collapsed in sleep even in a driving rain. "Never was I so tired as this night," George Hurlbut confided to his diary (April 7, 1862).

Plunged into the turmoil and terror of their first battle, the outcome of the volunteers' two-front war against their enemy and against their own fear was in doubt on both "fronts." Their social values and instinct pulled in opposite directions: the one to steadfastness and effective action, and the other toward flight and survival.

Despite the overwhelming terror inherent in the new environment of battle, some soldiers evinced active fighter attitudes such as calm, elation, or rage. Captain William Bradford was commanding Company A of the 57th Indiana as it joined in the Union counterattack of April 7. He told his wife, "I was perfectly astonished at myself. I never became excited, I do not know that it changed the beat of a pulse" (To wife, April 10, 1862). Others, such as Stanley, felt a sense of elation and aggressive excitement when the order to fix bayonets was given to the 6th Arkansas, and with it came the opportunity for release from the tension (Laurie 1985: 44; and B. I. Wiley 1978b: 72–73). Yet others such as George Gates became enraged and fought all the harder. When Gates saw the first comrade shot, he declared. "I was so enraged . . . I could have tore the heart of the rebel out could I have reached him" (To parents, April 8, 1862). Bradford's calm, Stanley's excitement, and Gates' anger were all positive responses to battle stress, and they all exemplified emotions that were associated with the third of the respondents of the men who expressed active-aggressive responses to their initiation in battle.

These responses were reinforced by certain situations. Among the most supportive were ties with friends and the sense of confidence they had in their territorially recruited units (Kellett 1982: 98, 286–87). This type of regiment embodied both political and community bonds with military traditions, such as esprit de corps and devotion to comrades. The volunteer regiment was thus a source of overlapping powerful loyalties. Lord Moran contended that good civilians made good soldiers. Fortitude in battle transcends military, organizational commitments. "Fortitude," he argued, "has its roots in morality." Responsible men who do their duty at home will also do so on the battlefield. Courage in battle is thus a character trait, a "moral quality." The individual volunteer's personal conscience and the choice he made between fight or flight determined his development as an effective soldier (Moran 1966: 160). By inference therefore, an army of volunteers composed of men who for a large part enlisted out of a sense of patriotic duty would be more resilient than an army of mercenaries or conscripts. Assistant Surgeon Samuel Eells typified such men. He was riveted so strongly to his place among his comrades that he did not notice the debacle unfolding around his 12th Michigan as Prentiss' division was surrounded. Eells wrote home, "I did not know but what I should get frightened in the first battle, but I believe I didn't, and if I had been . . . scared I don't think I could have run off and left our wounded crying for help" (To friends, April 13, 1862).

On the other hand, Bierce and his Hoosier outfit were encourged not so much by duty, as by the sight of artillery pulling up along side them. "There is something that inspires confidence in the line as a [field]gun dashes up to the front, shoving fifty or a hundred men to one aside as if it said, 'Permit me!' Then it squares its shoulders, calmly dislocates a joint in its back, sends away its twenty-four legs and settles down with a quiet rattle which says plainly as possible, 'I've come to stay.' There is a superb scorn in its defiant attitude" (1966: I, 252).

Some men were consumed by combat narcosis: a feeling of surging power and anger as they were swept along with their units. This sensation was facilitated by the relatively close formations of nineteenth-century warfare, in which collective emotions could spread more quickly. Olney experienced the feeling when his unit drove off a Confederate attack. The victory "exhilarated us," he recalled. It swept them up in a wave of savage excitement. "We had tasted blood and were thoroughly aroused. . . . The very madness of blood-thirstiness possessed us. To kill, to exterminate the beings in front of us, was our whole desire" (1885: 586). Victory also spurred on the elan of J. W. Green's Kentuckians as they swept the Union defenders before them. They plunged on thinking that "we would capture Grant's entire disorganized army," and were "greatly disappointed that we were not pushed forward" when evening wrung down the curtain (Diary, April 6, 1862).

The very dynamics of the fight that emboldened Green to wish to attack again also steeled Boyd of the 15th Iowa to make one last stand and yield no more (1953: 34). Boyd felt a sense of desperate determination as his unit deployed for the last time that day.

Yet underlying the active fighter's emotions was always a strong sense of patriotic commitment. There was a belief in "the cause." It was not formally articulated as an ideology, nor was it frequently mentioned, but it was there. Nationalism was such a powerful force that even recent immigrants had absorbed it. Leander Stillwell remembered asking his friend Charles Oberdieck, a recent arrival from Hanover, what he thought of the situation as their line collapsed along the Sunken Road. Was it all up, were they going to surrender at the landing, Stillwell asked Oberdieck. " 'I yoost tells you how I feels,' " replied the Hanoverian. " 'I no care anything about Charley [referring to himself]; he no haf wife nor children, fadder nor mudder, brudder nor sister; if Charley get killed, it makes no difference; dere vas nobody to cry for him, so I dinks about myselfs; but I tells, you I yoost den feels bad for de Cause!' " (Stillwell 1920: 50).

Emotional responses by the volunteers ran the gamut of human emotions from awed passivity to terror and panicky flight, to calm, exhilaration, and vengeful rage. Broadly speaking, the range of emotions can be divided into active-aggressive responses and passive-defensive responses. Among the fifty-one respondents in the three armies, Grant's army had the highest proportion of aggressive responses, Buell's men registered the lowest proportion of aggressive emotions, and A. S. Johnston's was in-between. The figures are puzzling, because Johnston's men had been the attackers and Buell's were probably the best trained, yet Grant's men evinced the most-frequent active-fighter emotions, despite the mauling they had sustained. However, Grant's men were the most successful of the three armies and they went into action with a higher feeling of confidence. When comparing the enlisted men and the officers, the results were not as surprising. The officers expressed aggressive reactions to the battle more frequently than the enlisted men.[10] This is attributable to the higher motivations and greater responsibilities that went with their rank. Officers, by necessity, could less afford to fall victim to passive emotions and abandon their responsibilities. The concerns for their command allowed them less occasion to think of their own fears, lapse into passivity, or let surprise paralyze them.

EMERGING FROM BATTLE

"Here," wrote Lieutenant Colonel W.D. Niles of the 16th Wisconsin, "I am surrounded with nothing but death. . . . It is very unhealthy here. . . . Some of the Rebs didn't get buried very deep, and there is quite a stench rises from the graves. We just made a business of killing the gray-backed rog[ue]s. O they laid thick for four miles" (Quiner, Reel No. 2, Vol. 5, pp. 251–52). The grim horror of the battlefield bore down on Niles' morale, because, as Bell I. Wiley so aptly put it, "The morrow of a battle . . . was in some respects more trying than the conflict itself" (1978b: 74; see also Marshall 1947: 179; Kellett 1982: 313). During the days that followed the engagement, those who held the field surveyed the corpses and wreckage that was strewn for five miles over the battleground. Living in the midst of such desolation weighed heavy on the men's spirit. This "after-scene . . . teaches the frailty of all things human, the extent of human suffering and the cost of 'glorious war,' " wrote a dispirited volunteer with the 18th Wisconsin (Quiner, Reel No. 2, Vol. 2, pp. 57–58). As the men emerged from the shock of their baptism of fire and looked around them, they found themselves surrounded by stink and misery. Picking his way among the bodies and destruction, Henry Clune described the environment. "Gentle winds of Springtime seem sighing over a thousand new-made graves" (To Maggie [wife], April 16, 1862). But behind the words was a harsher reality. For Clune and the Union victors who were left holding the field, the "spoils" consisted of wrecked wagons, shattered caissons, and several thousand tons of rotting flesh. In a way, the losing side was more fortunate, because they left the task of burying the dead and disposing of the wrecked equipment to the victors. But the defeated Confederates were not spared their own share of misery as they trudged the twenty miles back to Corinth. It was pitiable sight: the shambling wounded and wagons with groaning piles of maimed soldiers. At the end of this odyssey, Richard Pugh of the Washington Artillery screamed a heart cry in his letter to his beloved. "Oh May," he grieved, "war is a horrible thing and a battle field is torture" (Lathrop 1962: 383).

As their minds flashed between the cameos of combat horror seared into their memories and the terrible relics it left behind, a deep post-combat depression overwhelmed many of the soldiers. Their idea of war had changed; "since we left Fulton [probably Missouri]," wrote John Resley of the 11th Iowa, "we were playing Soldiers but now we know what it is to Soldier" (To Sarah, May 11, 1862). Pugh, the Louisiana artillerist, echoed his Northern counterpart when he told his wife, "I had no idea of war untill then, and would have given anything in the world if I could have been away" (Lathrop 1962: 378). A young officer in the 16th Wisconsin confessed, "I had no conception of [war] . . . no pen can describe, nor imagination conceive, the intensity of horror that has been presented us" (Quiner, Reel No. 2, Vol. 5, p. 227).

Robert Kimberly remarked on the change in mood that followed the engagement. There was no more music, the bands had stopped playing, and the entire drum corps had been mobilized as stretcher-bearers. Uniforms were soiled and the distinctions of rank less visible or emphasized (1897: 25–26). Music and parades suddenly seemed inappropriate with "so many men launched into eternity in so short a time," wrote a Confederate gunner with Captain Charles P. Gage's battery (LDG to parents, April 8, 1862).

The battlefield itself had a lot to do with the plummeting morale. A large majority of the men fell into despondency as they emerged from the battle: 72 percent of the sixty respondents who described their feelings after combat. As Wellington declared fifty years earlier, "Nothing except a battle lost can be half as melancholy as a battle won" (T. H. Williams 1962: 33). The sight of the "field of victory" accentuated the post-combat depression. Captain Andrew Hickenlooper, who commanded the 5th Ohio Battery at Shiloh and had seen four years of fighting, later maintained that "eyes [had never] rested on such a scene of human slaughter" (1903: 433). The men were in a state of shock, having been through something so awful that it would "dethrone reason or pervert the judgment," wrote Jim Blankinship, a Confederate trooper (To Livie, April 18, 1862; see also *The Seneca Advertiser*, May 30, 1862).

When the guns at last fell silent, the smell of putrefaction blanketed the surrounding countryside (G. Hurlbut, Diary, April 26, 1862). But ten days of cool, rainy weather slowed the decomposition (O. E. Cunningham 1966: 520). Juxtaposing the nascent spring to the situation on the battlefield, Henry Clune wrote that "the peach and apple trees are in full bloom and impart a delicious fragrance to every zephyr especially when mingled ... with the odor of decomposed horses" (To Maggie [wife], April 14, 1862). The men had to make haste in burying the corpses because the outbreak of typhus and gastric disorders was imminent (Cumming, 1866: Journal, April 22, 1862). The cool weather may have slowed the onset of an epidemic, but it had a deleterious effect on the survivors' morale. The dark uncomfortable weather lowered spirits. The men were uncomfortable outside and found it hard to move around the camp. "The rush of armed hosts and the constant moving of army teams over the ground, saturated with rains, have converted it into a quagmire" (*The Columbia City News*, April 29, 1862). To make things worse, many of the Army of the Tennessee's tents had been destroyed, leaving the exhausted men crowded into the ones that were still intact. Buell's men were no better off. They had left their equipage at Savannah and it took some time to bring it up (O. E. Cunningham 1966: 514; see also S. S. Howell, Diary, April 10, 1862).

The rain drove the men to their tents to brood amid the stench of decaying bodies. A soldier in the 16th Wisconsin wrote that "the men had gloomy thoughts caused by the loss of so many of their comrades, and as the weather was such as to prevent their moving from their tents, the low spirits and inactivity had a bad effect on the health of a good many" (Quiner, Reel No. 2, Vol. 5, p. 282). Enshrouded in his tent, listening to the patter of the rain, smelling the stench seeping through the canvas from outside, and hearing the shouts of the burial details as they went about their business, Cyrus Boyd cried out in despair: "Oh my God! can there be anything in the *future* that *compensates* for this slaughter" (1953: 38). There was no escaping the carnage. When Colonel David Stuart's brigade was relocated with the rest of its parent division (Sherman's) around Shiloh Meeting House, it was difficult to find a suitable campsite; "when we come to pitch our tents," wrote William Kennedy of the 55th Illinois, "we could not find ground enough without taking that where the dead were buried" (To wife, April 22, 1862). A soldier from the same regiment recorded that they were obliged to move their camp from location to location ever in search of a place on the battlefield where they would not have to share the campsite with dead men and dead horses, but alas, "this is one *graveyard* and," he desponded that "we shall never get out of it" (Boyd 1953: 44).

Those at work outside had less time to dwell on such things, but their spirits were also low. It was hard to imagine that the area had ever provided a livelihood to several dozen modest homesteads before the armies arrived. Now the order and humanity of a civilian presence had been raked off the land. "All the houses are deserted," wrote Assistant Surgeon Eells when he finally caught up with the backlog of wounded soldiers by late April and had a chance to explore the area of the fighting.

"The cattle run wild until they are caught by the soldiers and killed for food. The fences are burnt up for firewood and a great deal of the timber is cut down, or spoilt by the bark being taken off to make beds" (To aunt and uncle, April 28, 1862; see also William Innis to sister, April 16, 1862; William Brown to wife, April 10, 1862).

It was all terribly disheartening to the federal troops, especially when they had to pick their way among the corpses looking for distinguishing marks or articles of clothing to identify lost friends. Rolling them over, peering intently at each fly-specked heap, they completed their obligation to friends and relatives in their company and to their survivors back at home. William Richardson and his brother George had left Half Breed Tract, Missouri, to join the 6th Iowa, but now George was dead, and his brother wrote in despair, "Oh, if I could just see those this morning that were with us then" (To Mother, April 27, 1862). The gruesome obligation weighed heavy on H. H. Giesy, a junior officer in the 46th Ohio. "If you had been here yesterday and gone with me in my rounds to find my boys, you would have seen sights that would have chilled the blood of the most cold hearted" (To brother, sister, and mother, April 9, 1862).

"The carts for the dead are constantly running," Calvin Morley of the 18th Wisconsin told his wife (Quiner, Reel No. 2, Vol. 6, p. 56). Over a thousand men were assigned to disposing of the corpses and carcasses. "They dig holes and pile them in like dead cattle and have teams to draw them together like picking up pumpkins" (G. C. Meadows, Collection). Watching dead friends hitched to ropes and dragged to assembly areas and unceremoniously slung onto wagons to be carted to burial sites depressed the men terribly. It confronted them with the tenuousness of their own mortality, and worse yet, with their own expendability. They realized they were now cogs in the war machine. It was "dreadful," lamented a Hoosier survivor, "to see the poor soldier just thrown in a ditch and covered over without any box" (J. Hardin to Ress [sister], Letters, April 12, 1862). An Iowan was angered and depressed by the way the dead were disposed of without even a marker showing where they were buried. "Sometimes," he wrote, "our tents come over a little mound . . . where some unknown soldier has *died* for a principle[,] but his *survivors* have not even marked his last resting place or given him the burial of a *faithful dog*" (Boyd 1953: 44).

In some cases, "long trenches were dug about six feet wide and three to four deep. The dead were rolled on blankets and carried to the trench and laid heads and feet alternating so as to save space. Old blankets were thrown over the pile of bodies and the earth thrown on top" (G. R. Lee, Papers). In other cases, the teams used the terrain to advantage by simply rolling the dead down deep gullies. An Iowan described the grisly work to the folks back home. He took a perverse pleasure in driving home its realities, making sure that those at home shared the same horrors that their men had had to live through. He carefully detailed how the crews stamped about "on top of the *dead* straightening out their legs and arms and *tramping* them down so as to make the hole contain as many as possible. Other men on the hillside had ropes with a noose on one end and they would attach this to a man's foot or head and haul him down the hollow and roll him in" (Boyd 1953: 41–42). The task seemed never ending. According to R. M. Nichols, 6th Kentucky Infantry (U.S.A.), the grim work took four days, but others reported bodies still being interred a week later (R. M. Nichols to Brother and Sister, April 13, 1862; Quiner, Reel No. 2, Vol. 5, p. 240).

Rushing to dispose of the bodies to avoid an epidemic, the details worked haphazardly. The graves were too shallow, and the constant rain mocked the gravediggers' work, washing the sod off the cadavers. Bergun Brown found that the burial work had not hidden the horrors. Two weeks later, he wrote, "The battlefield . . . by this time is becoming rather offensive to people of delicate stomachs for it begins to smell old. It [is] a horrible state of affairs to live upon ground where horses and men are buried or rather covered up—feet sticking out or hands and head as the case may be. . . . Men are buried in some places on the surface—merely a few shovels of loose dirt upon them" (To folks at home, April 23, 1862). Jesse Connelley saw "bodies buried in shallow ravines where the washes had left the bodies with so little covering that with one the nose and part of the face was exposed; some with just a hand sticking out, and others, toes and so on" (Diary, May 19, 1862). In other areas, the dead were buried right where traffic had to pass, the rain and wagon wheels churning up the ghastly heaps beneath. "*Skulls* and *toes* are sticking from beneath the clay all around and the heavy wagons crush the bodies turning up the bodies of the buried, making this one vast Golgotha" (Boyd 1953: 44; see also similar descriptions in *The Fairfield Ledger*, May 6, 1862; A. F. Davis to F. D. Davis [brother], April 21, 1862; P. Dobbins to R. M. Banta, February 6, 1864).

But the hastily buried bodies were not left to rest in peace. The elements had already pried them up to mock the living. And later, family members on the battlefield reopened the graves and poked among the gore in search of the bodies of loved ones to take them home for burial. "We have seen lots of citizens here everyday since the battle," wrote William Kennedy, "they are digging up the dead and taking them home." He thought two-week-old corpses were better left alone for "they are so bad they are not fit to be seen." Kennedy added that "I would not want to see a friend of mine after being buried two weeks. You know," he explained, "they had to be buried without coffins and they look like a lott of mud" (To wife, April 22, 1862).

In the meantime, concern for the army's health grew acute. Within a week, units such as the 77th Pennsylvania and 31st Indiana had been forced by disease and stench to flee their camps. "If we're not moved from here soon," wrote Jim Drish, 32nd Illinois Infantry, "we will all die of sickness, for it will be awfull in a few days" (To wife, April 10, 1862; see also S. T. Davis, Journal, April 15, 1862; J. Connelley, Diary, May 4, 1862). Assistant Surgeon S. H. Eells of the 12th Michigan was soon complaining that Pittsburg Landing "is a very unhealthy place on account of the numerous graves and the filth that is all over the ground everywhere for miles, old foul clothes, rotting meat thrown away," and other detritus (To aunt and uncle, April 12, 1862). And Sergeant Edwin Payne, Company A, 34th Illinois Infantry, dismally concluded that "war is destruction. Not only in the few fierce hours of bloody contest which occasionally takes place, but in the quiet of the camp, where disease holds sway" (1902: 23).

The Union army's health was indeed plummeting with each day they remained on the battlefield. George Hurlbut, of Captain Jerome Burrows' 14th Ohio Battery, exemplified the physical and psychological effects of the pestilential environment when he confided to his diary, "feel very unwell again. . . . Shall have to give up, I am afraid soon, if I get no stronger. Have no news from the world at large, and feel lonesome." Ill and depressed he lay about camp "in a dreamy and lazy manner, unwell and out of humor" (Diary, April 27 and 29, 1862). "Its astonishing how the regiment [12th Michigan] has run down," Eells confided to his relatives. "Not much over 300 rank and file went forward in the advance [toward Corinth] and many of them were not fit to go forward" (To aunt and uncle, May 1 and 12, 1862).

While the Union troops tried to cope with the battlefield that they had inherited, the Confederates faced their own morale problems on the twenty-mile retreat back to their base at Corinth. Dragging what was left of the 5th Company of the Washington Artillery's guns back to Corinth, Robert Pugh told his wife that "everyone was hushed in sadness." Then he burst out plaintively, "Oh my wife 'twas a sad thing to return to our camp and miss the joyous voices and merry laugh of those we had left behind" (Lathrop 1962: 382). It had rained going in, and now as the haggard Confederate columns returned, it was raining going back. The mud churned up by the passing army a few days before, now tugged even more tenaciously as they headed home. "On our way back," Corporal J. E. Magee of Stanford's Mississippi Battery wrote, "[I] saw several wagons broke down—provisions thrown about in the mud." It was, he vouched, "the worst road I ever saw." In one "sink hole a mule was mired down half way up to his back" (Diary, April 10, 1862). By the time they reached Corinth the battery was exhausted and down to half-strength (J. E. Magee, Diary, May 26, 1862). The wagon capacity for the wounded was limited, many of the less seriously injured had to make their way back on foot. Morale was badly battered as the men collected themselves and set out searching the camps and hospitals to determine the fate of friends and kinsmen.

The mood of both armies veered from elation and excitement before the fight to gloom and despondency after the battle. "Almost all sick and the blues prevail in the most malignant form" a Hawk-eye infantryman reported (Boyd 1953: 43). Even two weeks after the engagement, the men seemed unable to break out of their despair. "How sad it is to see the boys looking down in the face and a 'want to go home' looking countenance on them," wrote George Hurlbut, as his battery tried to re-establish a camp routine (Diary, April 19, 1862). Youthful buoyancy evaporated, the men seemed old, tired, and sick as they went through the motions of camp life. Like ghosts, they glided among the heaps of dead and piles of wreckage. Cyrus Boyd recorded in his diary that "some of the men are sick and are so badly discouraged that nothing but the presence of death will make them move" (1953: 45). Many had had enough war, "I aint particular whether I see any more of the Elephant or no," an Ohioan admitted to his brother (C. Mitchell to Will, May 18, 1862).

Death imposed itself, it was no longer a remote idea, it was a real terrifying thing. Dying was not a heroic affair accompanied with dramatic posturing. Instead, it seized the stricken victim and fastened its grip so firmly that he was powerless to strike the heroic pose. Biology overwhelmed will; physical integrity was torn asunder and the victim left helpless, dazed, and convulsed, screaming in pain. The prospect of death shorn of all compensating romantic poses forced the soldiers to re-examine it in the new light.

Some attributed their survival to divine intervention. Augustus Mecklin reported that he saw to his salvation as the 15th Mississippi swept in to attack. "I thought of my own liability to fall victim perhaps in one more hour then came the momentous questions. Am I prepared. . . . Never before did I gaze so earnestly mentally into the dark unknown world and seek to the position I must occupy there. At this moment," he continued, "I made a sincere, honest surrender of myself to God." Having come through the ordeal unscathed, he sat down to his diary to "lift my heart in humble gratitude to the great father for all that He has bestowed upon me. My life has been spared and I have been sustained" (Diary, April 6 and 8, 1862). H. H. Giesy, a junior officer with the 46th Ohio, invoked similar religious convictions. "I can only say that it was through the mercy of God that my life was spared," he told his family (To brother, sister, and mother, April 9, 1862). Religious fatalism provided solace to the anxious soldiers and their kin. As Benjamin Guffey and the 18th Missouri (U.S.A.) resumed the march south to attack the enemy works at Corinth, he comforted his wife saying, "God only knows whether we shall meet on earth a gain, but after all what are the few short years we might have in the enjoyment of each others friendship here compared to the Eternity we shall spend together beyond the grave" (To Caroline, April 21, 1862).

For others, the cause was still worth sacrificing one's life for. Lieutenant Dewitt Loudon of the 70th Ohio told his wife that "for myself, I am not afraid to die. If my life can be of service to my country it is freely given." Should he however be killed, he left his wife with the following parting strictures. "Teach [the children]... to love their country & not to forget that their father gave his life for his country·that they among others might enjoy the blessings of Liberty, of Law & Order & good government" (To Hannah, May 3, 1862). The same day that Loudon pondered his fate, the 4th Tennessee's assistant surgeon, Lunsford Yandell, also wondered what was in store for him. "How many friends and associates have fallen around me since this war began... shall I go soon? Time alone can determine the question," he remarked fatalistically to his sister. And he added, "I hope I am prepared for my fate." However, he continued, "I have always had a sort of presentiment that I would not die young, that I had some mission to perform in the world" (To sister, May 3, 1862).

Some, however, reached the conclusion that they had had enough. "I have seen enough & am now very willing that peace may come, & I hope it will come soon," wrote Captain Charles Stewart, 21st Alabama Infantry. He was thankful that he had been spared, but he feared for the future realizing that "the next Battle may be my last" (To Julia, April 12, 1862). (Stewart was killed by an exploding cannon at Mobile.) Joseph Dill Alison was a surgeon at Shiloh and thus probably came closer to its horrors than many others. He, too, wrote, "I... have enough war to last me a lifetime" (1967: 46). And the 13th Iowa chaplain, John Steele, wanted no more of it either, confessing, "I would rejoice that the thing was closed that we could all return home to the quiet & peace of home" (To Mase, n.d. [probably April 1862]; see also John Ruckman to John Kinsel, April 12, 1862; Franklin Bailey to parents, April 8, 1862). Having fought at the Peach Orchard, Mecklin of the 15th Mississippi begged that "God grant that I may never be the partaker in such scenes again. My resolution is set... when released from this I shall ever be an advocate of peace" (Diary, April 7, 1862; see also J. D. Thompson to Mary [wife], April 10, 1862).

The volunteers proved themselves highly resilient despite Shiloh as the two armies began to shake themselves from their lethargy. By the second week after the battle they began to catch up with disposing of the dead and treating the wounded. Order began to emerge from the wreckage. Men were tallied, equipment inventoried and replaced, and the two armies began to prepare for the next round. Robert Pugh of the 5th Company of the Washington Artillery described the gradual metamorphosis of the army from despair to renewed determination. His diary entry for April 21 noted that the men had "recovered from the gloom and sadness thrown over [them] . . . by the battle. For a week or more after our return [to Corinth], everything was as quiet as if the whole country was around one church. The loss of friends, and the horrible scenes which they had just witnessed, together with their almost miraculous escape, seemed to quiet everyone. Neither drum nor fife could be heard," said the gunner. But two weeks after the fight, the despondency "was all worn away. The army is reorganized, the vacant places of the dead filled, and the past shut out in the thought of the future" (Lathrop 1962: 385). A Confederate Kentuckian exemplified the same resilience when he declared that "our fortifications are tolerable good and our army confident of victory" (J. W. Caldwell, Diary, May 5, 1862).

The surprising resilience of the volunteers and their resurgent morale so soon after such ghastly battle confirms Kellett's observation that heavy casualties do not necessarily reduce morale for long periods of time (1982: 265, 269). The ability to accommodate themselves to the butchery was one of the amazing things about the Shiloh volunteers. Charles Wright of the 81st Ohio demonstrated the ability to make the best of it. He and Company C were not so exhausted at the end of the battle as to forget that the sutler had fled and left behind his stocks. If the Confederates had not been too greedy, something might be left for a feast. Sure enough, they found plenty of pickled pigs' feet. "We got a lot of crackers," he continued, "and three or four of us went to the spring, bound on tasting pigs' feet and crackers. Griner [a comrade] filled his canteen with water and seating himself on the ground . . . commenced without form or ceremony to satisfy his craving for such luxuries. Suddenly he stopped eating, and heaved a deep sigh, exclaimed 'Well, I'm here yet!' " (Wright 1887: 46).

As the days passed, more and more letters lost their despondency and took a positive and active tone. Gunner George Hurlbut observed in his diary that "the troops seem inspired with recent successes and are pushing forward with vigor which bids fair to soon trap the rebellion and bring the war to a speedy and successful termination" (April 12, 1862). Colonel D. C. Loudon, an Ohio officer, who had also been in the worst of it as early as the initial attack told his wife that the rebels had shot his horse from under him; stolen his saddle, bridle, and holster; had plundered his camp; and taken all his clothing, but he had the satisfaction to know that "[he] . . . helped give the 'cusses' a most thorough drubbing . . . and [he was] . . . in good condition for another fight" (To Hannah, April 10 and 15, 1862).

NOTES

1. Among the most recent narratives of the battle are James Lee McDonough's *Shiloh—in Hell before Night* (1977), Wiley Sword's *Shiloh: Bloody April*

(1974), and the most detailed account, O. Edward Cunningham's "Shiloh and the Western Campaign of 1862" (1966). Dupuy and Dupuy (1970: 881) put Grant's and Buell's casualties at 13,000 of their 63,700 men in the field. Johnston lost 10,000 of his 40,000 troops.

2. The 14th Missouri Infantry in McArthur's brigade was armed with Henry breech-loading repeating rifles.

3. The element of surprise was repeated a hundred years later at the Battle of the Bulge. Here, too, an army that heretofore had been constantly on the offensive suddenly found itself on the defensive with inadequately trained troops (Blakeley 1965: 20).

4. Fifty-three soldiers left behind detailed accounts of the fighting.

5. O. E. Cunningham estimated that a regiment had sufficient ammunition to maintain a steady volume of fire for thirty to forty minutes (1966: 474). This is probably accurate for the average unit.

6. Wallace in Grant's army and Buell's three divisions (Alexander McCook's, William Nelson's, and Thomas J. Wood's) were only engaged on the second day.

7. Hence among those units where the losses were above 25 percent, 44 percent of the men emphasized casualties in their letters. On the other hand, 28 percent of those who were from units that suffered low casualties devoted their description to the sight of the dead and wounded.

8. In his seminal study of the reaction of 300 members of the Abraham Lincoln Brigade, John Dollard found that the vast majority of the men experienced fear in combat (1944). Dollard's sample of highly motivated Lincoln Brigade volunteers in the Spanish Civil War were, however, veterans with at least a year of fighting when they were polled (see also Marshall 1947: 149; Watson 1978: 213).

9. Thirty-six soldiers left behind descriptions of their emotions in battle.

10. Fifty men commented on this, with officers expressing active-aggressive reactions at almost twice the rate of the enlisted men.

5

Tactical Reappraisals

SOLDIERS' ASSESSMENT OF THEIR UNITS' PERFORMANCE AFTER THE BATTLE

Shiloh's volunteers had no rigorous training program to prepare them for their initiation to combat. Their military rite of passage was combat itself, and this crucible fostered their shared identity and unit pride. After battle studies have shown, most soldiers gain confidence in themselves and in their units' tactical abilities (R. Holmes 1986: 47, 218). Shiloh's soldiers were no exception. Their correspondence reflected a rising esteem for their regiments. Their letters lauded their units' achievements to the people back home so that they could share in its accomplishments. They also vigorously defended their regiment against any criticism in the hometown press. Finally, the soldiers expressed their new pride in their unit by their disdain for shirkers for letting the unit down and besmirching the regiment and their town.

Unit pride rose substantially after their baptism of fire, rising from two-thirds voicing plaudits for their regiment before the battle to nine out of ten afterward.[1] This corresponds with Stouffer's study of World War II infantry, where 92 percent of the men expressed pride in their units' accomplishments (1949: II, 140). In comparing the Confederate and Union armies, no significant difference distinguished the two forces. The Unionists were somewhat more boastful, but only a handful of Confederates left their remarks behind, preventing any firm inferences about their esprit de corps. Nevertheless, nothing appeared to suggest that Confederate morale was disintegrating after Shiloh.

Hoosier Jim Vanderbilt reflected the increasing unit pride. "The 23rd is some pumpkins in a fight not a man flinched but all were anxious for to get a shot or two at the rebels and we had the satisfaction of seeing the elephant" (To mother, April 16, 1862; see also A. Varian to Mary [sister?], April 13 [?], 1862: D. Ridley, Diary, April 13, 1862). To confirm their objectivity, the men frequently told the people at home that general so-and-so had complimented their regiment for its gallantry during the battle. Peter Pinder boasted that "the 52nd Ill. behaved most bravely, and received the congratulatory thanks of General Sweeney [Colonel Thomas W.], as well as Grant, who said we were the bravest of the brave in this fight, and that if all the regiments had stood fire as we did, we would have gained the day on Sunday" (*The Aurora Beacon*, April 17, 1862). Among the jauntiest affirmations of unit pride came from Lieutenant Colonel W.D. Niles of the 16th Wisconsin. Niles had taken command of his regiment during the fighting. The unit was in Prentiss' division and bore the brunt of the Confederate assault. The lieutenant colonel crowed home that the regiment "walked into their [the enemy's] affections most lively!" (Quiner, Reel No. 2, Vol. 5, pp. 251–52). Francis Johnson felt equal pride in his regiment, the 32nd Illinois Infantry, quoting a poem that one of his comrades (William Owen) composed to honor their regiment.

> It was on Shiloah's Bloody Field
> The 6th April Sixty Two
> The Rebels first Began to dread,
> The gallant Thirty two.
>   (F. Johnson Papers)

A Confederate Kentuckian named W.E. Minor, who was exiled from his hometown and unable to tell of his unit's (the 6th Kentucky Infantry) exploits to his local newspaper, vaunted its bravery to a Natchez paper. "Oh!" he exulted, "you ought to love us all—you ought to admire the bravery of the little band of Kentuckians that stood an iron wall against the batteries, musketry and gunboats of superior numbers" (*The Weekly Courier*, April 30, 1862). This pride in the accomplishments of the regiment was powerfully expressed by Lieutenant Colonel William P. Rogers, who lost a brother at Fort Donelson and who would lose his own life leading his 2nd Texas Rifles in trying to retake Corinth from the Union the following October. Rogers wrote to his wife, "The gallantry of our Regt. is spoken of by all—The last charge on Sunday evening and two on Monday were truly grand—These I led in person, on Monday carrying our battle flag. It has six holes through it on the staff." He then boasted that the "2nd Texas stands today ahead of all others in drill and discipline, and behind none in deeds of daring, valor and gallantry" (1929: 287, 290).

The men proudly told of their unit's decisive role in the outcome of the battle. Captain Hickenlooper, who commanded the 5th Ohio Battery, told how his unit "met and assisted in checking the first determined onslaught of the enemy, giving nearly two precious hours notice of the approaching danger to the still slumbering army" (1903: 404). William Bradford, for his part, believed that the "contest was still doubtful [on the second day] until" the 57th Indiana of Colonel George G. Wagner's 21st Brigade came on the scene and charged the enemy, "which," he boasted, "ended it at once" (To wife, April 10, 1862).

The volunteers also lauded their regiment's discipline, its orderly maneuvers, and its cohesion under adverse conditions. Richard Pugh, a Confederate enlistee with the 5th Company, Washington Artillery, wrote that it was no mean accomplishment to

march eighteen miles over bad count[r]y, take nothing but our blankets and three day's rations, lifting the cannon out of the mud and over hills, and meeting with every inconvenience which could possibly inconvenience an army, to go into the enemy's stronghold, where they had the advantage of knowledge of the count[r]y, having been there for weeks, meet them on their own ground and whip three times our number, then [to] retire, unmolested, being prevented by bad weather and the want of teams from bringing away everything we had captured (Lathrop 1962: 385)

On the Union side, Assistant Surgeon Sam Eells praised his 12th Michigan's conduct during the initial Confederate attack against Prentiss' line. He told friends at home that the regiment "retired slowly fighting as they went and doing splendidly for green troops" (April 13, 1862). At the other end of the line, taking the brunt of the first Confederate attacks, Lieutenant Colonel Dewitt Clinton Loudon of the 70th Ohio admired his command for maintaining cohesion throughout the battle. "We kept more men together than any other regt in the invasion." He went on to boast that so far as he could see his regiment had "as many men in ranks the second day as any other two regiments in the center brigades" of Sherman's division (To Hannah, April 15, 1862). During the second day's fighting, Colonel William H. Gibson thought his men had proved their combat skills in the battle when the regiment (the 49th Ohio) managed to change "front twice in perfect order, to meet a flank movement of the rebels," during which, he proudly declared, the "noble boys moved like veterans" (*The Tiffin Weekly Tribune*, April 18, 1862).

Others praised the way their regiments had "defiantly held their ground" (E. Hart 1864: 88), despite heavy odds that "war [were] at least 4 to 1 that Drove us Back" (James K. Lawrence to wife and children, April 8, 1862). Meanwhile, Alexander Varian bragged to the folks at home how the 1st Ohio did the community proud by capturing two "secesh flags" (To father, April 10, 1862). David Brand, a young Confederate, wanted his hometown to share his regimental pride. "I never saw, nor do I think there was ever braver men than our 21st (Alabama). I feel proud of the regiment. It has won a name that will be long remembered. No firmer or more determined men have [been] sent from any town in the Confederacy" (To brother, April 9, 1862).

The volunteers also justified their unit pride by describing how effective their fire had been during the engagement. This was especially true of the gunners. "Our mission," wrote George Lee of Battery E (Waterhouse's), 1st Illinois Light Artillery, "was to kill, and how well we performed it was shown by the awful heaps of dead that lay in front of our double shotted guns" (Papers). Captain Fry of Battery G, 1st Ohio Artillery fought around the Hornets' Nest and boasted of pumping 360 shells, 200 rounds of canister, and forty solid shot into the attacking Confederate lines "with excellent effect" (J. Barnett, Regimental History, n.d.). Voicing a similar professional pride on the Southern side, Richard Pugh, 5th Company, Washington Artillery, asserted that the Confederate artillery had been more accurate than the Northern gunners, arguing that "the enemy never silenced any of our batteries [but] . . . we silenced all of theirs . . . as we advanced, in many instances their batteries being almost entirely dismounted, whereas as far as I can learn not one of our guns was ever struck" (Lathrop 1962: 383).

The artillerists were also proud of having kept their guns out of the hands of the enemy. Losing guns in battle was a supreme humiliation. Military tradition requires artillerymen to stand by their guns; an ethos shared by gunners of all armies in all wars. The British observers, for example, marveled at the heroic effort of the Italian gunners in manhandling their guns through the mountains during the retreat after Caporetto in 1917 (R. Holmes 1986: 298). The same tradition manifested itself among the Confederate gunners, who took pride in extricating their batteries from difficult places often under enemy fire (A.G. Blakewell, Reminiscences).

The new veterans also justified their esteem for their regiment by noting the heavy losses that their unit sustained in comparison to other units. An officer proudly wrote to the regiment's hometown newspaper that "amongst all the regiments engaged in the fight, the 15th Ill. suffered most; two fifths of the men who went into action having been killed or wounded." The writer went on to add to his unit's laurels by declaring "the regiment was engaged in the thickest of the fight. . . . [And] on Monday its doubly decimated ranks dashed into the thickest of the fight [again]" (*The Freeport Bulletin*, April 24, 1862).[2]

In war, however, the object of the exercise is to kill more of the enemy than they of you, and several of the soldiers thought their regiment deserved special distinction for their effectiveness in achieving this. Among them was George Hamman of the 14th Illinois, who remarked that "nowhere lay the dead thicker, or were the trees more cut up, then [*sic*] at the place where our Regt. fought" (Diary, April 8, 1862). Captain James Lawrence was equally exultant over the lethality of the 61st Illinois Infantry's fire telling his wife and children, "we slew more in the Sunday fight than any other Ridgement" (To wife and children, April 8, 1862).

Finally, the men's regimental pride was reflected in their zealous defense of the regiment's reputation against critics. Virulent debates echoed in letters to the editor of their hometown newspaper. To insult the regiment was to cast aspersion on the community that sponsored it (*The Jacksonville Sentinel*, May 2, 1862; *The Dubuque Daily Times*, April 17, 1862). On the Union side, the Ohio boys got the worst reputation at Shiloh. They had the misfortune of fielding several units that disintegrated for no tactically acceptable reason. There was the conduct of the 53rd Ohio, which broke up after its colonel panicked, the 71st and 77nd also fled, along with Myer's Ohio Battery (O.E. Cunningham 1966: 302–3). The men of Jesse Appler's 53rd Ohio tried to justify themselves in their letters to the local newspaper. One officer explained that though the unit had broken on Sunday morning, its companies were later attached to other regiments and were in the rest of the fighting throughout the second day (*The Ironton Register*, May 15, 1862). Another 53rd Ohio man wrote to the editor that while it was "true, not near all the men were got together after the retreat, but most of them were, and done good fighting as any set of men. The fact was my dear sir, the whole attack was a complete surprise as could be," and the regiment should not be blamed under these circumstances. Another soldier of the 53rd blamed the unit's collapse on the cavalry, which "left us the bag to hold" (*The Ironton Register*, May 8, 1862). While yet another comrade insisted that it was all the fault of the artillery, namely Captain Samuel E.B. Waterhouse's battery, which "fell back . . . before the 53rd did, and that left our regiment without any support whatever; and if our regiment had staid two minutes longer they would have been taken prisoners or cut to pieces" (*The Ironton Register*, May 15, 1862).

Confederates were just as energetic in the defense of the good name of their regiment. Lieutenant Colonel William Rogers wrote home, "I would not have any of you speak of or allude to the slanders you have heard about the Reg. [2nd Texas] for you must see at once that they will recoil upon the hearts of the perpetrators." Rogers explained that on the second day the "Reg. did not run it fell back 2 or 3 hundred yards," and then ostensibly only to regroup so that they could counterattack. He added that he and his men "were all astounded to hear that the Reg. had been slandered by reports prejudicial to our gallantry, for we really thought we had fought well and our Generals thought so too for they have complimented us by authorising us to put Shiloh on our flag as a badge of *conspicuous gallantry* and as yet I am told no other Reg. engaged in that battle has a similar honor. So for then," Rogers averred, "the 2nd Texas is the Star Reg. of the army of the west" (W.P. Rogers, 1929: 290–1).

In defense of their unit's reputation, the men of both armies invoked several categories of explanation for its failures in the the field. Among the most frequent were those that blamed the regiment's lack of training and ineffective fire discipline. Gunner George Lee of Battery E, 1st Illinois Light Artillery (Waterhouse's) claimed that the men were "at a loss what to do and how to do it," during the initial stage of the fighting. "Three of these divisions were raw troops having had little if any drill, and some had received their arms but a few days before and were ignorant of their use" (Reminiscences). John K. Duke of the unfortunate 53rd Ohio recalled that "the regiment had not had a battalion drill when it went into the field," while others had never before even fired their weapons (1900: 39; see also Dawes 1969: 9).[3] The Illinois papers criticized the 16th Iowa, which had been attached to Prentiss' division and had forgotten to bring along ammunition to the battle and had to be sent back to the landing. And then once it got into the fight, it was accused of running "like sheep." Lieutenant J.F. Conyngham of the regiment's Company H angrily replied that it was all a lie, and tried to justify the unit's lack of effectiveness by pointing out to hometown readers that "our regiment were raw recruits, [and] never had any instructions in the manual of arms, all the instruction they had was firing half a dozen rounds Sunday morning before they marched into battle" (*The Dubuque Daily Times*, April 19, 1862). Its lieutenant colonel, Addison H. Sanders, bitterly complained, "we ought never to have been put in the field under such circumstances" (Throne 1954: 247).

Poor performance was often associated with a lack of fire discipline, a major problem in any engagement. Fire discipline is the bane of all armies—even veteran outfits. Marshal Saint-Cyr, who commanded Napoleon's veteran "grognards," estimated that a fourth of the French infantry's casualties were caused by the second line firing accidentally into the backs of the first line (R. Holmes 1986: 173). This occurred at Shiloh as well. An Iowan wrote home, "Some [of the men] . . . were given to firing some distance to the rear without thinking sufficiently who were in front, and in some instances wounded our own men." One of the men in Company H, 11th Iowa, "took position in front of a tree, having nothing between himself and the enemy, but a most excellent defense against the injudicious attacks of his own friends" (Sergeant Harold M. White cited in Throne 1954: 255). Private Elisha Stockwell, who was wounded twice on the second day at Shiloh while serving with the 14th Wisconsin, was almost the victim of his own comrades' fire.

The regiments had taken their position in the line and were ordered to open up on the Confederates. Ned, a pal, "stuck [his musket] . . . up in the air, shut both eyes, and fired at the tree tops, and Schnider did the same. But Schnider was in the rear rank behind Curly and he cut a lock of Curly's hair off just above his ear, and burned his neck. I thought Curly was going to strike him with his gun. He told him, 'You might have killed me.' and Schnider said, 'Makes me not much difference, I [never liked] . . . you very well anyhow' " (Abernathy 1958: 18).

Along with invoking lack of training and fire discipline, the soldiers of regiments that broke also replied to negative press reports by explaining that they had been taken by surprise. Private Robert H. Fleming who had fled with the 77th Ohio when the camp was overrun by the Confederates, nevertheless, defended his regiment, arguing that they would have "been bayoneted in their tents" if they had stayed. "Some cowardly correspondent of a Chicago paper, who probably got no nearer to the battlefield than Paducah, started the lie," he angrily retorted (1908: 145).

The most frequent defense that the volunteers invoked to justify their regiment's withdrawal was to claim that it had no choice but to retreat, because its flanks had been exposed by neighboring units. A Hawk-eye soldier-correspondent took exceptions to criticisms of the Iowa regiments as "prehdious" lies that were being spread by a "foe to the good name of the state," arguing that both the 15th and 16th regiments had been flanked and had no choice but to withdraw (*The Daily Democrat and News*, April 26, 1862; see also Sergeant A.J. Covill, Company I, 14th Wisconsin, to sister [Arvilla], April 12, 1862, Wilson S. Covill Collection). Sometimes it was supposed to be only a case of mistaken identity. "I hear," Captain N.W. Edwards of Company H of the 15th Iowa wrote, "that some charge the reg. with cowardice, but they confounded us with the 15th Michigan" (*The Council Bluffs Nonpareil*, May 3, 1862).

One arm often blamed the other for a precipitous retreat. The infantry often blamed the cavalry or the artillery, which was supposed to anchor each stretch of the line (J.E. Magee, Diary, April 7, 1862). On the other hand, the artillery blamed the infantry for failing to protect the batteries (*The Jackson Standard*, May 2, 1862; G. Hurlbut, Diary, April 6, 1862).

Yet others blamed rebel perfidy. Lieutenant Conyngham of the 16th Iowa claimed that his regiment was taken by surprise because "the rebels . . . displayed the American flag, and we were ordered to cease firing." They then "flanked our right by pouring in a deadly cross fire into our ranks," and the men had to withdraw (*The Dubuque Daily Times*, April 24, 1862).

The good name of the regiment was jeopardized by reports in the press of thousands of Union shirkers who crowded at the landing during the first day's fight. George McBride of the 15th Michigan felt an "utter

contempt for those great burly creatures . . . hiding . . . while their comrades were out yonder, breasting the storm" (1894: 10). This contempt
was sarcastically reaffirmed by another veteran of Shiloh, Ambrose
Bierce, who contended, "An army's bravest men are its cowards. The
death of which they would not meet at the hands of the enemy they
will meet at the hands of their officers, with never a flinching" (1966: I,
245). Yet the "right" of a soldier to run from battle is one of those things
that makes a battle endurable (Keegan 1976: 309). The option to flee in
order to survive and fight another day provides resilience to army morale. It impedes fatalism, passive acceptance, surrender, and thus, useless destruction of an army when resistance may be totally pointless and
where incompetent commanders may not be willing to accept the reality
of the situation. Bull Run already showed that running from battle does
not destroy a volunteer army, and Shiloh confirmed the point. At Shiloh,
many of the shirkers who had accumulated at the riverbank on the first
day were back in the line on the second.

But the men in the line did not have such a detached view of the
phenomenon. Their comments after the battle ranged from derision to
outright hostility. This differentiated them from World War II veterans.
Stouffer found that World War II soldiers were far more tolerant of
shirkers (1949: II, 140–41). The Second World War soldier, however, was
not a member of a territorially recruited regiment with close community
ties, except for the National Guard units, although they too were frequently broken up and their officers transferred out. Shiloh's soldiers
believed that such behavior let their comrades down and gave a bad
name to their town (Folmar 1981: 57). "Cravens with pale faces and livid
lips" John Ellis of the 16th Louisiana called them (To mother, April 29,
1862). "The scum of battles" and "dastard bullet dodgers" was the way
Lance Sergeant E.R. Kellogg of Company B, 1st Battalion, 16th U.S.
Infantry, referred to them (Recollections). William Stimson shared Kellogg's anger, "I felt ashamed to see men run as they did throwing away
there guns and accutriments" (To wife, April 10, 1862). As the 57th
Indiana went into action on the second day, one of the men staggered
out of line claiming he was sick and had to stop. William Bradford,
marching next to him, reacted angrily. "I replied to him that if he did
[step out of line] I would kill him" (To wife, April 10, 1862).

Others vented their resentment at the shirkers by humiliating them
and making derisive remarks. Sam Watkins' 1st Tennessee came up in
support of an Alabama outfit that had broken under fire and was fleeing
to the rear. He remembered how the Tennesseans laughed at them for
running (1962: 41). When the 11th Iowa passed fleeing deserters on its
way to the front Sergeant Harold White of Company H caustically
evoked the scene. "One frightened fugitive . . . exclaimed, 'Give them
h-ll, boys. I gave them h-ll as long as I could.' Whether he had really

given them any," reflected White, "I cannot say, but assuredly he gave them everything else he possessed, including his gun, cartridgebox, coat and hat" (Throne 1954: 254).

When comrades failed in their duty, they besmirched the regiment and the parent community. The people had every right to know who had let the regiment and community down. While most soldiers escaped military sanctions for shirking, they did not escape what awaited them back at home. The same strong bonds between home and front existed in the Australian army, which was also manned by territorially recruited volunteers. During the Gallipoli campaign of 1915, the Australian commander used social coercion to make sure that the troops behaved. The general reported home the names of men who failed in their duty at the front. At Shiloh, such denunciations to the homefront were not left to generals. The volunteers themselves reported on shirkers. They kept track of who was in the line and who was not, recording this in their diaries and letters. Second Lieutenant William Vaught of the 5th Company Louisiana's Washington Artillery gave his mother the name of one of the men in his unit, who had "skipped away" during the fighting (To mother, April 19, 1862). On the other side, the diary of an unidentified soldier in Company A of the 14th Illinois included a report on the behavior of the men, keeping track of twenty-two of them, who "left [their] . . . company in the field with out orders," while the rest of the company "performed like . . . vetteron[s]" and in a "manner worthy of a son of Illinois" ("J," Journal of Company A, 14th Illinois, April 14, 1862).

In fact, desertion was not as big a problem as is often claimed about Shiloh. If civilian contract employees such as the teamsters of the army and division train, the sutlers, and the visitors were excluded from the count, the proportion of shirkers at the landing was approximately 10 to 20 percent of Grant's effectives.[4] This is not an exceptional rate of desertion compared to European armies, where the rates climbed as high as 20 percent in Napoleon's forces or the French army in Italy in 1859. Even the elite Prussian *Regiment de Garde* had desertion rates that approached those of the mass army at Shiloh (R. Holmes 1986: 84). Generally, the regiments all did well. No unit panicked to a man. Every unit reported killed and wounded after the battle. This suggests that all units had men who remained in the firing line or returned to it in companies or platoons.

Several factors went into creating regimental pride and strengthened the cohesion of the volunteer regiments after the battle. First, there was the strong identity that linked the regiment to the community. The men obviously were bound by their national allegiance, but this was a political and intellectual commitment. On the other hand, their ties to their state and community were of a more fundamental sort, they were emotional, deep felt, and very strong. They transposed these civilian ties to their regiment and company, which in turn reinforced the unit's cohesion. The community-regiment link was articulated by a young officer in his report to the local newspaper on the behavior of the 16th Iowa during the battle. "The boys fought nobly. Our motto on entering the field was 'Keep up the good name of Iowa!' " (*The Waterloo Courier*, April 30, 1862). State and community ties and national commitments were not mutually exclusive. They, in fact, reinforced each other. They worked on different levels: the former, at the emotional level, and the latter, at the political level. The national ties provided the issue and the incentive to join up and go to the war, while the community attachments served to buttress regimental pride and cohesion. Kellett correctly maintained that a longtime association among members of a unit reinforced cohesion (1982: 23). These long associations, which underpinned a regiment's cohesion, predated the Civil War. They were grounded in the traditions of the community.

A second element that fostered pride in the regiment and forged a strong sense of cohesion among its soldiers was the battle experience itself. Marshall noted that working together in tactical situations created a "sympathetic understanding" among the men in World War II outfits. The men got to know each other under the most stressful conditions imaginable and their comrades' deportment under these conditions created bonds of mutual confidence and dependence, and ultimately, an esprit de corps. Because as Marshall wrote, the average soldier is unwilling "to risk danger on behalf of men with whom he has no social identity" and in whom he has no trust (1947: 150, 153). Kellett also emphasized the importance of the primary group in the formation of strong unit loyalty through the primary group's provision of mutual support in combat (1982: 41–42; see also Janowitz 1959: 66).[5] Janowitz's, Marshall's, and Kellett's views are illustrated by Archibald Stinson's post-combat change in attitude toward his comrades in Company I, 30th Indiana Infantry, when he wrote, "Our Boys all fought like Brave soldiers. . . . I was a little doubtful of our Reg . . . but now I am not. . . . Now I would not be afraid to trust them under any circumstances" (To Cousin Mollie, April 28, 1862).

Another element that helped forge unit pride and cohesion at the Battle of Shiloh was associated with the tactical doctrines that prevailed. Ironically, while close-order formations caused high casualties, they also reinforced unit pride and cohesion. Men fought shoulder to shoulder with their comrades; their conduct was in full view of the company. There were no isolated foxholes to hide in. Shirking was always visible! The men were subjected to intense social pressures. If a man broke and ran, such behavior was clearly visible to those whose esteem he most cherished. Better to risk life and limb than be perceived as a shirker by one's comrades and one's community when such behavior was reported to the people back home.

There were also social pressures inherent in close-order formation fighting. This may explain why the men actively and almost uniformly fired their weapons as rapidly as possible. They were eager to give the impression to their comrades that they were active fighters. The frequent need to bring up more munitions to the firing line attests to their readiness to shoot and their eagerness to show they were good fighters. This raises questions about Marshall's suggestion that 75 percent of an army's soldiers do not fire their weapons and will not fight (1947: 50, 74–75).[6] Janowitz explained that battle paralysis may be attributed to a sense of isolation and passivity among the men spread out in loose-formation fighting from concealed positions (1959: 76–77). But at Shiloh, tactical doctrine imposed dense formations and may explain why the Civil War troops produced such intensive fire in comparison to infantrymen in World War II. Civil War soldiers were fighting in full view of their comrades and this reduced the sense of isolation that threatens cohesion in combat.

Finally, regimental pride and unit cohesion increased after the battle because of the kind of recruits who manned the early armies of the Civil War. Lieutenant H.C. Wright, 32nd Illinois Infantry, described his men. "Co. H is composed of as good fighting material as any in the service, and turned out more men on the day of the battle in proportion than any company in the Regiment" and was in the hottest of the fight" (*The Jacksonville Sentinel*, May 2, 1862). They were volunteers, basically good men who were prepared to make a commitment to their country's cause and, later, to their comrades and their regiment. Their courage and commitment was founded in their morality. Moran's argument states that courage and fortitude are rooted in family and community upbringing. These qualities are what make good soldiers.[7] Character had to supplement inadequate training while the troops learned their new profession through experience. This held the armies together during the first year of the war.

A pattern of development began to emerge in molding the morale of Shiloh's recruits. It followed three stages. In the first stage, as the army was being constructed, morale was grounded in patriotic exhortation. It inspired the men to join and it sustained them during the initial phase of organization. Once the volunteers took the field, new motivations were grafted to their patriotism. During this phase, the men became acquainted with their messmates and army life, and they formed attachments and commitments to their comrades and their units. In the third stage, an esprit de corps was forged in battle, gaining importance in motivating the men. It did not replace their patriotism and communal

ties; it, too, was bonded onto the earlier motivations and in turn reinforced them. Ties to regiment coincided with community links and ultimately patriotic loyalty. This territorial recruitment served as the
foundation of morale by combining the two most powerful sources of
combat motivation: patriotism and unit pride.[8] It made possible the
recruits' emergence from the fighting with new confidence in their ability
to stand up to enemy. This transformation was reflected in Colonel D.C.
Loudon's comments to his wife after the battle. "I begin to think," he
wrote, "I will do pretty well for a soldier. . . . I dont feel half as nervous
& timid as I used to when I had to speak at a college exhibition. I . . .
listened to the cannon thundering in our front, as great deal more cool
than I did then waiting for my turn on the programme" (To Hannah,
May 3, 1862).

POST-COMBAT ASSESSMENT OF THE LEADERSHIP

While the rank and file of both sides came out of the engagement at
Pittsburg Landing proud of their regiment and more confident about
their own ability to withstand fire, they were not very sure that the
generals had stood the test. For example, the Northern soldiers believed
that Grant was incompetent and Buell had pulled Grant's chestnuts out
of the fire. A rumor circulated of a conversation between Buell and Grant
at the height of the crisis. The conversation was not true, but its content,
recorded by Payson Shumway, reflected the army's image of Grant, and
it was hardly favorable.

Buell—"What are all these men doing here at the Landing" (meaning those who
    had fled to the river bank panic stricken).

Grant—"They wont fight"

Buell—"It is the fault of their damned officers . . . .My troops will soon be here.
    Can you hold the rebels one hour?"

Grant—"No."

Buell—"Can you hold them in check half an hour."

Grant—"No."

Buell—"Can you hold them in check fifteen minutes?"

Grant—"No."

Buell—"Can you hold them back at *all*."

Grant—"No *I cant*."

Buell—"Then by God I can."

"Buell," according to the rumor, immediately "took command . . . and
a disgracefull surrender prevented" (Diary, May 1, 1862).

The battle weeded out more bad officers. None was spared his men's severe appraisal, and many were driven to resign. Most, however, passed the test in their men's eyes and gained their men's loyalty and affection. Sam Watkins said of the 1st Tennessee's colonel, George Maney, "A child or a dog would make up with him on first sight," adding that he was fearless having "no nerves" (1962: 52).

The battle did not appreciably shake the men's confidence in their company and regimental commanders. Their standards for assessing their colonels and captains shifted after the battle. Tactical competence now came to outweigh personality traits in judging officers. The portion of the respondents who stressed tactical competence doubled after the battle. This is not surprising, because combat forced the men to realize that while an officer's personality might be a bane, his incompetence could be fatal.[9]

After the battle, the rank and file were divided over the quality of the leadership. Captain William Bradford of Company J, 57th Indiana, sensed the rising discontent and told his wife in "my opinion . . . of the present commissioned officers there will be a good many of them home before a great while" (To Lucie, April 24, 1862). A fellow Union officer, Assistant Surgeon Samuel Eells, thought that his colonel, Francis Quinn of the 12th Michigan, would surely be driven from the ranks and into premature retirement. "The Col.," wrote Eells, "had hardly any friends in the regiment among the officers or the men." And he added, "a good many of the officers have resigned or intend to do so" (To Uncle & Aunt, May 12, 1862).

At the top of the Union army, the high command was still untested before the battle. Of Grant's six divisional commanders, only Sherman was a professional officer (O.E. Cunningham 1966: 106). The Union troops assailed their divisional commanders for not taking countermeasures against a surprise attack. The following poem circulated among the Union rank and file.

> At Pittsburg Landing, then,
> With thirty thousand men,
> The arrival of Buell we awaited;
> But enterprising Joe
> Did n't wait for us you know—
> Sidney Johnston a surprise contemplated
> (C. Wright 1887: 31).

An unnamed soldier-correspondent reported to his hometown editor that "if our Generals here had had their eyes open, they might have saved 1,000 lives" (*The Ironton Register*, May 8, 1862). Corporal Alexander Varian serving with 1st Ohio in Buell's command wrote home, "Grant was whipped on Sunday & if it had not been for part of Buell's Army coming up Monday morning they would have all been taken prisoner" (To Mary, April 1862).

The federal rank and file also began to complain again about the high command's lethargic advance on Corinth. "We certainly have forces enough to secure a victory," wrote a Hoosier captain. "But if our generals permit them to escape Corinth and go South without giving them battle I will think it a great lack of generalship or else cowardice . . . [e]qualed only by McClellan letting them get away from Manassas with their wooden battery" (William Bradford to Lucie [wife], April 24, 1862). And when the Confederates did manage to escape from Corinth, the reaction among some of the rank and file was vociferous. W.G. Munson of the 16th Wisconsin Infantry wrote a scathing letter to the local newspaper editor about the alleged incompetence of the Union high command. "General [Henry W.] Halleck has allowed this army, which has spent so many weeks creeping upon [the Confederate forces at Corinth], to leave by running all the [railroad] cars they could muster during the whole of the last three days and four nights, and that while we were so near as to be kept up at night by the whistling of the engines" (Quiner, Reel No. 2, Vol. 5, p. 286).

The main complaint against the way the high command conducted the battle centered on the lack of overall command and control. "The fight was a free one; the Generals . . . seemed to have no system; gave very few orders," leaving the field-grade officers to run the show. The regimental commanders fought "as near on their hook as ever you saw," wrote a Buck-eye soldier to the local newspaper (*The Ironton Register*, May 8, 1862). Illinois infantryman Z.P. Shumway noted that "There seems to be but little Generalship displayed, as the Enemy out-flanked us at the very outset" (Diary, April 7, 1862; see also *The Jacksonville Sentinel*, May 2, 1862; Dugan 1863: 100). Prisoner of war Amos Currier of the 8th Iowa wrote from Mobile, "Our forces were not organized for battle and hence entered the fight as units rather than as a compact mass. Under such circumstances it was foolish to attempt the maintenance of our extended line[,] but a tenable position should have been at once selected and the forces withdrawn within it. On the contrary our forces formed a weak line which was repeatedly broken" (Journal, April 17, 1862).

Of the two Union army commanders, Grant came in for the most criticism. If anticipation is the major part of the art of command, then Grant could not but bear the burden of the near disaster (Marhall 1947: 187). A cascade of letters burst upon the homefront from the rank and file condemning the high command, in general, and Grant, in particular, for "this great disaster" (Boyd 1953: 42). Grant "had been rather careless" (A.F. Davis to F.D. Davis [brother], April 21, 1862), and was "hated and despised by all the men and cursed ever since" (Boyd 1953: 47). An unnamed Iowan outlined the rank and file's indictment of Grant's generalship. "I think Gen. Grant fell short of his duty. He knew or might have known, that the rebels were coming to attack us, and he staid at Savannah until after they commenced their work, and when they did come he did nothing to aid in checking their advance" (*The Daily Democrat and News*, April 21, 1862). Another damned Grant as an "embecile" who had "bungled the whole thing" (T. Blaisdell, Collection and letter to Sisters & Bros., April 12, 1862). A correspondent of the 72nd Ohio told the hometown editor that "Grant is strongly suspicioned and I think him guilty, for he allowed us to be surprised, without, making any preparations whatever" (*The Seneca Advertiser*, April 25, 1862).

Another Ohioan blamed all the generals, because they "did not have any pickets out more than half a mile, and on Saturday night the rebels lay within three-fourths of a mile of our camp" (*The Ironton Register*, May 8, 1862). Peter Pinder in the 52nd Illinois told his hometown newspaper that even though prisoners taken on April 4 had warned of an impending attack, "our officers gave no heed to the omens, thinking it a hoax, and took no measures to guard against surprise, expecting as much to see the devil himself as to see the rebels come and attack us in our own camp" (*The Aurora Beacon*, April 24, 1862). As a result, the enemy "found us sleeping," and for the ensuing "great loss of life in this battle Genl Grant is a great degree responsible" (Z.P. Shumway, Diary, April 1862; see also L.M. Blakeley cited in Throne 1954: 243; Boyd 1953: 42; A. Currier, Journal, April 17, 1862; *The Jackson Standard*, May 2, 1862; *The Daily Democrat and News*, April 21, 1862). The men in the line also resented the fact that Grant had set up his headquarters nine miles from the army, taking over a posh mansion with all the comforts of home, including a liquor cabinet. (Z.P. Shumway, Diary, April 1862). "So little did Gen. Grant know about matters and things," reported an unnamed correspondent to his hometown newspaper, "that he was quietly snoozing down at Savannah . . . and did not git on the field till after noon; and then was drunk" (*The Ironton Register*, May 8, 1862).[10]

By contrast, the troops lionized Buell. Samuel N. Buford, an aide-de-camp with Buell's army, told his brother, "Grant's share is very small. . . . Grant was badly whipped and if we hadn't have come to his relief when we did his entire Army would have been taken prisoners or drownd into the Tennessee river" (To Charlie, April 21, 1862). Even Grant's own men believed that Buell had saved the day. Sergeant Cyrus Boyd, 15th Iowa Infantry, thought Buell's arrival "was all that saved Grant's Army" (Boyd 1953: 34). Buell appeared to be the better general, for while the Confederates had defeated Grant on Sunday, Buell "showed [them] something different" the next day. Another Iowan, Sergeant Harold White of the 11th Regiment in Grant's army, believed that Buell's presence alone was worth as much as his entire army. For while Grant commanded on Sunday, "chance seemed to rule the hour," but once Buell arrived "the change seemed to be miraculous." White explained to a friend, "Regiments the day before had gone into battle with no idea of what they were to do: without support and with no provision for following up their success, or recovering what they had lost. To-day it was different and for the first time we could perceive the difference between a soldier, for such Buell assuredly is, and an imbecile" (Throne 1954: 257). Moreover, the men believed that Buell had actually taken overall command from Grant on the next day, and a rumor circulated that Buell had let Grant know in no uncertain terms what he thought of his leadership. The rumor was recorded as follows. "Buell told Grant that he could blow his generalship to h-ll with a thimble of powder, and that he had his men scattered over ground enough for 700,000 men" (*The Daily Democrat and News*, April 21, 1862).

Less was said about specific divisional and brigade commanders. However, among those who came in for criticism was Colonel Jesse Hildebrand, who commanded one of Sherman's brigades. It was said that he had "never mastered the intricacies of Hardee," and took no part in trying to coordinate the operations of his brigade (Duke 1900: 40). An adjutant in his brigade recalled an encounter with the old man. According to the adjutant, he was more an observer than a participant. "I saw Colonel Hildebrand sitting on his horse by an old barn, intently watching the swaying lines and waving banners of the troops, fighting across a long open field south. . . . I went to the colonel and said to the Colonel, where is the brigade?—'I don't know;' he replied, 'go along down that road and I guess you will find some of them.'—Why don't you come with us, get the men together and do something?—I said.—'Go along down that road' he answered sharply, 'I want to watch this fight' " (Duke 1900: 51). Sherman was also criticized especially by the men of the 53rd Ohio, who he had publicly rebuked for breaking under fire. An anonymous correspondent wrote to the local newspaper that it was unfair to blame the 53rd for being routed, because Sherman had not responded promptly to the crisis and had not taken measures to provide support to the threatened line. "So little did General Sherman know of matters and things, that when we sent [a courier] to him, and told him the rebels turning our left, and in a few minutes we would be flanked completely, he would not believe it, and would not allow his orderly to disturb his repose! and," he added, "the fight had been raging one and a half hours before he got a piece of artillery to protect our Brigade" (*The Ironton Register*, May 8, 1862).

On the other side, major generals Hardee and Bragg were unpopular with many of the men. Hardee was shot at by his own men (Kellett 1982: 109), and Bragg was disliked as an unfeeling martinet. He was called "the great autocrat," who loved "to crush the spirit of the men." A Tennessean wrote that the more "hang-dog look they had" the more Bragg was pleased, and he ventured that "not a single soldier in the whole army ever loved or respected him" (Watkins 1962: 49). However, the Confederate rank and file loved and respected General Albert Sidney Johnston. "No braver soldier ever gave his life to the Confederacy," wrote Captain D. Sullins of the 19th Tennessee Infantry (1910: 225). He was a "towering military genius . . . with far seeing military insight," wrote another (McMurray 1904: 212). Many were convinced that his death prevented total victory. "The people of the North [can never] pay the debt they owe to the private Federal soldier who fired the shot" that caused his death, wrote one of Johnston's men (McMurray 1904: 212–13). G.W. Jones of Stanford's Mississippi Battery wrote in his diary, "what a pity that General A.S. Johnston was killed. If he had not received that fatal wound, Grant and his army would have been either killed, drowned in the Tennessee River, or taken prisoners" (Spradlin 1981:7.)

If any battle of the Civil War was a field-officers' battle, it was Shiloh. The soldiers' attitude toward their company and regimental officers varied from man to man and from unit to unit. Some were extremely unpopular. The men of the 15th Iowa reported there was "much dissatisfaction . . . in regard to our field officers. Some of whom are notoriously incompetent. The Col[.] does not know the difference between file right and file left and is as ignorant of Military Maneuvers as a Child." And the lieutenant colonel drilled the regiment "under the *inspiration* of about a quart of old Comissary" (Boyd 1953: 45). There were cases of drunken officers trying to command regiments in battle. Lieutenant D.F. Vail remembered his 16th Wisconsin trying to defend a position that was already being flanked, because a drunken adjutant would not change orders (1897: 3–4).

Along with incompetence and drunkenness, the men of some of the regiments had to put up with a leader's cowardice. One was called an "arrant coward," who avoided combat by calling sick "though his cheeks looked as red as ever" (J.K. Newton to parents, May 26, 1862). In another sector, near the Peach Orchard, a volunteer recalled that once the fighting started, "shoulder-straps and gay uniforms did not appear to be so plentiful and so dashing as upon parades or reviews" (Dugan 1863: 100). William C. Robinson told his friend back home that the "1st Lt. was soon put 'hors de combat' by the whiz . . . of a cannon ball. He fell fainting to the ground and was carried off the field" (To Charlie [Abbott], April 19, 1862). Another soldier told how his Captain "runn and left his Company," when things got tough. "He was a coward, [and] he has been under arrest ever since" (W.J. Kennedy to wife, April 1862).

As many soldiers came away from the fighting with a high regard for their officers; "i think we have a Splendid Kearnel he was rite on hand all the time," a Hoosier in Company E, of the 57th Regiment, told his family (J. Jones to father and mother, April 13, 1862). Others were more specific in describing their leaders' actions under fire. "Our Col.," wrote one recruit, "rode over the field smoking his pipe as calmly as in his tent" (A. Currier, Journal, April 17, 1862). Another admired how his colonel (Edward N. Kirk, 34th Illinois) rallied his regiment after it was badly shaken by a Confederate attack (Payne 1902: 21). A gunner with Captain Felix H. Robertson's Alabama Battery told the local press that the men so admired the commander that "not a man in our battery would think of retiring until Capt. Robertson says 'its time' " (*The Mobile Advertiser and Register*, April 29, 1862). Another butternut soldier declared, "I would rather risk him to fight seven days in the week from daylight until dark than any soldier I ever knew" (McMurray 1904: 213; see also T.C. Robertson to mother, April 9, 1862).

Rank was of little significance in the line once the unit was under fire. Mutual respect between officers and men replaced hierarchical constraints (John Ellis 1980: 348). The volunteers wanted officers who were right up there alongside them when things got hot. They expected their officers to share the risks with them. In this sense, they were no different than their counterparts in World War II. Infantrymen have always liked officers who lead out front and not from behind (Stouffer 1949: II, 124–25). "One of Many" wrote to his local editor that Lieutenant Colonel Hall of the 11th Iowa was "a pugnacious little hero," who was right in the thick of it alongside his men (Throne 1954: 250). There was also Leander Stillwell's old Captain Reddish of the 61st Illinois, who "went in . . . took his place in the ranks, and fought like a common soldier." He may not have known drill very well or other military arts, but the old man certainly inspired the men's confidence by his willingness to lead them and share the risk with them. Stillwell told how "he picked up the musket of some dead or wounded man, and filled his pockets with cartridges and gun caps. . . . He unbuckled his sword from the belt, and laid it in the scabbard at his feet, and proceeded to give undivided attention to the enemy. I can now see the old man in my mind's eye," Stillwell recalled, "as he stood in the ranks loading and firing, his blue-gray eyes flashing. . . . Colonel [Jacob] Fry happened to be near us at one time, and I hear old Capt. John yell at him: 'Injun fightin, Colonel! Jest like Injun fighting!' " (1920: 61). Levi Wagner's Colonel Ben Smith of the 1st Ohio was known for his drinking, but Wagner recalled affectionately that when "little Col. Smith was offered a drink of whiskey . . . his reply was, 'No Sir. When I go into a battle I go in sober.' That was heroic," Wagner affirmed, "for a man who liked his drinks" (Reminiscences, in Papers).

T.A. Taylor of the 4th Tennessee in his reaction to regimental elections just after the battle summed things up pretty well when he observed, "I don't like some of the new officers, but can stand what the company can" (Diary, Taylor Collection, April 29, 1862). For the fact was that the men's confidence in their ability to withstand fire and their trust in their comrades led many to believe that even if some of the officers were not up to standards, the rank and file could hold its own. "The truth was," wrote a private in the 77th Ohio, "the men in the line were equal, if not superior, in average intelligence . . . to the officers in immediate command" (Fleming 1908: 141). Many of the men had already seen enlisted men fill a leadership void that an officer had left during the battle. One such was a veteran in the 17th Illinois who had already seen action at Fort Donelson. He somehow came over to the green, frightened recruits of the 53rd Ohio, whose colonel had abandoned them, and he helped them respond to the first Confederate rush. "He was a brave, cool man," one witness recollected. "First, he found some Enfield rifle cartridges. . . . Next he went along the line, telling the men he had seen the elephant before, and had learned that the way to meet him was to keep cool, shoot slow and aim low. He, [told them] 'why, it's just like shooting squirrels—only these squirrels have guns, that's all.' Pretty soon he called out: 'Good-bye' and as he hurried to rejoin his own company" (Duke 1900: 48). He was never seen again.

POST-COMBAT ASSESSMENTS OF ENEMY COMBAT PERFORMANCE

"I could not help but admire their courage," wrote Payson Shumway, an Illinois soldier, in describing the combat performance of the enemy (To wife [Hattie], April 13, 1862). Shumway's assessment of Confederate effectiveness weighed in the balance of factors influencing morale. The large majority of the soldiers shared Shumway's newfound respect for the adversary's courage.[11] Both Confederates and Unionists emerged from the battle with a newly wrought—though often grudging—respect for their enemy's fighting ability. Responses on both sides were remarkably similar reinforcing the argument that the Western armies shared more similarities than differences. The resemblance was not accidental. A Hoosier with Wagner's brigade recalled comrades in Ohio and Kentucky regiments who had found their Confederate brothers dead on the battlefield (A.F. Davis to F.D. [brother], April 21, 1862). Not surprisingly, the respect for the enemy increased in proportion to the losses that the men's unit sustained; i.e., the higher the losses the higher the esteem for the fighting ability of the enemy. The men from units that suffered above average casualties noted the enemy's effectiveness twice as frequently as men from lightly engaged regiments and batteries.

The recruits assessed each other's capability using two criteria. First, they judged the enemy according to the quality of the weapons and supplies that they used in the battle. Second, they evaluated the enemy's fighting prowess. The quality and abundance of the food and equipment that the North provided to its men left a deep impression on the Confederates when they seized the Union camps on the first day. A quick inventory of the booty brought home the power and the wealth that the federal government had available to suppress the rebellion. J.P. Barnes, an ambulance driver with the Mobile "Continentals" in Chalmers' brigade, had never seen an army "so liberally supplied with all the implements of war and the comforts of life as these men seemed to be" (*The Mobile Advertiser and Register*, April 16, 1862). On a lighter note, a Tennessean with the 1st Regiment recalled how "the boys were in clover" as the men helped themselves to the Union booty. "The harvest was great and the laborers were not few," he reminisced happily (Watkins 1962: 43). A gunner in Captain William H. Ketchum's Alabama battery shared the wonder at the treasures of the Yankee camps. "Such a splendidly provisioned army I never heard of," he remarked before providing an inventory to the people back home of the items that the Yankees took along with them on a campaign. There were "pickled oysters, pig's feet, lemons, [and] sweet meats of all kinds," he marveled (*The Mobile Advertiser and Register*, April 11, 1862). Sam Houston, Jr., of the 2nd Texas was equally impressed with the Union camps. "I won't say the place boasted waterworks or a central park," he declared, "but doubtless there would have been such improvements, had we left the inhabitants unmolested for a few additional weeks. As it was, they certainly had everything calculated to render camp-life pleasant" (1930–31: 329).

The Confederates "expropriated" the bounty in short order exchanging their flintlocks and shotguns for Union-issue arms (O.E. Cunningham 1966: 459). W.S. Dillon of the 4th Tennessee commented that "the enemy have better arms than we have, most of our men are armed with the old musket but the enemy have Enfield rifles and rifled muskets" (Diary, April 7, 1862). Then they returned to the luxuries. "We had a hearty supper from the Yankee stores," recalled Jim Griffin. He and the 5th Company of the Washington Artillery took time out to enjoy the "excellence of [the Union] . . . Commissary Department" and do "justice to the provisioner" (*The New Orleans Daily Crescent*, April 19, 1862).

On the Union side, an infantryman with the 16th Wisconsin of Prentiss' division looked over some Confederate prisoners taken at Corinth and found them to be "stout, healthy, fine looking fellows," who appeared well supplied (Quiner, Reel No. 3, Vol. 6, p. 278). According to Chester A. Buckland of the 72nd Ohio Infantry, they were "well dressed and pretty well armed" (*The Fremont Daily Journal*, April 25, 1862). Other Union volunteers, however, found them a rather "hard looking set" (Quiner, Reel No. 2, Vol. 5, p. 245), who were "indifferently clad and unkempt in appearance" (Hickenlooper 1903: 411). Most wore only "butternut jeans" (W. Bradford to wife, April 10, 1862) and they appeared bedraggled; but one thing they had in common was that they "generally bore a determined and defiant air" (Hickenlooper 1903: 411). Ephraim Kimberly of the 41st Ohio, Colonel William B. Hazen's brigade, found the Southerners generally primitive, their backwardness denoted by the type of sidearm they took with them into battle. They carried large knives suggesting that "crude notions of war found lodgment among the fiery Southerners" (Kimberly and Holloway 1897: 25). Kimberly made the mistaken assumption, like his forefathers' British foes a century earlier, that such "primitives" would never be able to fight a modern war effectively.

Overall, the Northerners expressed a healthy respect for their opponents; however, it was often grudging. They attributed Confederate impetuosity to a dose of whiskey laced with gunpowder, the story being that this brew was what gave the Confederates such elan. The proof was in the faces of the Confederate dead and in their canteens. When the men of the 15th Illinois turned their attention to burying the rebel corpses, one infantryman testified that "We noticed that the faces were black. On examination, we found that their canteens contained whiskey and gunpowder which was, no doubt, the cause of [their courage]. It seems," he surmised, "that this had been given to them just before going into battle to make them fight." This, he argued, was the real reason why they fought like "demons" the first day (Barber 1894: 60–61). Union surgeons supposedly confirmed the coloration of the Confederate dead as being attributable to the ferocious concoction. Why else, the story continued, were they seen to throw away their guns and "rush upon the artillery with closed fists and wild screams and laughter" (*The Columbia City News*, April 29, 1862).

Other detractors of Confederate bravery attributed their vigorous attacks to the allegation that "the rebels had their cavalry behind their infantry, just driving them, so they could not go back" (*The Ironton Register*, May 8, 1862). Some also thought that the Southern performance was an act of desperation in a lost cause. "I don't believe the rebels will ever fight as long or as hard again, as they did here," wrote one Union soldier a week after the battle (Quiner, Reel No. 2, Vol. 5, p. 57; see also *The Council Bluffs Nonpareil*, May 3, 1862). A few bluecoats also believed that their own fire was far more accurate. L.M. Garrigus reported to the local newspaper editor in Kokomo, Indiana, that "a very large porportion [of the Union troops] are slightly wounded in arms feet and legs," because, he believed, "the rebel shot very low." On the other hand, "our men killed most of them, but we had most wounded" (*The Howard Tribune*, April 29, 1862). Corroboration came from Jim Newton who wrote that "a good many of the boys" in the 14th Wisconsin came out of the battle with the conclusion that the "Secesh shot awful careless with their guns" (J.K. Newton 1961: 16; see also J.K. Newton to father and mother, Abdel D. Newton Papers, April 12, 1862).

Such was not the attitude of the majority of Union troops. George F. Lee of Waterhouse's battery (Battery E, 1st Illinois Light Artillery), told a friend back home, "If we ever had a notion in our heads that those fellows couldn't shoot we had it dispelled" (To Nesbitt, n.d.). Lee's attitude was more typical of the Union troops regarding the enemy's fighting ability. He, like most of the Northern volunteers, came out of the fight with grudging respect for the courage of their Confederate opponents. Their impetuosity came as a surprise to the men after the easy victory at Fort Donelson. Timothy Blaisdell, an Illinois gunner, explained the difference by suggesting the enemy at Donelson were "rabble" whereas at Shiloh they had "met the flower of the Southern army" (To family, April 12, 1862). E.R. Kellogg of the 77th Pennsylvania concurred, "There was no lack of gallantry on the part of the Confederates" (Recollections). "They fought bravely and . . . the attack was sudden and able," judged another Northerner, Lieutenant Colonel Addison H. Sanders of the 15th Iowa (Throne 1954: 247; see also J. Ufford to brother, April 8, 1862; W.R. Stimson to wife, April 10, 1862). Sergeant Harold M. White, Company H, 11th Iowa, rated his opponents "A Number One" and went on to report that "one look at them was enough to convince a man that courage and discipline are virtues peculiar to neither North or South" (Throne 1954: 253). When the bluecoats came in contact with enemy captives, the Unionist troops found that the Confederates were just as highly motivated as they were, and that the Southerners had the misapprehension that the North was fighting the war to abolish slavery. This assumption surprised the Northerners, because most of them had initially enrolled only to restore the Union. When Amos Currier, a prisoner of the Confederates, told his guards that no such idea as abolition motivated the Northern army, the Southerners were skeptical, replying that they did not see "how we can fight merely to sustain [the] . . . government" (Diary, April 17, 1862). Mobilizing for such a legal abstraction could hardly inspire the North. The Southerners, in contrast, fought for a high revolutionary purpose, national independence, and they assumed that only another equally powerful revolutionary ideal could inspire the North—a goal such as the abolition of slavery. A soldier with the 15th Michigan never forgot the first conversation he had with a Confederate, a wounded fourteen-year-old sitting against a tree, who shouted at the passing enemy, " 'Well, if you are going to kill me—kill me. . . . What you'se come down to fight we-uns for? If you want the niggers, I wisht you had all of them. I haven't got any' " (Ruff 1943: 299).

The men on both sides wrote home warning their friends and kinfolk not to underestimate the enemy's courage. William Ross of the 40th Illinois told his parents "never did I see such men fight. When ever you heare . . . a man say they wont fight tell him he nows nothing bout them for wen our cannons would mow them down by hundreds others would follow and take their plase and fight like demons" (To father April 10, 1862; see also W. Richardson to father and mother, April 13, 1862). John Mosley of the 16th Wisconsin joined in the surge of admonishment, "People may talk about the cowardice of Southern soldiers; [but] they are only deceiving themselves. Soldiers never fought better than those who fought us here," he admitted in a letter (Quiner, Reel No. 2, Vol. 5, p. 253). There was also Lieutenant II.C. Wright, Company H, 32nd Illinois, who advised a friend, "Just for my sake, when you hear republicans say the secesh will not fight, tell them that I say they lie, and are a set of cowards, or they would not stay at home and talk in that way; and if they [the Confederates] only had the republicans to fight they could make a crop at the same time and keep them whipped. I judge by the fighting done by the republican troops of Ohio, Wisconsin, and Michigan" (*The Jacksonville Sentinel*, May 2, 1862; see also *The Ohio Repository*, April 8, 1862).

The Confederate army failure led many Union soldiers to mistakenly assume that the Southern troops had been demoralized, despite their heroic efforts. "The rebels can make but one more stand, and their cause is done for," said Captain N.W. Edwards of Company H, 15th Iowa Infantry to his friends and neighbors in Council Bluffs (*Council Bluffs Nonpareil*, May 3, 1862). "They are loosing confidence in their Commander, and they are almost at mutiny now." The word was out that "many Regiments would leave if they could only get out on Picket, but they keep all suspicious Regiments within their lines as mutch as possible" (Samuel Sheperdson to sister, May 13, 1862). The belief was confirmed for many when Southern soldiers were reported to have begun drifting into the Union lines around Corinth. Rumors circulated around the camp fires of Company G of the 30th Indiana Infantry that "one whole Brigade gave themselves up" (Samuel Sheperdson to sister, May 13, 1862; see also *The Ohio Repository*, April 9, 1862). Jim Newton expected that his 14th Wisconsin would soon return home, telling his kin, "I hope that I shall be on hand to help you make [maple sugar] . . . by the time another spring comes around," adding the proviso, "that is if we get 'Uncle Sams thrashing' done by that time (J.K. Newton to father and mother, Abdel D. Newton Papers, May 3, 1862).

The Confederates also tended to be grudging in their praise of Northern fighting prowess. Colonel Rogers of the 2nd Texas Infantry still believed that the Confederates were better fighters, but he was discouraged by the size of the enemy forces. "Two to one we can whip them but if we contend with greater odds the result will be doubtful"

(1929: 287). W.S. Dillon of the 4th Tennessee argued that the only thing that saved the Union army was its superior logistics. "I think," he asserted, "if their army was fed and clothed like ours they could not keep it in the field for six months" (Diary, April 6, 1862). Robert T. Moore of the 19th Alabama was not impressed by the Yankees either. He had been watching them hastily throw up breastworks around Corinth and had been to Mobile and had seen the Northern prisoners from Shiloh. Mirroring an erroneous assumption prevailing in Union camps as well, Southerners believed the Shiloh bloodbath had crippled their enemy's fighting spirit. Serving in the works defending Corinth, Lieutenant Bill Vaught of the Washington Artillery did not attribute much staying power to the Union host, writing home that "200 of their cavalry deliberately rode into our lines . . . & were surrounded . . . *they said* [they] *had lost their way* & did not know where they were going" (To sister, May 17, 1862).

MEDICAL SERVICES

Stories also circulated in the hospital wards of Corinth that the federal musketry was especially effective, because the Unionists had poisoned their bullets. "The doctors seem to think that the enemy poisoned their balls, as wounds inflame terrible," wrote Kate Cumming, a volunteer nurse (*Journal* 1866: April 23, 1862). But lack of proper antiseptic measures was obviously the real cause of the high infection rate, not poisoned bullets. An Alabamian in Chalmers' brigade wrote home about another form of Union perfidy. He accused them of using explosive bullets, wrongly assuming that this was what caused such gaping wounds. "I don't know anything about it—but I saw a bullet (Minnie) that was hollow, and contained some white substance that resembled powder; whether it was imagination or not, many of our boys say they heard bullets exploding in the air" (*The Mobile Advertiser and Register*, April 18, 1862). One such bullet was found and analyzed in Memphis and discovered only to have clay in the cavity. The horrendous mutilation caused by the musket balls was attributable to the soft lead balls, up to 0.75 caliber, that were fired with such kinetic energy that they deformed and spread when they struck a bone, making a great exit hole, tearing everything on the way out.

The ferocity of the fighting and the lethality of the weapons turned the men's attention to the medical support services that they could expect if they fell victim. What they saw had a demoralizing impact. This was one of the darkest aspects of the Battle of Shiloh, and one of the most corrosive morale factors; the men dwelt at length on it in their letters and diaries. "It is impossible to say what the wounded of our army may be obliged to undergo," James Griffin of the Washington Artillery wrote to his father, after seeing the state of the Confederate medical facilities at Corinth (*The New Orleans Daily Crescent*, April 19, 1862). Parson Sullins of the 19th Tennessee believed that the horrors he witnessed in the field hospitals affected him far more than the fighting itself. "Battle can but dimly be recalled, and is by no means stamped on the mind as . . . the long line of wounded and dying men on the way to the surgeon's station; the trickling blood from the improvised stretcher; the white upturned face . . . the quick breath and far-away look; the effort to tell you something . . . the amputated legs and arms laid in a tangled heap . . . these and such like are never forgotten. O, how I have wished I could forget! I still shut my eyes sometimes in an effort to shut it all out—but in vain; it is all there still" (Sullins 1910: 217–18).

Medical care at Shiloh was an "unqualified failure." Whatever organization had been put in place before the fighting fell apart once the battle started (G.W. Adams 1952: 81). The death rate among Union troops was 13.6 percent from gunshot wounds during the Civil War (G.W. Adams 1952: 123), and given the disorganized state of the services at Shiloh, it must have been even higher. Contrary to their World War II counterparts (Stouffer 1949: II, 145), the immense majority of whom thought that medical service was very good, the Shiloh troops were nearly unanimous in condemning the surgeons and hospital orderlies. Although Grant and A.S. Johnston had already begun to reorganize the medical services after the fighting at Fort Donelson, these measures had not been implemented yet. A.H. Stephens a surgeon with the 6th Ohio testified angrily that the medical horrors "occurred principally from the totally unprepared condition of the medical department for the proper care of the wounded. This would not have been the case had our commanders had the slightest idea of a battle occurring at this point. The consequence was that over five thousand wounded men were to be cared for, for whom not a tent had been pitched" (Quiner, Reel No. 2, Vol. 5, pp. 275–76). There were supposed to be three ambulances and two wagons per regiment in the Army of the Tennessee, which meant that Grant should have had approximately 400 wagons available for moving the wounded. But over half his train was driven by contracted civilian teamsters. Many of them probably abandoned their equipment during the battle. The others, the military teamsters, were probably called to other duties such as hauling up ammunition, so that very few wagons or ambulances were available for evacuating the wounded. Furthermore, being a spacious and comfortable vehicle, the four-wheeled ambulance was prized by the upper echelons for transporting their personal belongs.

There is not much evidence to confirm that there were many units with designated ambulances and attendants available. From Hildebrand's brigade of Sherman's division, Lieutenant Colonel E.C. Dawes reported that "no orders had been issued in our brigade [before the battle] as to the care of the wounded. No stretcher-bearers had been detailed" (Duke 1900: 48–49). The same report came from Assistant Surgeon S.H. Eells of the 121th Michigan in Prentiss' division. He too confirmed that the regiment did not have any ambulances available for evacuating the wounded (To aunt and uncle, May 1, 1862).

There was also a shortage of surgeons and supplies at the field hospitals. D.M. Cook, surgeon of the 3rd Iowa, had written to his home state a month before the battle pleading for more surgeons and instruments, but none had been sent (*The Dubuque Daily Times*, May 29, 1862). Nor did the men deem the competence of the surgeons as adequate to the task. They found them ignorant and callous. G.W. Adams has pointed out that troops at Shiloh came from states that had the lowest appointment standards for surgeons. Indiana was a notorious example. In 1862, the state's governor, Oliver P. Morton, sought to put through someone whose sole qualification was brief service as an attendant in a field hospital and one year's reading in a local physician's office. Wisconsin did not even have an examining board, leaving the selection process to regimental commanders (G.W. Adams 1952: 10). Much the same situation existed on the Confederate side (B.I. Wiley 1978b: 267–68).

The poor quality of the medical personnel elicited angry soldiers' denunciations. A volunteer of the 16th Wisconsin wrote to his hometown editor about the departure of an incompetent regimental surgeon. "We have a change of Doctors in our regiment. . . . Well, our sick will not mourn their departure; [and] the graves of our bravest and strongest men will not become more numerous" (Quiner, Reel No. 2, Vol. 5, p. 281). A Union infantryman told his kin, "I have not taken any of the Doctors medicine since I have enlisted and do not calculate to unless I am obliged to. Others that have been doing so are dropping like sheep" (D.G. James to parents, April 28, 1862).

The first line of medical service were the stretcher-bearers and assistant surgeons who were supposed to evacuate the wounded and provide first aid (B.I. Wiley 1978a: 144, 1978b; 262–63). It appears from the tenor of the comments that there was no established procedure for evacuating the men. There may very well have been members of the rank and file, such as bandsmen, who would have been designated stretcher-bearers, but there was no reference to such orders in any of the correspondence. More likely, such decisions were made during the battle. For example, the 6th Ohio's surgeon, A.H. Stephens, had no designated attendants before the battle and had to rush among the men to get people to help him just before the regiment went into action. "From the very great state of excitment that prevailed among the soldiers, it was almost impossible to procure attendants," he complained (Quiner, Reel No. 2, Vol. 5, pp. 275–76). The large number of wounded left on the battlefield on the first night attested to the lack of stretcher-bearers and ambulances (Baird 1978: 47; see also O.E. Cunningham 1966: 504). One of the soldiers who survived the ordeal, Martin Donahue of the 12th Michigan, said in his diary that he had lain where he had fallen for two days before he finally received attention (Diary, April 27, 1862). This coincided with the testimony of Surgeon D.M. Cook, who wrote home that for lack of help, he still had wounded men who had not reached his hospital four days after the battle began (*The Dubuque Daily Times*, May 29, 1862).

The second stage in the system of medical aid was removal to a field hospital, usually consisting of a group of tents or whatever other shelter could be requisitioned by the regimental surgeons. But the regimental hospitals would serve only their own men, and the brigade and division surgeons did not have the authority to shift medical personnel to where they were needed. Here at least, the Union army had an advantage by holding the field after the battle and by having access to river transportation at Pittsburg Landing. Evacuation to the rear, to Savannah and beyond, was far easier, and supplies and help could arrive more quickly. The Union wounded were spared the torture of a jolting freight wagon ride over twenty miles of churned roads to Corinth. The Confederate medical situation there was even worse; the Southern forces had lost many of the captured Union medical stores. Not only that, but as Buell and Grant's counteroffensive rolled them back, many of their surgeons remained behind to tend the wounded who could not be evacuated; therefore, their own surgeons' services were lost (G.W. Adams 1952: 82). James Williams of the 21st Alabama lamented the lost of Dr. Redwood, the regiment's surgeon. "There is no doubt," wrote Williams, "that he deliberately allowed himself to fall into the enemy's hands, rather than desert our wounded men on the field" (Folmar 1981: 59–60).

As the Confederate army began its retreat, the Union surgeons who were captured on the first day quickly made an *ad hoc* arrangement with their Confederate confreres. The Confederates were desperately short of ambulances and could not take their wounded back with them to Corinth. Samuel Eells, a captured assistant surgeon of the 12th Michigan, participated in the negotiations. "It was agreed," he wrote home, "that the wounded should be left where they were until they could be carried away & then they should go each to their own party without hindrance from the troops of either side, & their Surgeons & attendants should go with them" (To friends, April 13, 1862).

Behind the Confederate lines the situation was chaotic, few buildings were available, only some Union tents. First-aid kits were in short supply, despite Medical Director David Yandell's special order for improving evacuation and field hospitals. This order, issued over a month before, had not yet been implemented. Antiseptics were unknown and the surgeons probed the wounds with unwashed fingers, resorting to brandy and opium to reduce the pain—if they were available. William Thompson of the 6th Mississippi described the scene at a field hospital, it was a 'sight' I would like to forget. Piles of dead soldiers . . . in rows were others who were dying. . . . Screams from the operation table. . . . They were being unloaded like so many butchered hogs . . . the wagon beds were streaming blood" (1964: 21). "Merciful Heaven," a Confederate captain confided to his diary, "what a sight. . . . The sympathy of my nature which had been comparatively inactive amid the hurricane of destruction . . . was now fully aroused and 'my heart bled' for my noble boys" (J.W. Caldwell, Diary, April 6, 1862). "It was a pitiful sight I can tell you," wrote Assistant Surgeon Samuel Eells. "Such groans and cries for help. . . . I hope I never see the like again." As the Union Line collapsed, Eells worked feverishly in his improvised ward, when "General [Thomas C.] Hindman of Arkansas rode up and placed a guard over us and assured us we should not be molested though we must consider ourselves prisoners. Two rebel Surgeons came up too and established their hospitals right by ours and made liberal use of our medicines and hospital stores. There we worked all day upon rebel wounded and our own," he told a friend (To friends, April 13, 1862). Eells later made his way back to the Union lines.

Grant had lost many of the medical supplies, when the Confederates captured the camps, and Buell had left his train far behind as he rushed to Grant's aid (B.I. Wiley 1978a: 143). A litany of horrors surrounded the field hospitals around the landing. "By Wednesday," complained Surgeon A.H. Stephens (6th Ohio) to the editor of *The Cincinnati Lancet and Observer*, "I had forty dead on my hands; these for want of room were carried off—left outside the house, and I did not succeed in getting them buried until some of the corpses gave . . . evidence of decay. I could not get more buried until many of the mangled corpses were far gone in putrefaction, and the alternate rain and sunshine, with the great moving crowd around the house, caused bodies to be sunk or covered partially . . . in the mud, which with the mangled and severed limbs scattered promiscuously gave a picture not overly pleasing" (Quiner, Reel No. 2, Vol. 5, pp. 275–76; see also J. Connelley, Diary, April 9, 1862). Surgeon James R. Zearing of the 57th Illinois described the situation at the landing during the first two days. "You may imagine the scene of from two to three thousand wounded men at one point calling to have their wounds dressed. We worked to the best advantage we could, but the absence of extensive preparations for such an event, caused a great deal of suffering, that might have been prevented" (To Puss, April 8, 1862).

The complaints about the medical service poured homeward. The men of one regiment reported that the "first surgeon . . . ran off leaving the sick and wounded in the hospital" (Quiner, Reel No. 2, Vol. 5, p. 274). And even after the emergency of the first few days, the indictments continued to stream homeward. Lieutenant D.F. Vail never forgave the army medical services for the loss of a friend because of the inadequate medical care. "It was two weeks before anything was done, and then," he wrote bitterly, "it was too late" (1897: 5). The men accused the hospital staff of callousness and incompetence and believed that many of the orderlies were thieves. "The boys in the hospital are starved," complained a wounded soldier of the 16th Wisconsin. "The waiters and hangers around drink the liquors and eat the dainties that are furnished to the sick. . . . Hundreds of our brave boys who gallantly stood up in the defense of their country have sank into untimely graves through the neglect of our villanous surgeons, who instead of attending to the wounded, spent their time riding up and down the river on the boats, drinking their wine and enjoying their meals" (Quiner, Reel No. 2, Vol. 5, p. 274). By contrast, the civilian nurses who arrived to lend a hand were much appreciated when compared to the army attendants, though a Wisconsonian wrote home that the "nurses . . . are all very well in a humanitarian way," but "not much in the line of attraction." The convalescent lamented over the "gaunt females, over thirty years old" that had been inflicted on the boys (Quiner, Reel No. 2, Vol. 5, p. 275).

As late as two weeks after the battle, reports from Pittsburg Landing continued to detail the woeful medical situation. Hospitals still lacked beds; the wounded were bedded on the wet ground (W.J. Kennedy to wife, April 22, 1862). And when General Halleck decided to move the hospitals upstream to be nearer to Corinth (in anticipation of the siege), the tents and supplies did not keep up, leaving the men lying along the bank of the river without shelter or beds once again (B.I. Wiley 1978a: 140).

Evacuation to the rear was a better alternative. Savannah, a few miles upriver, was a small town with more shelter for the wounded, but there were not enough steamboats available to transport the wounded and simultaneously move up supplies and reinforcements. Other steamers were jammed with wounded and there were no facilities available to receive them, thus rendering the boats unavailable for evacuation duties (O.E. Cunningham 1966: 436). One of the steamers that helped in evacuating the wounded was the *Continental*. "The scene upon the boat was heart-rending—men wounded and mangled in every conceivable way," according to William Swain, Company G, 11th Iowa, who was among them. "The dead and dying [were] lying in masses, some with arms, legs, and even their jaws shot off, bleeding to death, and no one to wait upon them or dress their wounds—no surgeon to attend us." Not only did the boat lack medical personnel, but the captain and crew showed no sympathy for the men's plight. There were about 1,200 thrown on board, and there they lay for some unexplained reason from Sunday night until Wednesday afternoon. During the entire period, claimed Swain, the men were without water or rations. "Some begged the Captain to broach the Commissary Stores on the boat, but he would not allow them to be taken without a requisition! Many tried to buy or beg food, each time the gong sounded summoning the crew to their meals. But the Captain replied that he had nothing to sell!" (Throne 1954: 263). The situation was no better on the *Mound City*, where pillow cases and sheets were ripped from the passenger compartments and used for bandages, reported Surgeon Andrew Rankin (Army Record). The medical situation was a disaster. Cyrus Boyd of the 15th Iowa expressed his anger. "If the people at home know how the sick soldiers are treated in this Army there would be such a howl of indignation and cussing as would make the country tremble" (1953: 40).

Among the Confederates, the same disaster was occurring. The men were evacuated as quickly as possible in the face of the Monday counterattacks. After cursory treatment, the wounded were loaded on ambulances and sent rearward (Baird 1978: 47). Emergency facilities were set up just north of the Tennessee-Mississippi line at Monterey, where eventually 2,800 sick and wounded accumulated. It was a makeshift installation that oozed signs of tragedy. Charles Wright described it as follows. "The sick and wounded at this place could not receive the attention they deserved on account of the scarcity of physicians and nurses. These gallant men died at the rate of eight or ten per day" (1887: 38). Most, however, were sent on to Corinth. The small town was transformed into a receiving station, where nearly every building became a ward with a yellow flag fluttering forlornly above. Men were sprawled everywhere, with the attendants and physicians leaping from one to the other mutually entangled in a catastrophe beyond their means (Baird 1978: 47; see also J.E. Magee, Diary, May 25, 1862).

J.W. Cullom of the 24th Tennessee was assigned to help in a hospital and was horrified by the scenes. "I carried out my arms full of legs and arms and saw pieces of human flesh lying around like beef" (To Mary, April 10, 1862). The center of it all was the Tishimingo Hotel and the railroad siding in front of it. It was here that volunteer nurse Kate Cumming came to lend a hand. She was shocked by the sight. At the Tishimingo, men and freight accumulated in front, while in the backyard, piles of cut-off limbs were stacked up. "Nothing," she wrote, "that I had ever heard or read had given me the faintest idea of the horrors witnessed here" (*Journal*, April 11 and 12, 1862). Wounded and dead were everywhere; sometimes there was no place to even lay the wounded and no one to bury them either. Captain John Caldwell had his arm broken in the battle and had trudged the twenty miles to Corinth in search of succor. When he dragged himself in, no one would help; his was not considered an urgent enough case. Turned away from one hospital after another, he lapsed into helpless despair. "I sat down by a tree in the rain. . . . I wished myself most dead" (Diary, April 7, 1862).

Inside one of the wards, Nurse Cumming watched man after man head for the amputation room facing excruciating pain and realizing that it was all for naught because most would not survive anyway; the poor wounded were not even allowed to die unmolested. Cumming recounted the last tormented days of a youth, named Fuquet, who knew he was to have his arm cut off. "Poor fellow!" she recorded in her diary, "I am doing all that I can to cheer him. He says that he knows he will die, as all who have had limbs amputated in this hospital" (*Journal*, April 23, 1862). It was to be done on a table at the end of the hall. Cumming confided to her diary that "when an operation is to be performed, I keep as far away from it as possible. To-day, just as they had got through with Mr. Fuquet, I was compelled to pass the place, and the sight I . . . beheld made me shudder and sick at heart. A stream of blood ran from the table into a tub in which was the arm. It had been taken off at the socket, and the hand . . . was hanging over the edge of the tub." She explained her presence in the amputation room without realizing the implicit grotesqueness of the hospital butchery, by adding that "the passage to the kitchen leads directly past the amputating room" (*Journal*, April 24, 1862). Working amid the carnage, Assistant Surgeon Lunsford Yandell could bear no more of the horror after two weeks in the wards at Corinth. "I am sick of being a medical officer," he wrote home. "I wish to go into the cavalry as a private and may yet do so. It is my earnest wish, the anxiety—the mental anguish which I suffer, when with the wounded is almost unbearable. . . . I suffer I believe almost as much as my patients do. I fear I have mistaken my calling" (To sister [Sally], April 21, 1862).

To alleviate the overburdened facilities at Corinth, the authorities tried to organize rail transport to other places, such as Tallassee, Alabama; Holly Springs, Oxford, or Okolona, Mississippi; but the railroads were snarled up. "One of the surgeons complained bitterly of the bad management of the railroad, and said that its managers should be punished, as they were the cause of a great unnecessary suffering. . . . They take their own time to transport the wounded, and it is impossible to depend upon them" (Cumming, *Journal*, April 17, 1862). Kate Cumming described the scene at the depot. "We saw a whole Mississippi regiment sick, awaiting transportation. They looked very badly, and nearly all had a cough." And further along the track "within a short distance of the hospital [a doctor] heard groans; went to the place from which they proceeded, and found a box-car, that had been switched off the track, filled with wounded men, some dead and others dying, and not a soul with them to do anything for them" (*Journal*, May 11, 1862).

While Corinth had trouble bringing in supplies from the hinterland, Northern states responded with varying alacrity to the appeals of their troops. Lieutenant Colonel D.C. Loudon asked his wife to act on behalf of the 70th Ohio Infantry to marshal hometown help. Loudon complained that the aid had heretofore not gotten through from the state or federal authorities. Loudon blamed it on the state bureaucracies. "Supplies have to pass through too many hands" (To Hannah, April 24, 1862). However, E.C. Milgate, who was wounded in the side by a musket ball while serving with the 52nd Illinois, was taken under the wing of an Ohio aid society and then shipped to the 3rd Military Hospital in Cincinnati. He reported to the hometown newspaper in Aurora, Illinois, that the Ohioans had treated him well; far better than the medical personnel in the crowded wards of Savannah. There he had lain for twenty days before the ball was finally extracted. By contrast, "Cincinnati justly deserves all the praise she has received and more for the manner in which she has treated the wounded. The boat [the *Tycoon*] which brought us here was fitted out and manned by the citizens of this place . . . acting as nurses and deck-hands, and the supplies were furnished by the Ladies' Aid Society of this place" (*The Aurora Beacon*, May 15, 1862).

Thanks to the regiments' territorial recruiting base, they could call on their home states and counties for help when their army's medical services were overwhelmed by the flood of wounded. The letters and reports from the front were not filled with heroic euphemisms to spare the population the truth of war. They reported the unvarnished truth about the slaughter. Thus the people back home were quickly made aware of the disaster and were able to respond.

Responses varied. Many Northern communities chartered steamers and sent teams of civilian volunteers with medical supplies and doctors to help their outfits. They helped evacuate hundreds of men back to hospitals in their home states. Townsfolk in Alabama and Mississippi sent volunteers and supplies on every available train to evacuate as many men as they could to their regimental home bases. Where the communities responded effectively to the calls of their soldiers, they tightened the bonds to their regiments.

However, some states responded lethargically to their soldiers' needs. D.M. Cook, surgeon of the 3rd Iowa, wrote scathingly to his hometown newspaper of the lack of support. "We suffered much more here than we would have done, had there been as much energy manifested on the part of our State authorities, as there was by those of Illinois, Indiana, and Ohio, and other States which had wounded here to care for." Cook had brought men down to the riverbank to have them evacuated, but the captains would not take aboard the Iowa troops, not even the worst cases. The captain of the *Blackhawk* refused to take any but Illinois men, because that state had chartered the steamer and Governor Richard Yates himself was on board supervising the operation. The Hawk-eye surgeon declared, "I felt disgusted with all things human on board that boat, and was compelled to take my brave and suffering wounded boys back to camp." He went on to indict the shoddy treatment of the men by the people of his home state, accusing them of breaking the contract between the men in the army and the people in the community. "After fighting and suffering as they did at Pittsburg, and then to be neglected in the way they were, it has not made a favorable impression on their minds and feelings toward the rulers of our State. . . . While we are fighting for their homes and firesides, it is their bounden duty, to make our cares sufferings and dangers as small as possible" (*The Dubuque Daily Times,* May 29, 1862).

One bright spot in a generally dark picture was Assistant Surgeon Bernard J.D. Irwin of Brigadier General William Nelson's staff. Irwin gathered tents and surgeons into one location at Colonel David Stuart's former encampment. There he organized wards and coordinated medical service. His measure served as a model for Union field hospitals later in the war (Sword 1974: 420).

REACTIONS TO DEATH AND SUFFERING

The butchery on the battlefield and in the field hospitals hardened the men and confronted them with killing another human being. The dilemma between civilian prohibitions against killing and a military ethos demanding the contrary is closely related to combat motivations of Shiloh's soldiers. Whenever possible the soldiers preferred to avoid coming to grips with the dilemma. "I do not now have any conclusive knowledge that during my entire term of service I ever killed, or wounded, a single man," reminisced an Illinois soldier years later. "It is more than probable that some of my shots were fatal, but I don't know, and am thankful for the ignorance" (Stillwell 1920: 60–61). It is no surprise then that few of the volunteers discussed the topipc in their diaries and letters.

Marshall has argued, in a study of twentieth-century soldiers, that the fear of killing was the most common cause of battle failure; the horror of committing homicide even exceeded the threat of being killed (1947: 78). However, Ashworth contended that there was "little evidence in the personal documents [of World War I trench fighters] . . . that soldiers experienced either fear of aggression or temporary paralysis. Many expressions of revulsion against war exist in the sources; but these did

not make men inert" (1980: 215). The latter interpretation more accurately reflects the reaction of Shiloh's soldiers. Obviously, the soldiers
would not have wanted to admit to their communities that they had not
done their duty by refusing to fire at the enemy. Nevertheless, not even
one, among hundreds of soldiers' letters, diaries, and reminiscences,
expressed recalcitrance to shooting at the enemy. The only restraint they
mentioned was simply the lack of targets.

Gradually, civilian values were compartmentalized from the new military ones. Dulled by proximity of death and suffering on the battlefield,
their working value system became one characterized by callous non-
chalance to the idea of death and killing. It was founded, in the workaday
world of the front-line soldier, on the simple statement that all things
being equal it was better to kill than to be killed. The process of coming
to terms with death and killing and the resulting callousness that characterized the veterans began to develop during the early months of
campaign, as the recruits saw friends and acquaintances die by accident
and disease. Saul Howell vividly remembered when he first witnessed
someone's death. It happened in Missouri in July 1861.

A musket report from Company C [3rd Iowa]. . . . Great commotion. . . . It was
announced that it was corporal H.H. Sherman. The ball entered one of the
testicles and passed through the whole length of the body, lodging in the right
breast near the surface, at the collar bone. . . . It was a mournful, impressive
scene to behold betokening the deep feeling of . . . sorrow and affection. [Sher-
man] spoke a few times, speaking of having come forth to fight the battle of his
country. Also of the flag of our country, and of his mother. . . . He suffered
dreadfully till eased by chloroform. . . . This affiar cast a gloom over the whole
camp (Journal, July 24, 1861).

Death was not yet banal. It occasioned individual funerals and collective
expressions of grief. When a well-liked officer in the Natchez Rifles died
of illness, a committee was formed and a resolution was drafted and
sent home extolling his virtue and mourning his loss (*The Natchez Daily
Courier*, February 28, 1862).

But with the rising losses to disease and death, the men learned to
live with it. They regretted a friend's passing but went on with their
own lives. "It is a right sad thing to die in camp," wrote an Alabamian,
"that is to the man who is doing the dying. [But] the happening of such
an event interferes in no way with a game of euchre that may be going
on in the next tent, and interests no one but those detailed to bury the
body" (*The Mobile Advertiser and Register*, September 1, 1861). Later, death
became even more banal, eliciting more and more callous comments.
Killing the enemy was described like a sporting event. A Hoosier wrote
home about one of his first chances to shoot at the enemy. "I fired my

musket at them twice but did not hit them for they was to far off. I would," he added sportingly, "like to kill one of them but maybe I will get a chance yet" (J. Vanderbilt to mother, January 26, 1862). Bill Warren, Company H, 13th Iowa, also wanted to get a chance to shoot at the enemy, but lamented, "the only thing I hav killed since I caim here [Jefferson City, Missouri] was a mule [that] broke its legg" (To wife, January 23, 1862).

Shiloh served as catalyst for the brutalization process. "War is *hell* broke *loose* and benumbs all the tender feelings of men and makes them *brutes*," Cyrus Boyd confided sadly to his diary two days after the battle (Boyd 1953: 42). The flood of horrors was sloughed off. Ambrose Bierce came across the remains of an Illinois regiment that had refused to surrender when caught in a ravine. The men were systematically mowed down, the brush caught fire, and the survivors and corpses consumed by the flames. Looking into the ravine, the Hoosier cynically shrugged off the sight. "Faugh! I cannot catalogue the charms of these gallant gentlemen who had got what they enlisted for" (1966: Vol. 1, p. 262).

To overcome their initial reticence to the idea of killing, they resorted to the perfectly valid rationalization that Edgar Embley of the 61st Illinois invoked when he first saw the Confederates advancing on them. Embley reasoned that "fore evry secesh that we killed there would be one less to shoot at us" (To family, April 28, 1862). Amos Currier, the New Hampshireman with the 11th Iowa and the selfsame soldier who earned a degree in the humanities, was shocked at his transformation. "I saw men fall around me and others lying dead with scarcely an emotion" (Diary, April 17, 1862). A lad with the 12th Michigan told his family, "I didn't think any more of seeing a man shot down than you would of seeing a dumb beast killed" (Franklin Bailey to parents, April 8, 1862).

Shooting at other people turned out to be a lot easier than a civilian could perhaps imagine. "It is surprising with what satisfaction opposing forces will shoot at each other," wrote Lieutenant D.F. Vail of the 16th Wisconsin, directly contradicting Marshall (Vail 1897: 2). A Louisianian told his brother how he killed his first Yankee, with no remorse whatsoever. "I gave it to one blue belly about where his suspenders crossed sending him to eternity in less time than I taks to tell it" (B.F. Wilkinson to brother, April 16, 1862). The men learned to kill remorselessly, and some grew to see it as a sport, much like a hometown turkey shoot. Lieutenant William Vaught, the Louisiana gunner, bragged to his kin how he exploded a shell in the face of an annoying Union rifleman and admitted that "I have become passionately fond of gunnery, and have attained to great skill. In action I frequently train the guns myself, though it is none of my business [as section commander]." He boasted how he "fired at a wagon which was galloping across my position a mile off. The shot," he chortled, "carried off the head of the saddle horse" (To sister, May 17, 1862). The same attitude was voiced by a volunteer with the 14th Wisconsin who wrote home airily that he had "the pleasure of shooting at a number of rebels," and ended with "love to all inquiring females" (Quiner, Reel No. 2, Vol. 5, p. 133). Saul Howell admitted to his diary that "it was fun to see them running when we fired" (Journal, April 7, 1862).

Death had become so familiar to the men after two days' fighting that corpses were simply part of the flotsam and jetsam that littered the area. "Men chat carelessly with dying and dead men around them. Corpses lie almost unnoticed in the mud, teamsters driving almost over them, and the crowd, surging to and fro hardly stopping to look at them," reported a soldier-correspondent (*The Columbia City News*, April 29, 1862). The description was echoed by a Union captain. "I ate my dinner . . . within six paces of a rebel in four pieces. Both legs were blown off. His pelvis was the third piece, and his head and chest were the fourth. . . . Myself and other amateur anatomists would . . . examine the internal structure of man. We would examine brains, heart, stomach, layers of muscles, structures of bones etc., for there was every form of mutilation. At home," he concluded, "I used to wince at the sight of a wound or of a corpse; but here in one day, I learned to be among the scenes describing them without emotion" (Wheeler 1976: 102). Howell also admitted that he was "getting indifferent while gazing at the ghastly corpses" (Journal, April 9, 1862). Burying them was simply one more detail among the many in sprucing up the camp after the battle. Cushman served with a unit of sappers and miners who dug the large pits into which the Confederate corpses would tumble, about 150 per hole. He observed with some surprise how they "cover them with as little unconcern as I would bury a dead dog" (To brother, April 13, 1862). The dead were a nuisance, and few saw any use for them once their pockets had been rifled for anything of value (W.R. Stimson to wife, May [?] 1862). Besides burial, a corpse was otherwise of interest as an object of humor. J.M. Long of the 9th Texas recalled one corpse who had "his head upon a knapsack, and his hands folded upon his breast, a cob pipe placed in his mouth, as if 'the pipe of peace.' I never dreamed or believed the soldiers could have indulged in such levity on the battlefield, in the presence of death" (Long 1893: 279).

NOTES

1. Fifty-eight volunteers wrote assessments of their unit's performance after the battle or commented on this topic in their diaries. There were also published comments in their memoirs and letters to the editor. A cross-tabulation showed that they tended to laud their unit in public to avoid hometown displeasure and were more candid in their intimate correspondence. A chi-square yielded 2.00 with a chance of error of 16 percent and one degree of freedom.

2. A cross-tabulation of the green regiments in the Union army who suffered 40 percent or more casualties during the engagement revealed that the 18th Missouri (U.S.A.), the 55th Illinois, and the 3rd Iowa shared this distinction. A cross-tabulation of the Confederate outfits showed that the 22nd Alabama; the 6th Mississippi; and 4th, 23rd, and 24th Tennessee sustained losses of over 40 percent. Casualty figures were not, however, always complete or accurate for many of the units engaged.

3. The 53rd Ohio had been organized barely a month before the battle. It had received its weapons only the previous week and had had no serious drill or instruction (Dawes 1969: 5).

4. Colonel Jacob Ammen estimated the number at the landing to be 10,000 to 15,000 (McDonough 1977: 178), of whom some 2,000 to 3,000 would have been rear-echelon military personnel and civilians such as private contract teamsters with the army train, visiting civilians, sutlers, etc.

5. During the airborne landings in Normandy, it was found that it was almost impossible for non-commissioned officers to lead a group into combat if the members of the group did not know each other. This was also found to be true in the Ardennes offensive (Janowitz 1959: 68).

6. Harris found that soldiers in the Eastern theater were not reluctant when it came to using their weapons. For example, the 20th Maine with 358 effectives fired 20,000 rounds between 4:30 in the afternoon and the early evening at Little Round Top on the second day of the Battle of Gettysburg. An inventory of supplies showed that the regiment had used up all its munitions (1983: 63–64).

Ashworth's study of World War I trench fighting also challenged Marshall's assumption that the infantrymen were immobilized by an instinctive revulsion to the idea of killing. Ashworth contended that while most people tend to find the idea of killing hardly gratifying, it does not imply *ipso facto* that they will not go about it when trained and ordered to do so. Although he found that revulsion and paralysis occurred in hand-to-hand encounters in the trenches, in conformity with Marshall's thesis, he found no such restraints when the fighting consisted of firing weapons at the enemy (1980: 214–16).

7. Fortitude in war has its roots in morality; that selection is a search for character, and that war itself but one more test. . . . Courage can be judged apart from danger only if social significance and meaning of courage is known to us, namely that a man of character in peace becomes a man of courage in war. . . . Character as Aristotle taught is a habit, the choice of right instead of wrong; it is a moral quality which grows to maturity in peace and is not suddenly developed on the outbreak of war. . . . Man's fate in battle is worked out before war begins. For his acts in war are dictated not by courage nor by fear, but by conscience, of which war is the final test. . . . If you know a man in peace, you know him in war (Moran 1966: 160)

8. Wesbrook provides one of the most succinct explanations of the elements that go into making morale (1980: 266). See also Stouffer (1949: II, 137) for a discussion of the nature and formation of group loyalty.

9. Twenty-six men commented about their officers after the battle.

10. The men from the Ironton, Ohio, area were probably from the 53rd Regiment, the one that had been disgraced for breaking up after its colonel panicked

and deserted his men during the initial attack. Sherman had dressed them down and the men were bitter. They vented their spleen on the high command in the local paper.

Among those who came to Grant's defense over the drunkenness charge was Colonel Jacob Ammen, who was one of Buell's brigade commanders and who, therefore, had no vested interest in saving Grant's or the Army of the Tennessee's reputation. Ammen noted in his diary that "I am satisfied Genl Grant was not under the influence of liquor, either of the times I saw him" (Copy Diary, April 8, 1862).

11. Of the thirty-seven volunteers who left behind their opinions on this topic, 76 percent emerged from the battle with a healthy respect for their opponents' effectiveness and courage. This list of respondents is not inclusive. Numerous other soldiers' comments were used, but, again, there was not enough information on these men to include them in the statistical profiles.

6

Strategic and Political Assessment

WHO WON AND HOW MUCH LONGER WOULD IT LAST?

"This is the hardest faugh Battle Ever faugh on this Contanent," or for added emphasis, "in Erope," Captain Jim Lawrence, 61st Illinois, wrote about assessing the scope of the engagement (To wife and children, April 8, 1862). The letters and diaries are replete with allusions to the enormity of the battle. An Alabamian boasted that it was said to be "the bloodest battle ever was fought. The manases battle is not a circustance to it" (J.M. Stevens to Mary [wife], April 8, 1862). By comparison, Fort Donelson was merely described as an "interesting fight . . . a mear skrimishe to what this was hear," wrote Jacob Behm from the camp of the 48th Illinois (To brother and sister, April 27, 1862). "Shiloh was the most stupendous battle in the nations history, maybe in the history of the world" (J.W. Davis to brother [George], April 11, 1862; see also D.C. Loudon to Hannah [wife], April 10, 1862; Z.P. Shumway to wife [Hattie], April 8, 1862; J. Jones to father and mother, April 13, 1862; W.P. Rogers 1929: 287; W. Innis to wife, April 10, 1862; J. Connelley, Diary, April 9, 1862).

The men assumed there was proportionality between the battle's scope and its strategic significance. A Hoosier infantryman proclaimed in most dramatic terms, "The quiet of the Tennessee has been disturbed, the Waterloo of America has been fought, and the death blow to secession has been struck" (J. Connelley, Diary, April 9, 1862). A Hoosier agreed, writing to his hometown paper in Kokomo, Indiana, that "we will certainly wind up the rebellion in this quarter" (*The Howard Tribune*, April 29, 1862). The apocalyptic scale of the battle had to match its significance. This had been the decisive battle of the war, in which the lives of both the volunteers and the country were at stake (J.F. Drish to wife, April 10, 1862). To add to the dramatic scope and significance of the struggle, the new veterans made sure to point up how near a thing the battle had been. "If we only had had two more hours daylight," lamented a New Orleans gunner, "we could have driven them right in to river . . . and the rout would have been more complete than at Manasses" (Lathrop 1962: 379). Unionists concurred, admitting that "had not night fallen upon us at this time it is terrible to think what might have followed" (*The Lima Weekly Gazette*, April 23, 1862; see also S.S. Howell, Journal, April 7, 1862).

Such a great battle and its attendant losses demanded a victorious outcome. Both sides' soldiers came away arguing that they had won.[1] Each side desperately wanted to believe that so costly a battle had not been in vain. So much had been sacrificed, so much was at stake, that to admit defeat would have been unthinkable for the men in the ranks.

While Unionists conceded that their enemies had got the better of them the first day, they believed that they more than evened the score on the second. Most of their letters unequiovcally claimed Shiloh as a victory. George Levally, of the 13th Ohio Light Artillery, was typical, when he exclaimed, "They beat us on Sunday but we give them fits on Monday" (To father, April 12, 1862; see also *The Fremont Daily Journal*, April 25, 1862; J. Lawrence to wife and children, April 8, 1862; H.H. Giesy to brother, sister, and mother, April 9, 1862; D.C. Loudon to Hannah [wife], April 10, 1862).

The Confederate reaction was more tempered. They realized that they had not destroyed the Northern army and they knew they had been obliged to return to their base, but they still argued they had wrought havoc among the Unionists on the first day and had proven themselves on the second day by stubbornly resisting against heavy odds. If nothing else, they had successfully carried out a massive raid that had crippled the Northern forces. Actually A.S. Johnston and P.G.T. Beauregard may not have viewed the battle the same way. Johnston definitely saw Shiloh as a battle of annihilation, but Beauregard may have seen it as simply a large raid to do as much damage as possible to the enemy and delay its advance on Corinth.[2] Beauregard's interpretation of the objectives was echoed by some of the men. Richard Pugh of the 5th Company, Washington Artillery also saw it as a great raid, insisting that even if they had had to retire, it was a great Confederate victory. To "meet them on their own ground and whip nearly three times our number, then retire, unmolested, being prevented by bad weather and want of teams from bringing away everything we had captured" was a major military achievement (Lathrop 1962: 385). W.E. Minor of the 6th Kentucky (C.S.A.) exulted in the Army of the Mississippi's achievements to a friend. "The battle of Shiloh sends a thrill of electric fire through the entire South" (*The Weekly Courier*, April 30, 1862). But some were more equivocal in assessing the outcome. An Alabamian admitted, "I can't say whether we are whiped or not though I don't think we arc or will be" (J.M. Stevens to wife [Mary], April 8, 1862). A young medical officer voiced the same restrained sentiment, although more articulately, when he affirmed that "our army and the Federal army both suffered severely. I dont think either can claim a victory. . . . Our losses [are] fearful" (L. Yandell to father, April 10, 1862).

In assessing the outcome of a battle, the Civil War soldier made a judgment that was influenced by personal and political considerations and this colored his estimate of the result. This was his first major engagement, and as a volunteer and a politicized soldier, the recruit saw himself at center stage of the unfolding historical drama, whose fortuitous outcome he desperately sought and for which he had risked his life willingly. His assessment could not but be tendentious.[3]

The men obviously had a difficult time grasping the "big picture" through the turmoil of the battle. Although direct participants, they felt in the dark about the overall situation, and they desperately wanted confirmation of their success. They pleaded with the people back home to rush newspapers to them. They were interested in the strategic situation of their army and wanted to know how the war was going with John Pope at Island No. 10, David Farragut at New Orleans, and George McClellan on the peninsula (W. Richardson to father and mother, May 31, 1862; see also J.K. Newton to father and mother, April 12, 1862, Abdel D. Newton Papers; W. Bradford to Lucie [wife], April 24, 1862).

True enough, the ordinary volunteer did not know very much about the situation after the battle, besides the fact that the Union army held the field and the Southerners had pulled back. However, they knew just about as much as their commanders. A Hoosier infantryman declared that the common soldiers "have their own opinion about these things and the officers have theirs and a soldiers opinion is as good in this case as the greatest of men" (W. Innis to wife, April 27, 1862). The rank and file based their assessment of who won the battle by using three criteria. First, they used strategic indicators, such as who held the field and who had retired without gaining their objectives. Second, they compared the material losses incurred by each side, including equipment and men. And third, they gaged the impact on enemy morale and the level of cohesion that the adversary managed to maintain after the fight.

The reason each side thought they had won at Shiloh was that the men on each side conveniently emphasized different benchmarks favorable to their side for determining the victor. Hence, while both sides assumed the other had sustained heavier losses, the Confederates emphasized the demoralization of the Unionists on the first day, especially the capture of men and matériel during the first day's attack. On the other hand, the Federals stressed the strategic fact that they had driven the Southerners back and managed to hold on to the battlefield. The strategic indicator of success was voiced, for example, by an Ohioan who trumpeted, "Victory is Ours! . . . the enemy repulsed and the Stars and Stripes still float over our encampment" (*The Seneca Advertiser*, April 25, 1862). Jabiel Lyon of the 1st Ohio invoked the same criterion, but even more succinctly, noting "[we] did a fight with the rebles . . . drove them back through the day and all night" (Diary, April 7, 1862).

While the Union troops made exclusive reference to the strategic criterion of holding the field for judging the outcome of the battle, the Confederates, for their part, emphasized a second criterion for judging who won. They noted the psychological and organizational dimension of the struggle, the effect that their surprise attack had had on the unsuspecting and complacent Union army. Grant's army had been completely disrupted and ended up a jumbled mass of men cringing at Pittsburg Landing by the end of the first day. The shock of the attack had surprised and demoralized the enemy. Both sides, however, invoked the enemy's heavy losses to justify their claim to victory. Each believed the other had suffered more heavily. In point of fact, however, both sides suffered great losses: 10,699 for the Confederates and 13,047 for the combined Union forces. A casualty rate of 24 percent for Johnston's army and 20 percent for the Federals (Marsh 1975: 43; Grant 1982: 190–91; O.E. Cunningham 1966: 43). The reason both sides assumed that the other had lost more heavily is probably attributable to the fact that they each fought from defensive positions on one of the two days of the battle. Troops fighting from defensive positions usually assume that they inflict greater losses on the enemy, because they do not have to expose themselves to fire as much as the attacker. A Union soldier wrote in his diary, "I think they must have lost more largely than we as they fought on their feet while we hardly ever fired standing" (A. Currier, Journal, April 17, 1862). Also, each side assumed that they had fought against superior numbers. George Hamman of the 14th Illinois was convinced that his side had only 38,000 men to hold off 115,000 Confederates, and even when Buell arrived, he believed this only brought Union effectives up to 78,000. Furthermore, the Union soldiers thought that the Confederates had been reinforced by Van Dorn with an additional 20,000 (G. Hamman, Diary, April 8, 1862). At the same time, the Confederates assumed they were fighting double their own numbers when Buell arrived on the second day.

As the Federals advanced over the battlefield on Monday, they came across huge numbers of dead and wounded Confederates; they supposed that the South had sustained a very costly defeat. This led H.O.

Hadley of the 16th Wisconsin to remark that "the enemy's loss is estimated at three that of ours." He went on to guess that "the way the dead rebels were piled up . . . ought to be a 'caution' to 'Secesh' " (Quiner, Reel No. 2, Vol. 5, p. 245). A corporal with the 40th Illinois put the enemy losses at 35,000 killed and wounded, while estimating Union casualties at 20,000 (W.H. Ross to father, April 10, 1862). Jim Vanderbilt, 23rd Indiana Infantry, was somewhat more accurate, telling the folks at home "we buried 4,013 rebels and we have been burring all the week and they ain't burried yet" (To mother, April 13, 1862). That still left a lot of supposed rebel dead unaccounted for. A Hoosier with the 39th Infantry, who went on a patrol along the Corinth Road, explained the discrepancy between the estimates of dead and those actually buried. "They [the Confederates] halled wagon loades after wagon loades a way . . . [also] we found dead rebbels for 5 or 6 miles long the road as far as we went and no telling how much farther the dead was strowed" (W. Innis to wife, April 16, 1862; see also J.F. Drish to wife, April 10, 1862; *The Ironton Register*, April 24, 1862).

Contrary to the Northerners' assumption, the Confederates were far from demoralized. A member of the "Williamson Grays" (Company D, 1st Tennessee Infantry), chortled that they had returned to Corinth with booty and "vermin galore" (W.M. Pollard, Diary, n.d.). They saw it as a successful raid that had caused havoc among the Union defenders and resulted in the seizure of large quantities of Union supplies. The Confederates believed themselves victorious, having "captured several thousand prisoners and all their ordnance, and stores, etc." The captain of the "Tom Weldon Rebels" (Mississippi) also added for emphasis, "We slept in their tents" (*The Natchez Daily Courier*, April 15, 1862). William Moore, an Alabamian, shared the belief that victory belonged to the South, basing his assumption on the tremendous losses that Grant and Buell had sustained. "I don't think that the Yankees will ever fight us anymore, I think they are tiard of it. It is said that we lost twenty five hundred men, and the yankees lost twenty thousand" (1961: 300–301).

Despite the ferocity of the fighting, belief in an early victory remained strong.[4] The conviction that the war could not last much longer was founded on the assumption that the war was turning into a bloodbath that neither side could sustain for more than a year (Rogers 1929: 288). The Northern troops also believed that the rebel army's spirit was broken. "It can't last much longer," wrote an infantryman in the 14th Illinois, "as the rebels cannot sustain many more defeats without losing all the confidence their soldiers ever had" (Z.P. Shumway to wife [Hattie], April 27, 1862). A Missourian with Company B, 18th Infantry Regiment, believed that with the loss of Corinth "they ar geten tired of the fun . . . if we drive them a nother time or two . . . I think they will get tired of hit" (D. Pollock to William [brother], May 31, 1862; see also Z.P. Shumway to wife [Hattie], April 13, 1862; McEathron 1938: 4).

Union belief in approaching victory had strengthened, though gone was the exhilaration of the early months of the war. "The Federal troops seem inspired with the recent successes, and are pushing forward with vigor which bids fair to soon trap the rebellion & and bring the war to a speedy and successful termination," wrote a Union gunner (G. Hurlbut, April 12, 1862). News was also reaching the lines of other Union victories, which strengthened the belief that the war would soon end. Sergeant F.J. Beck of the 30th Indiana voiced these sentiments in a letter to the hometown newspaper. "The recent victory at New Orleans, and the reported victories of McClellan have an enlivening influence on the army. They feel that our armies are invincible. . . . I never hear the remark, 'If we are victorious at Corinth.' It is 'When we have taken Corinth.' It is true that the opinions of soldiers have little to do in deciding a battle, but men do fight better when they are confident of victory" (*The Indiana True Republican*, May 29, 1862; see also *The Aurora Beacon*, May 1, 1862). Wilbur Hinman of the 65th Ohio also believed victory was near. "Things indicate that a speedy close of the war is at hand and you cannot imagine how eagerly we watch each glimmering ray of hope. We hear . . . of the capture of Richmond and Norfolk, the blowing up of the Merrimac and the defeat of the rebel gunboats on the Mississippi" (To friends, May 13, 1862). The two largest armies of the Confederacy had been driven back and were gradually surrounded—one bottled up at Corinth, and the other pushed into Richmond. Also, rumor had it that General Pope was on his way from his triumph at Island No. 10. The word was that he had crossed the Mississippi on April 24 and was on his way with 30,000 more men to help finish off the rebels. A captain in the 57th Indiana was so confident that the forces at hand were more than adequate that he believed that "we don't need them here" (W. Bradford to Lucie, April 24, 1862). The overall strategic situation led Albert Carpenter, serving in an Illinois regiment, to write to his brother, "I think the war is about wound up; Island No. 10 is ours, and if we can clean this gang out we will be all hunk" (Quiner, Reel No. 2, Vol. 5, p. 242).

But victory would have to be complete. The South must be brought to its knees through unconditional surrender. "In a few Days," an Illinois soldier confidently foretold, "you will [see] We took Corrinth and if Uncle McClellan has good Success at York Town the fighting is Nearly Done with and you will see a lot of Dirty Ragged Lousy Good for Nothin Chaps [home again] (G.W. Russell to Betty, April 28, 1862; see also Mungo Murray, Reminiscences). In the meantime, Russell demanded retribution for the losses he and his comrades of the 55th Illinois sustained when the Confederates plundered their camps at Shiloh. "I must pay a visit to Jeff Davis and get my Knapsack and a good many of other trinkets worth more than 2 cents . . . and come home with plenty of money" (G.W. Russell to Betty, April 28, 1862).

However, a few of the volunteers on both sides were not as sure as the majority of their comrades that the war was going to end so soon. "Some of the men think that we will be home by the first of July," wrote John V. Mosley of the 16th Wisconsin. "I hope so but I think differently. This rebellion is too deeply seated to be so soon eradicated. The South must not only be conquered, but held. Down here, where you find one Union man, you will find thousand secessionists" (Quiner, Reel No. 2, Vol. 5, p. 253). On the Confederate side, the 4th Tennessee's assistant surgeon was as darkly prescient. "God grant that it may end soon, and yet I do not see any ray of hope for its early termination. The future grows darker. Those persons who reason themselves into the belief that peace will soon come or at least that the war will soon cease, are blinded and mislead by their wishes" (L. Yandell to sister [Sally], April 21, 1862).

STILL WILLING TO FIGHT ON?

Huddling beneath the shelter of his tent as the rain poured down on Corinth, Assistant Surgeon Lunsford Yandell wondered if it was all worth it. "O! Dear me! I wonder if I shall ever be repaid for the privations and hardships which I am . . . to endure as a soldier? I wonder too, if posterity will justly appreciate the blessings we shall have conferred upon them when we achieve freedom from the Yankees" (To sister, April 25, 1862). Despite the suffering and horror they had been through, the vast majority of the men were ready to fight on. They had not used up what Lord Moran called the soldier's quotient of courage (1966: 62). The men remained surprisingly game after their encounter with the elephant. An Ohioan wrote to his father, "I must confess that having one day's experience in dodging balls & shells & listening to the whistling bullets, I am not at all anxious to go into another fight. Still," he added, "if we do go into battle again you may rest assured I will do my duty faithfully" (A. Varian to father, April 21, 1862). In fact, the troops of both sides were as ready to go into action again as they had been before the battle. Nine out of ten of the men who left behind their thoughts about the prospect of seeing action in another fight expressed the determination to see it through. Strikingly, there was virtually no change in the level of determination before and after combat in both armies.[5] But their attitude had changed from an almost light-hearted eagerness before the battle to grim determination to see it through afterward.

The letters were replete with assertions of the men's willingness to persevere. "I shall fight hard and nothing but the Bullets can ever make any Difference," a member of the 55th Illinois vowed (G.W. Russell to Betty, April 28, 1862). Jesse Connelley and the 31st Indiana had been pulled back from the front for a while because of illness in the ranks, yet Connelley remarked in his diary that the boom of cannon seemed to beckon the men back. "As quickly as a squad gets well, it goes to the front," he wrote and added, "hope I shall go soon" (Diary, May 4, 1862). Samuel Eells, the 12th Michigan's assistant surgeon, resented it when his badly mauled regiment was sent back to Pittsburg Landing to build fortifications. He and the others saw it as a disgrace to the regiment (To aunt and uncle, May 12, 1862). The same spirit was echoed in other letters and diaries. "You can hardly imagine how eager the troops are," wrote a soldier with the 6th Iowa, bragging "it doesn't suit an army of western boys to lie still and have [the] ugly devils so close to us and not have an opportunity to making a general rush and settle the question as soon as possible so we can return" (W. Richardson to father and mother, May 18, 1862; see also *The Fremont Daily Journal,* April 25, 1862; M.P. Murray, Papers).

Within the perimeter at Corinth, Dixie's volunteers voiced the same determination. There were men such as Rufus Catin who had now been driven from his home. New Orleans' fall had orphaned Catin and the men of the 19th Louisiana. "Our communications with home is entirely cut off.... How dreadful the suspense of the long silence that must ensue." But he declared, *"for the cause* we must endure it. We must fight the harder" (To cousin Fannie, May 24, 1862). With the loss of Tennessee, George Blakemore of the 23rd Regiment had nowhere to return either, nonetheless, he, too, vowed: "I am willing to do anything for my country" (Diary, April 29, 1862). Another homeless Tennessean, this one with the 24th Regiment, pledged in a letter to his wife, "I am willing to do my part until the last" (Mott 1946: 247). The same determination was voiced by still another soldier of an orphaned regiment, the 6th Kentucky. W.E. Minor wrote to a friend that "the North don't understand our spirit. They mistake for what we are fighting. They had as well try to quench the fire of life—as to try to subjugate those who are satisfied they are fighting for their mothers,, fathers, sisters, kindred, and the tender ones of their hearts" (*The Weekly Courier,* April 30, 1862).

As the days turned to weeks following the battle, the soldiers on both sides realized that Shiloh had not decided the issue after all. "The way things is turned out, I cannot tell," a Hoosier of the 39th concluded, but it was beginning to look like "we will have to fight those rebbels" one more time (W. Innis to wife, April 16, 1862), despite all the sacrifices and the appalling slaughter at Shiloh. The people at home came to the same realization. "Everybody is anxious to hear the result of the forthcoming battle at Corinth. Well I don't blame them," wrote soldier-correspondent E.M. Newcomb of the 16th Iowa in reply to queries from the local editor. "We, too, are anxious to have the affair settled; and had much rather settle it here, and now, than be compelled to penetrate farther into this unhealthy climate" (*The Dubuque Daily Times*, May 16, 1862). If there would have to be one more big fight, "the boys are all anxious to clean out the rebels this time and go home," said another in his letter home (Quiner, Reel No. 2, Vol. 5, p. 28). The Union soldiers expressed the same confidence in the outcome. The rebels would not be allowed to get away on this occasion and the Confederate army and the rebellion would be ended in one swoop in a short war. "I do not fear for the morrow this time as I did when I went in to the field at Shiloh. There it seemed to me like desperation here [Corinth] it seems like marching to certain victory," wrote Captain Madison Walden of Company D, 6th Iowa Infantry (To wife, May 20, 1862).

Their opponents were equally convinced that victory for the South was still possible. "The enemy are gradually closing in upon us. [But] We are ready and confident," a gunner told his family (W. Vaught to sister, May 5, 1862). A Tennessean heroically recorded in his diary, "Our soldiers all seem eager for the fight tis victory or death with the southerners at their post" (G.T. Blakemore, Diary, May 3, 1862). Rufus Catin of the 19th Louisiana shared his resolution, writing home that "if we have anything like fair play you may rest assured we will send back the obnoxious hirelings of Lincolndom howling to the shelter of their ironclad boats [at Pittsburg Landing]" (To cousin Fannie, May 24, 1862). The patriotic surge had taken a more muted form, but it was strengthened now that the men were fighting with their backs to the wall. A Tennessean vowed to his wife, "Our lives must be sacrified to save our Country. . . . I don't think the yanks will ever be able to reach this place if they do they will have to walk over our ded bodies. . . . [We] will . . . die before Corinth . . . will be surrendered up to Yankeedom" (W.H. Williams to wife [Susan], May 19, 1862). Others not only believed Corinth was untakeable, but even thought that when the army finally evacuated the city, it was not fleeing, but instead was going back on the offensive to regain Tennessee. Captain Stewart of the 21st Alabama packed his kit for action and told his wife, "When we commence moving I hope we will not stop until we get into Kentucky" (To Julia, May 20, 1862). George Blakemore a Tennessean himself was even more convinced that the objective remained his home state. Despite the Shiloh setback, he remained confident that a new offensive was in the offing when his 23rd Tennessee was sent out seven miles. "I feel proud," he confided to his diary, "that I am outside the main line of our army. I . . . will be back in old Tennessee in less than three weeks" (Diary, May 28, 1862).

Other Confederates were less optimistic, but equally resolute to persist in the struggle despite what they had gone through at Shiloh. "God grant that peace may be given—not to one Caesar, but to the rival Caesars . . . for peace can never exist with them as one Nation," wrote W.E. Minor of the 6th Kentucky Confederate Infantry. "But," he vowed ominously, "if the North do not wish peace, they can have war—*desparate war*" (*The Weekly Courier*, April 30, 1862). There was already speculation in parts of the western Confederacy about the feasibility of "partisan warfare" (*The Arkansas State Gazette*, May 3, 1862).[6] Others were already resisting as prisoners of the Northern forces. James Crozier had been wounded at Shiloh and was in a wagon train headed for Corinth when he was captured by Union cavalry. While many of the men in his regiment, the 3rd Kentucky Infantry, were willing to swear an oath of allegiance to the federal government in exchange for their freedom, Crozier refused. "I look on any one taking the oath [to the Union] as nothing but a deserter," he declared. The next day as the parolees left him behind, he admitted to his diary, "I feel very low spirited about it, but I am *determined to go my own way*, and to stick to my oath [to the Confederacy], let the consequences be what they may" (Diary, April 14 and 15, 1862). Hence, despite imprisonment, death, and wounds at Shiloh, the men on both sides remained resolved to carry on.

The determination to solider on despite all that had happened to them at Shiloh testifies to the resilience and commitment of the young volunteers. These troops withstood the withering impact of Shiloh and were ready to continue their military odyssey. From the trauma of "seeing the elephant" for the first time, they emerged with greater confidence in their own ability to withstand fire and with a growing esprit de corps. Immobility, bad weather, short rations, and disease had a more corrosive effect on morale than the fighting itself, yet they remained undeterred. The men's ardor seemed intact, even among the Confederates. They remained ready to push on to finish the fight with yet one more decisive battle facing them. In the face of the trauma of Shiloh, defeats, conscription, and the unhealthy situation around Corinth, the volunteers' resilience was indeed surprising.

The combination of motivations for continuing the struggle evolved as a result of their first combat experience. The commitment remained firm, but the mix of motivation was more complex and more tempered. Surveying the mass graves around Shiloh, Cyrus Boyd noted bitterly in his diary, "What a mockery these lines seem—'Blest are the brave who sink to rest, with all their Country's wishes blest' " (1953: 44). None could challenge such a reaction to the slaughter. These thoughts were echoed on the other side by a Kentuckian. "I sometimes doubt if it was ever wise to go to war on any account. Life is but a brief affair, and people are I expect about as happy under one form of government as another." Yet in the next line he wrote, "Liberty purchased at the price of war, is dearly bought. . . . [But] I expect to serve in the army till the war is over" (L. Yandell to sister [Sally], April 21, 1862). A similar sentiment was expressed by an Iowan of the 15th Regiment as he observed the graves in every direction, some within twenty feet of his tent. He wrote in his diary that as dreadful as it all was, "the Union must be preserved" (H. McArthur, Journal, April 15, 1862). It was a fight to sustain the Union for the North, it was a struggle "for the right" (A. Currier, Journal, April 17, 1862; see also Barber 1894: 51). The terrible price had to be paid, though; "war is a most devastating institution, a great calamity at best; but of all the horrors, civil war is the worst. . . . But the Constitution and the Laws must be upheld, cost what blood and treasure it will," wrote a Union soldier-correspondent (*The Ironton Register*, May 8, 1862).

The patriotism was still a major factor after Shiloh, but it was more muted. It took a defensive tone, such as preservation of the Union, defense of one's home, etc. It was less frequently expressed in lofty phrases. Furthermore, the patriotic commitment was now frequently juxtaposed with the costs of the war. There were no more eloquent pronunciamentos, instead there were sad declarations of commitment to see it through despite the tremendous costs. The veterans did not express the exhortative patriotic theme as frequently as they had before the battle. There was less talk of "the cause," "the preservation of the Union," the struggle against "subjugation by Lincolndom," the "upholding of the Constitution," etc. Before Shiloh, two-thirds of the men voiced such patriotic declarations, however, this proportion dropped by half after their first engagement.[7] The reason for fighting was voiced less explicitly, less ideologically, less fervently, and less zealously.

Other considerations came to the fore. The men became far more hostile toward the enemy after combat. The proportion expressing hatred toward the enemy increased fivefold.[8] As many were fighting out of hatred of the enemy as were fighting for the initial patriotic reasons invoked during the mobilization. The enemy and the war had become real to the men; they had lost too many friends to the foe. There were many Confederates who had been driven from their homes in Missouri, Kentucky, and Tennessee. Not only their homes, but their own lives were at stake. It was no longer theater, drama, or glory; it was a hard business of killing foes. The enemy had become the "Hessians," they were "fiendish," they had to be "cleaned out and scoured" from the land like vermin. It would be a war of extermination, a total war against traitors and the confiscation of their property, and if it took more killing, so be it. One soldier even expressed pleasure at the sight of more rebel dead. Killing could be done more easily if the enemy was demonized or if some other reason for disliking him could be mustered in justification of the butchery.

Although Kellett (1982: 193) argued that in the context of the modern battlefield the enemy is largely invisible and that it is thus difficult to arouse sustained hatred of the enemy, the fighting conditions of the nineteenth century were different. The enemy was nearer and frequently visible; the ranges of the weaponry required direct fire at relatively short distances to inflict losses. Hence, the killing zone was quite narrow. Furthermore, the number of men packed in the combat area and the need to fire standing up meant the enemy was clearly seen as numerous and threatening, while the effects of their fire were visible and direct. The enemy was not anonymous; the source of harm was not impersonal.

Thus, contrary to Stouffer's (1949: II, 157) findings, regarding World War II infantry, that "combat did not increase the hatred of the enemy which men felt initially," the obverse occurred among Shiloh's soldiers.[9] Instead of being diminished by combat, animosity toward the enemy became more intense after the battle. This effect is in agreement with B.I. Wiley's contention that among many Southern troops, "antipathy toward ordinary Yankees was deep and pervasive" (1978b: 314). William Swain, Company G, 3rd Iowa, recalled passing a column of prisoners on his way to the front and hearing them curse the regiment, calling them " 'damned Yankees,' and swearing that they would give us enough of 'Dixie's land' before that day's work was over." He angrily wrote to his father, "I never felt more like shooting a rebel" (Throne 1954: 259).

Swain's reaction begs the question whether the Union troops were equally disposed to their enemies. B.I. Wiley contended that the Yankees harbored less hostile feelings toward the Southerners, that they even had "amicable inclinations" toward them (1978a: 351). This was not the case with Shiloh's bluecoats, who were just as hostile to the enemy as their Southern counterparts. The newspapers also kindled hatred toward the enemy. For example, a report circulated to the effect that Union men in Tennessee were being crucified by Tennessee troops, that spikes were driven through their hands and they were left to die (*The Jackson Standard*, May 22, 1862). V.E. Young of the 14th Wisconsin wrote to the local editor that "there is a most vindictive hatred existing between the two armies of the West, which cannot be extinguished for generations to come." He saw a long vengeful war ahead as a result of the rising hatred. "We shall destroy their army organizations, but," he feared, "we shall not capture them and the war will become a fierce guerilla warfare that can only be ended by the total annihilation of the one party or the other" (Quiner, Reel No. 2, Vol. 5, p. 148).

While the slavery issue had been the vehicle that divided the nation, the Northern soldiers did not enlist to abolish it, nor did they change their neutral attitude toward slavery after the battle. Generally, the soldiers appeared to believe that slavery was inefficient, harsh on its victims, and a drag on the South. But it was not a sufficient reason to go to war. These troops were all Westerners, and many came from states with a long tradition of support for abolition, such as Michigan and Ohio, which had strong Republican constituencies and which were among the few states that elected Free Soil party and Liberty party congressmen in 1844, 1846, and 1848. Yet, among the troops, Amos Currier was the only volunteer who actually came out against slavery in the post-battle sample, and he did not express a strong aversion to the system. He merely argued that the situation of the slaves was not the one presented to the public. "My small opportunities for observation," he wrote from a prisoner of war camp at Cahaba, Alabama, "make me certain that their thoughtful moments are embittered with sadness" (Journal, May 1, 1862). Currier, by the way, was not a native of Iowa, but was born in New Hampshire and had obtained a degree at Dartmouth, emigrating to Iowa in adulthood. More typical of Westerners' attitudes to the black population was the reaction of an Illinois soldier, Corporal William Ross of the 40th Infantry. Although his comments were made a few months later, they are, nevertheless, included for their clarity and frankness. When Ross' brother suggested enlisting, the elder brother wrote back from the front advising against it and giving the following reasons. "For Gods sake do not volunteer till this negro question is settled, for the Devil is going to be kicked up be for Long for the soldiers are Swaring that they will stack their arms, Desert, or go to the confederate army or any thing be for they will fight to free the negroes" (W. Ross to Levi [brother], September 30, 1862).

While research on combat motivation during World War II and the Vietnam War has argued that the main motivational factor was the men's attachment to their comrades and their units, this was not the case among Shiloh's volunteers (Marshall 1947: 42, 159; Gabriel 1978: 41, 70; Hauser 1980: 192). The only outright affirmation of unit loyalty to justify fighting on was made by an Alabama lieutenant of the 21st Regiment in a letter to his wife when he declared, "I do not wish to leave my own regiment; indeed I do not know that I would accept a place in any other; I helped it win an honorable name, and to leave it would seem like selling my birthright for a mess of pottage" (Folmar 1981: 62).

However, the most important reason for continuing to fight was the men's sense of duty. This broad concept merged self-esteem, obligation to comrades, and loyalty to one's community and country (in other words, patriotism). When these three elements are combined in the broad notion of "duty," the Shiloh volunteers were no different than Stouffer's sample of World War II soldiers.[10] Most men fought on for an amalgam of overlapping reasons, a rationale that probably merged patriotic obligation, personal pride, and the avoidance of besmirching their own and their family's reputation as well as a sense of loyalty to comrades and regiment. The motives were imprecise and hopelessly intertwined, making it difficult to make any but the broadest inferences. The range of variations in the expression of sense of obligation is reflected by some of the following comments. Tom Honnell, 15th Ohio, wrote to his friend, "I do not wish to shrink from my duty which I owe to My God My Country & My friends & if the majority of our company goes I expect I will go too" (To friend [Ben Epler], May 21, 1862). A Confederate echoed Honnell's combination of priorities when he wrote home, "I have had a hard road to travel. I cant blame nobody but my self, I think it is my duty to be here and do all I can to help save our Country and recover our liberties. . . . I dont know that I will be benefited in any respect but I feel if I gain our Country and our liberties you and the children would be benefited" (W.H. Williams to wife [Susan] May 19, 1862). The ties linking duty to the soldier and his family came across in a Union officer's letter home, "I dont have any desire to be shot or even shot at, but I believe you may feel satisfied that you will not have to blush nor our children to feel that they have been disgraced by my running away [from battle]" (D.C. Loudon to Hannah [wife], May 3, 1862). Amos Currier echoed this same sense of honor and obligation to family, self, and country when he refused to foreswear taking up arms again against the Confederacy in exchange for release from the prisoner of war camp at Columbus, Georgia. It had been a long way from Shiloh, but he was determined to continue to do his duty. "I should like," he wrote in his diary, "to leave this place and especially to see my friends but I shall purchase neither by such an oath. . . . I mean to return with integrity unblemished and honor unstained or not return at all" (Journal, May 19, 1862).

However, the commitment to soldier on was conditional on support from home. Any shirking at home, any reluctance to enlist and share the burden had a deleterious effect on morale. This tacit contract between home and front was evoked in a soldier-correspondent's letter to the hometown newspaper, in which he also summed up his own feelings about soldiering on. "Well," he wrote, "I have had as much of fighting as I want. I had some curiosity to be in a battle to try my metal, but I have no such curiosity now. If nothing else will do but more fighting, I will try it again; but indeed, I would be willing for some others who never have tried, or like it better than I do, to try it" (*The Ironton Register*, May 16, 1862).

The letters and diaries of the men who fought at Shiloh reveal, as B.I. Wiley said, that they were "people of integrity" (1961: 80–81) or, as Barton (1981) wrote, "good men." Despite all the horrors to which they had been subjected and despite appalling conditions at Shiloh and Corinth after the battle, the majority of the men on both sides were prepared to carry on. Their reasons were complex and intermingled. Patriotic sentiments were more muted and were less frequently proclaimed. On the other hand, the fighting had embittered a large minority of the men against their enemies. Too much blood had been spilled at Shiloh and too many comrades maimed and killed by the enemy to put it all aside. Slavery was hardly mentioned or for that matter were explicit loyalties to unit. But duty was becoming an important factor in continuing, and if envisaged in the most inclusive sense (i.e., including country and thus patriotism, loyalty to the unit, and a sense of honor and family pride), it became the most important reason for fighting on.

This suggests that the Civil War volunteer who saw action for the first time at Shiloh was probably not very differently motivated than his modern counterpart. He was, perhaps, more forthcoming in expressing his sense of duty to home and country, but that may have been more a reflection of the style of the time. Yet there was one difference—it was a political one. The Civil War was a struggle between two mutually exclusive national alternatives: union or secession. Futhermore, despite the lack of training, the soldier was able to maintain his morale through his attachment to and support from the community from which his territorially recruited regiment had been mobilized. Today's soldier, often fighting in large amorphous units in foreign wars for a vague national interest and often lacking a clear notion of the country's stake in the conflict, musters his commitment in a more muted form. Futhermore, if the cause is not right, he falls back on the outfit as his source of obligation to fight. Patriotism is only invoked when the soldier sees a clear and present danger to his country; wars over far away geopolitical interests do not merit such an encompassing powerful reason for fighting. We suggest that if given a cause that is clearly perceived by both soldiers and homefront as involving the nation's survival, the modern American soldier's reasons for fighting would not be much different from Shiloh's volunteers and their communally recruited regiments. One last point: these early volunteers disproved the assumption with which this project was begun—that seeing the elephant would be such a wrenching experience that they would be forever transformed by its horrors. Their initiation to combat did not change them as much as would have been expected, because they fought on into the second year of the war essentially the same citizen-soldiers as they were before.

NOTES

1. Thirty-two soldiers in the data set discussed the outcome of the battle, twenty-three were Unionists and nine were Confederates. Interestingly, both sides came out of the engagement convinced that they were victorious: 89 percent of the Confederates thought they had won and 83 percent of the Northerners believed they had defeated their opponents. Chi-square yielded 11.22 with a

probability of chance of only 0.01 percent and one degree of freedom, inferring that nationality had a strong impact on which side the soldiers thought won the battle. A parametric score with phi yielded 0.59 and a non-parametric score of 0.51 (contingency coefficient).

2. William Preston Johnston in *Battles and Leaders* (1956: I, 552–53) cited a telegram sent by his father, Albert Sidney Johnston, to President Davis stating his method of attack. This appears to support the idea of a hard smashing blow against the Union force. In the *Official Records, War of the Rebellion, Series I* (Vol. X, Part 1, p. 397), A.S. Johnston's memorandum to the corps commanders states his aim. "Throw him [Grant] back on Owl Creek, where he will be obliged to surrender." This also indicates that A.S. Johnston intended to destroy the Union army at Pittsburg Landing. However, in the same volume (pp. 392–95), in Special Order No. 8, written by Colonel Thomas Jordan (for A.S. Johnston, but under Beauregard's direction), a battle plan is laid out that is designed to capture supplies and force the enemy back in a massive raid, rather than to cut the enemy off and surround them.

3. For a discussion of the difference between a soldier's assessment of the battle and the way the leaders perceive it, see Keegan (1976: 47) and Baynes (1967: 83).

4. Of the twenty-four men who commented after the battle on the duration of the war, twenty-one still thought that it would soon be over. This is only slightly lower than before the battle.

5. Forty-two recruits left behind records of their attitude about the prospect of facing the combat again: 88 percent of them were prepared to soldier on in spite of the shock of their baptism of fire as compared to 95 percent before Shiloh. When the men of the two sides were compared, the Union troops showed a somewhat higher readiness to continue, 95 percent as opposed to the Confederates of whom 81 percent declared that they were ready to keep up the fight. This is striking considering that Beauregard's troops had known nothing but defeat and had only recently been thrown together as a fighting force. This data is from the letters and diaries for the period between April 6 and May 31.

6. *The Arkansas State Gazette* (May 3, 1862), for example, advised against such a strategy arguing that there was no advantage in it, because it would lead to reprisals so that "our friends will suffer."

7. Sixty-eight percent of the men voiced patriotic reasons before the engagement, dropping to 39 percent afterward.

8. It rose from 8 percent before Shiloh to 39 percent after the engagement.

9. Racial factors apparently affected the attitude of the World War II infantrymen toward their enemy. While Sledge (1981: 38), who fought in the Pacific against the Japanese, told of an abiding hatred toward the enemy, Ellis (1980: 317–18), who wrote on combat in Europe, found that there was little hatred toward the Germans, although he added darkly that surrendering troops had a fifty-fifty chance of being killed.

10. Seen in this light, the 13 percent who expressed this sentiment might be combined with other categories of related responses such as unit loyalty (3 percent) and even patriotism as duty to country (39 percent), raising the proportion of those fighting out of a very broad sense of duty to 55 percent of the

soldiers. The fluidity and intangibility of human motivations obviously renders such manipulations and inferences from them very tentative at best. Thus, it is difficult to go much further with categories that have had to be molded *ex post facto* from the men's correspondence. World War II psychologists were not constrained by the same problems; Stouffer did a survey of infantry veterans and found that 52 percent of the enlisted men and officers evoked notions related to duty ("ending the task," "solidarity with group," and "self-respect") as justifications for soldiering on (1949: II, 108), which suggested that, at least as far as duty was concerned, the American soldier's sense of obligation as a motivating factor had not changed much over the century.

Bibliography

MANUSCRIPTS AND UNPUBLISHED MATERIALS

Adams, Henry Clay. Civil War Journals, 1861–65. University of Iowa Library.

Ammen, Jacob. Diary (Copy). Collection. Indiana Historical Society.

———. Diary (Microfilm). Ohio Historical Society.

Armes, Thomas. Civil War Diary—1862. Indiana State Library.

Backus, Henry E. Diary, 1861–64 (Microfilm). Illinois State Historical Library.

Bailey, Franklin. Manuscript (Copy). Shiloh National Military Park.

Bailey, Peter P. McCulloch Papers. Indiana University.

Baker, Francis R. Memoirs (Typed). Illinois State Historical Library.

Bakewell, A. Gordon. Reminiscences, 5th Company. Battalion of the Washington Artillery Collection. Tulane University.

Barnes, J.P. Ketchum's-Garrity's Battery Folder. Alabama Department of Archives and History.

Barnett, James. Regimental History of 1st Ohio Light Artillery, Battery G. Western Reserve Historical Society.

Beach, John. Memoirs. Illinois State Historical Library.

Behm, Jacob. Collection. U.S. Army Military History Institute.

Bersetter, J. Griffith Family Papers. Iowa State Historical Department.

Blaisdell, Timothy M. Collection. U.S. Army Military History Institute.

Blakemore, George Thompson. Diary. Tennessee State Library and Archives.

Blankinship, Jim. Manuscript (Copy). Shiloh National Military Park.

Bradford, William S. Letters. Indiana State Library.

Brand, David. Twenty-first Alabama Folder. Alabama Department of Archives and History.

Brant, J.L. Manuscript. Shiloh National Military Park.

Brenton, R.A. Papers. Indiana State Library.

Brewer, William. Collection. State Historical Society of Wisconsin.

Brown, Bergun H. Papers. Indiana Historical Society Library.

Brown, William. Collection. State Historical Society of Wisconsin.

Bruce, Francis H. Bruce Family War Letters. Illinois State Historical Library.

Brucker, Magnus. Letters. Indiana Historical Society Library.

Buck, T.C. Manuscript. Shiloh National Military Park.

Buford, Samuel M. Charles Buford Collection. Library of Congress.

Burt, Andrew S. Collection. U.S. Army Military History Institute.

Caldwell, John W. Diary (Typed). U.S. Army Military History Institute.

Cam, William B. Letter. Logan Uriah Reavis Papers. Chicago Historical Society.

Campbell, William W. Diary (Copy). State Historical Society of Wisconsin.

Carr, I.W. Diary. Iowa State Historical Society.

Catin, Rufus W. Papers. Library of Congress.

Cato, John A. Papers. Mississippi Department of Archives and History.

Clampitt, Eli H. Papers. Indiana State Library.

Claver, Charles. Diary. Iowa State Historical Library.

Clune, Henry. Papers. Shiloh National Military Park.

Cole, James M. Papers. Illinois State Historical Library.

Coleman, John M. Robert B. Hanna Collection. Indiana Historical Society Library.

Coleman, W.E. Papers. Tennessee Department of Archives.

Connelley, Jesse B. Diary. Indiana State Library.

Covill, Wilson S. Collection. Wisconsin Historical Society.

Craft, John A. Papers. Indiana Historical Society Library.

Crary, Judson R. Collection. Chicago Historical Society.

Crozier, James. Civil War Diary, 1861–63 (Typed transcript). Filson Club, Louisville, Ky.

Cullom, J.W. Letters. Shiloh National Military Park.

Cunningham, Josephus. Letters. Iowa State Historical Department.

Cunningham, O. Edward. "Shiloh and the Western Campaign of 1862." Ph.D. dissertation, Louisiana State University, 1966.

Currier, Amos N. Collection, 1832–1909 (includes Journal). Iowa State Historical Society.

Curtis, Erastus. Private Diary. Ohio Historical Society.

Cushman, Gustavas H. Civil War Letters. Iowa State Historical Department.

Davis, A.F. Letters, 1862. State Historical Society of Missouri.

Davis, Andrew. Papers. U.S. Army Military History Institute.

Davis, Jacob Weaver. Letter. Western Kentucky University Library.

Davis, Samuel Thomas. Civil War Journal. Western Kentucky University Library.

Devore, Cornelius. Griffith Family Papers. Iowa State Historical Department.

Dillon, William Sylvester. Diary. University of Mississippi.

Dobbins, Peter B. Manuscript (Copy). Shiloh National Military Park.

Doll, William. Reminiscences and Biography. Indiana State Library.

Donahue, Martin. Diary and Letter, from Donahue to Wife (Typed copy). Shiloh National Military Park.

Drish, James F. Letters. Illinois State Historical Library.

Eells, Samuel Henry. Collection. Library of Congress.

Ellis, John. Collection. Louisiana State University Archives.

Embley, Edgar. Papers. U.S. Army Military History Institute.

Fagg, William. Diary. State Historical Society of Wisconsin.

Fairchild, Cassius. Correspondence, October 1861–June 1862. Wisconsin State Historical Society.

Fee, James Frank. Letters. Indiana Historical Society Library.

Filbeck, Nicholas. "History of the 32nd Regiment," Indiana Infantry. Indiana University.

Fletcher, William Baldwin. Memoirs, April 13–June 27, 1861. Indiana University.

Foxworth, Jobe M. Diary and Account Book and Letters. Mississippi Department of Archives and History.

Franklin, Samuel B. "Memoirs of a Civil War Veteran." U.S. Army Military History Institute.

Gates, F.S. Papers. Shiloh National Military Park.

Giesy, H.H. Hartford Collection. Western Kentucky University Library.

Godwin, D.G. Papers. Tennessee Department of Archives and History.

Grebe, Balzer. Autobiography and Civil War Diary. Illinois State Historical Library.

Green, John Williams. Diary, 1861–65. Filson Club, Louisville, Kentucky.

Griffin, [Unknown]. Papers. Shiloh National Military Park.

Griffith, Abel P. Griffith Family Papers. Iowa State Historical Department.

Guffey, Benjamin. Letters, 1862–64. State Historical Society of Missouri.

Guthrie, Leroy. Letters. Shiloh National Military Park.

Hamman, George. Diary, 1861–62. Illinois State Historical Library.

Hanaford, Frank. "Civil War Reminiscences." Illinois State Historical Library.

Hannum, Sharon. "Confederate Cavaliers." Ph.D. dissertation, Rice University, 1965.

Hardin, J.A. Cravens Collection. Indiana University.

Hardin, John J. Civil War Letters. Indiana Historical Society Library.

Harrington, Abdel D. Papers. U.S. Army Military History Institute.

Harris, John L. Correspondence. Illinois State Historical Library.

Harrison, Thomas J. Civil War Letters in Bishop Collection. Indiana Historical Society Library.

Hart, Albert Gaillard. Papers. Western Reserve Historical Society.

Harvey, William. "Notes taken from Diary" (Copy). Shiloh National Military Park.

Haydel, E.C. Michel Thomassin Andry Collection. Louisiana State University Archives.

Henderson, William. Letter. Indiana Historical Society Library.

Hinman, Wilbur F. Papers. Western Reserve Historical Society.

Honnell, Thomas C. Letters. Ohio Historical Society.

Hotze, Peter. Diary. Arkansas Department of Archives and History.

Hovey, Alvin. Collection. Indiana University.

Howard, W.A. Manuscript (Copy). Shiloh National Military Park.

Howell, Saul Sylvester. Daily Journal (Diary). April 1861–November 9, 1862 (Copy). Iowa State Historical Society.

Hurlbut, George. Diary, 1862. Western Reserve Historical Society.

"H.W.H." Mrs. M.L. Kirkpatrick's Scrapbook, Vol. I. Alabama Department of Archives and History.

Innis, William. Jean Simmonds Papers. Indiana State Library.

"J." Journal of Company A, 14th Illinois Volunteer Infantry. Illinois State History Library.

James, David Goodrich. Papers. Wisconsin Historical Society.

Jayne, Seeley. Civil War Letters. Indiana State Library.

Jetton, R.A. Letters. Confederate Collection. Tennessee State Library and Archives.

Johnson, Charles. Papers. Shiloh National Military Park.

Johnson, Francis M. Reminiscences (Typed copy). Illinois State Library.

Johnson, George W. Correspondence, 1861–62. Kentucky Historical Society.

Johnson, Thomas. "My War Experiences." Indiana Historical Society Library.

Jones, James H. Civil War Letters. Indiana Historical Society Library.

Kellogg, E.R. Recollections. U.S. Army Military History Institute.

Kennedy, William J. Letters. Illinois State Historical Library.

King, Jeptha. Civil War Letters. Indiana Historical Society Library.

Kirkpatrick, James N. Civil War Letters. Indiana Historical Society Library.

Knighton, James O. Papers. Louisiana State University Archives.

La Brant, Jonathan L. Papers. U.S. Army Military History Institute.

Lawrence, James. Collection. Chicago Historical Society.

"L.D.G." Letter to parents, April 8, 1862. Charles P. Gage's Battery File. Alabama Department of Archives and History.

Lee, George R. Papers. U.S. Army Military History Institute.

Levally, George W. Papers. Shiloh National Military Park.

Loudon, Dewitt Clinton. Papers. Ohio Historical Society.

Lyon, Jabiel. Diary. Ohio Historical Society.

McArthur, Henry C. Papers (include Journal). Iowa State Historical Department.

McMurry, S.J. Papers. Confederate Collection. Tennessee Department of Archives and History.

McWhirter, James. Letters. Filson Club, Louisville, Kentucky.

Magee, J.E. Diary. Duke University Library.

Mahan, Leonard H. Diary (Copy). Indiana State Library.

Mallory, Silas S. "Not in a Useless Cause: The Journal of Events during my Career as a Soldier in the Union Army" (Typed). Ohio Historical Society.

Mansfield. Mansfield Collection (n.d.). Arkansas Department of Archives and History.

Markle, Richard. Letters. Illinois State Historical Library.

Marks, David R. Journal, 1862–67. Illinois State Historical Library.

"Mart." William B. Mitchell Papers. Ohio Historical Society.

Martin, Parkhurst T. Collection. Illinois State Historical Library.

Matthews, John L. Letters, 1861–89. Iowa State Historical Society.

Meadows, George C. Collection. U.S. Army Military History Institute.

Mecklin, Augustus Harvey. Diary. Mississippi Department of Archives and History.

Millar, William. Robert Thompson Van Horn Papers, 1855–1907. State Historical Society of Missouri.

Minkler, Levi. Diary (Copy). Shiloh National Military Park.

———. "The Short Military Career of a Union Soldier Captured at the Battle of Shiloh." Kendy Baselt Collection. Alabama Department of Archives and History.

Mitchell, C. William B. Mitchell Papers. Ohio Historical Society.

Mitchell, Kenneth, ed. Service of William Mitchell and the 31st Indiana Volunteer Infantry in the Civil War, manuscript written in 1960, based on his diary. Indiana State Library.

Mock, Martin. Letter. Ohio Historical Society.

Moore, Robert T. Papers. Nineteenth Alabama Folder. Alabama Department of Archives and History.

Murfee, Hardy. Papers. Confederate Collection. Tennessee Department of Archives and History.

Murray, Mungo P. Papers (include Reminiscences). U.S. Army Military History Institute.

Newton, James K. Abdel D. Newton Papers. Wisconsin Historical Society.

Nicholls, W. Papers. Shiloh National Military Park.

Nichols, R.M. Letters. Shiloh National Military Park.

Nixon, L.I. Diary. Shiloh National Military Park.

Oliphant, M. Todd. Diary. Ohio Historical Society.

Pase, Jack F. Civil War Letters. Indiana State Historical Society Library.

Pfaw, George. Papers. Tennessee Department of Archives and History.

Pollard, William M. Diary. Tennessee State Library and Archives.

Pollock, David Wilson. Letters, 1861–63. State Historical Society of Missouri.

Post, William H. Post Family Letters. Illinois State Historical Library.

Power, Julius and Jacob B. Papers. Indiana State Historical Society Library.

Pugh, Richard. Papers. Louisiana State University Archives.

Quiner, E.B. "Correspondence of Wisconsin Volunteers." Microfilms, Reels 2 and 3, Vols. 5, 6, and 9. Wisconsin Historical Society.

Rankin, Andrew C. "Army Record of A.C. Rankin, M.D." Chicago Historical Society.

Reddick, James M. Papers. Indiana Historical Society Library.

Resley, John R. Civil War Letters. Iowa State Historical Society.

Reynolds, Edward H. Memoir-Diary. U.S. Army Military History Institute.

Rice, Mortimer. Civil War Diary. Illinois State Historical Library.

Richard, Thomas P. Papers. Louisiana State University Archives.

Richardson, George S. and William A. Civil War Letters (Typed copy). Iowa State Historical Society.

Ridley, D. Letters and Diary. Shiloh National Military Park.

Robertson, Thomas C. Papers. Louisiana State University Archives.

Robinson, William Culbertson. Manuscript. Illinois State Historical Library.

Ross, William H. Collection. Chicago Historical Society.

Ruckman, John. Papers. Shiloh National Military Park.

Russell, George W. Letters. Illinois State Historical Library.

Sackett, Edwin C. Sackett Letters. Illinois State Historical Library.

Sampson, Terah W. Letters. Filson Club, Louisville, Kentucky.

Schermerhorn, Winfield Scott. Letter. Iowa State Historical Department.

Sheperd, Thomas E. George W. Lambert Papers. Indiana Historical Society Library.

Sheperdson, Samuel. Family Papers. Indiana State Library.

Shumway, Z. Payson. Civil War Diary and Letters. Illinois State Historical Library.

Skinner, Calvin. David Shockley Papers. Indiana Historical Society Library.

Skinner, William. Papers. Shiloh National Military Park.

Slack, John. Juliet Starbuck Civil War Collection. Indiana Historical Society Library.

Small, Thomas M. Civil War Diary. Indiana Historical Society Library.

Snell, James P. Papers. Illinois State Historical Library.

Soners, George. Scribner Letters. Ohio Historical Society.

Spencer, Judith Ann. "The Faltering Footsteps: Hardships Suffered by the Confederate Civilians on the Homefront in the American Civil War of 1861–1865." Masters thesis, North Texas State University, 1977.

Steele, John. Steele-Boyd Family Collection. U.S. Army Military History Institute.

Stevens, J.M. Manuscript (Copy). Shiloh National Military Park.

Stewart, Charles. Papers. U.S. Army Military History Institute.

Stimson, William R. Papers. Library of Congress.

Stinson, Archibald D. Papers. Indiana Historical Society Library.

Stratton, David W. Civil War Diary (Copy). Indiana State Library.

Sullivan, Peter J. Papers. Shiloh National Military Park.

Taylor, T.L. Diary, Taylor Collection. Shiloh National Military Park.

Thompson, Joseph Dimmit. Diary and Letters. Tennessee Department of Archives and History.

Thornton, John J. Thornton Scrapbook. Mississippi Department of Archives and History.

Ticherer, I. Papers. Seventeenth Alabama Folder. Alabama Department of Archives and History.

Todd, Oliphant Monroe. Diary. Library of Congress.

Turnbull, David C. Papers and Letters, 1836–89. Indiana State Library.

Ufford, John. Letters. Iowa State Historical Department.

Unknown. Journal of the Orleans Guard. Walton-Ghenny Family Papers. Historic New Orleans Collection.

Unknown. Phrased Testimonies Contacted by the History Department (Copy). Shiloh National Military Park.

Unknown. Reminiscences Regarding the 5th Company, Washington Artillery Battalion. Collection. Tulane University.

Unknown (34th Illinois Infantry). Diary (Typed transcript). Illinois State Historical.

Vanderbilt, James C. Civil War Letters. Indiana State Library.

Varian, Alexander, Jr. Letters (Copy). Western Reserve Historical Society.

Vaught, William S. Papers. Historic New Orleans Collection.

Vieira, Augustine. Papers. Illinois State Historical Library.

Wagner, Levi. Recollections. U.S. Army Military History Institute.

Walden, Madison M. Civil War Letters. Iowa State Historical Society.

Walker, Andrew J. Papers. Library of Congress.

Walker, T.J. "Reminiscences of the Civil War," received from Mrs. Charles B. Reaves, Sunspot, N.M.

Walter, David S. Letter. Indiana Historical Society Library.

Ward, Williamson D. Diary and Letter. Bower Papers. Indiana Historical Society Library.

Warner, Herschel Jaspel. Letter (Typed copy). Indiana State Library.
Warren, William H. Civil War Letters. Iowa State Historical Society.
Watkins, Thomas C. Papers. U.S. Army Military History Institute.
Watts, Harry. Civil War Reminiscences (Copy). Indiana State Library.
Wayne, Harley. Letters (Copy). Illinois State Historical Library.
Weisner, Reuben E. Diary. Illinois State Historical Library.
Weller, John H. Letters. Filson Club, Louisville, Kentucky.
Werly, Stephen. Diary, 1862–64. State Historical Society of Missouri.
Wiley, Aquila. Papers. Western Reserve Historical Society.
Wiley, J.H. Letters. Shiloh National Military Park.
Wilkinson, Michajah and B.F.W. Papers. Louisiana State University Archives.
Williams, Maurice J. Diary (Typed copy). Shiloh National Military Park.
Williams, W.H. Letter. Confederate Collection. Tennessee State Library and
    Archives.
Winchester, Edwin F. Collection. Wisconsin Historical Society.
Winslow, R. Hoyt. Diary. U.S. Army Military History Institute.
Winton, George P., Jr. "Anti-Bellum Military Instruction of West Point Officers
    and Its Influence upon Confederate Military Organization." Ph.D. dis-
    sertation, University of South Carolina, 1972.
Word, W.S. Scribner Letters. Ohio Historical Society.
Yandell, David Wendel. Letter, Yandell to Johnston (Typed copy of the original
    at the Filson Club, Louisville, Kentucky), Baird Collection. Western Ken-
    tucky University Library.
———. Letters from David W. Yandell to William Preston Johnston, Mrs. Mason
    Barret Collection of the Albert Sidney Johnston Papers. Tulane University.
———. Yandell Collection. Filson Club, Louisville, Kentucky.
———. Yandell Collection (Copy). Western Kentucky. University Library.
Zearing, James Roberts. Collection. Chicago Historical Society.

NEWSPAPERS

L'Abeille de la Nouvelle-Orleans/The New Orleans Bee, June 1, 1861–April 26, 1862.
The Arkansas State Gazette (Little Rock), June 1, 1861–May 3, 1862.
The Athens Messenger (Athens, Ohio), June 1, 1861–May 30, 1862.
The Aurora Beacon (Aurora, Ill.), January 16 and 23, March 6, 20, 27, April 17
    and 24, May 1 and 15, 1862.
The Belleville Democrat (Belleville, Ill.), December 14, 1861.
The Belvidere Standard (Belvidere, Ill.), July 2 and 16, 1861.
The Burlington Daily Hawk-eye (Burlington, Iowa), June 1, 1861–June 1, 1862.
The Clairborne Southerner (Clairborne, Ala.), June 1–December 1, 1861.
The Columbia City News (Columbia, Ind.), June 4, 1861–June 3, 1862.
The Council Bluffs Nonpareil (Council Bluffs, Iowa), May 1, 1861–June 1, 1862.
The Daily Capital City Fact (Columbus, Ohio), June 1, 1861–May 31, 1862.
The Daily Commercial Register (Sandusky, Ohio), June 1, 1861–May 7, 1862.
The Daily Democrat and News (Davenport, Iowa), June 1–October 23, 1861; March
    27–June 1, 1862.
The Daily Gate City (Keokuk, Iowa), June 1, 1861–June 1, 1862.
The Daily State Sentinel (Indianapolis, Ind.), June 1, 1861–May 31, 1862.

The Daily Steubenville Herald (Steubenville, Ohio), June 1, 1861–May 30, 1862.
The Decorah Republic (Decorah, Iowa), June 1, 1861–June 1, 1862.
The Dubuque Daily Times (Dubuque, Iowa), January 1–May 31, 1862.
The Dubuque Herald (Dubuque, Iowa), April 5–June 3, 1862.
The Eastern Clarion (Paulding, Miss.), July 19, 1861–June 1, 1862.
The Elyria Independent Democrat (Elyria, Ohio), June 5, 1861–May 28, 1862.
The Fairfield Ledger (Fairfield, Iowa), June 1, 1861–May 31, 1862.
The Freeport Bulletin (Freeport, Ill.), July 4, 1861; January 30, April 24, 1862.
The Fremont Daily Journal (Fremont, Ohio), June 1, 1861–June 1, 1862.
The Hancock Democrat (Greenfield, Ind.), June 5, 1861–May 31, 1862.
The Howard Tribune (Kokomo, Ind.), June 4, 1861–June 1, 1862.
The Indiana True Republican (Centreville, Ind.), June 1, 1861–May 29, 1862.
The Ironton Register (Ironton, Ohio), June 6, 1861–May 29, 1862.
The Jackson Standard (Jackson, Ohio), June 6, 1861–May 29, 1862.
The Jacksonville Sentinel (Jacksonville, Ill.), May 2, 1862.
The Lima Weekly Gazette (Lima, Ohio), July 3, 1861–May 28, 1862.
The Lincoln Herald (Lincoln, Ill.), May 8, 1862.
The Louisville Daily Courier (Louisville, Ky.), June 1–December 13, 1861.
The Mahoning Sentinel (Youngstown, Ohio), June 5–October 30, 1861; July 9, 1862.
The Memphis Daily Appeal (Memphis, Tenn.), January 1–June 1, 1862.
The Mobile Advertiser and Register (Mobile, Ala.), June 15, 1861–June 1, 1862.
The Nashville Union and American (Nashville, Tenn.), June 1, 1861–February 1, 1862.
The Natchez Daily Courier (Natchez, Miss.), June 1, 1861–June 1, 1862 (except March).
The New Orleans Commercial Bulletin (New Orleans, La.), June 1, 1861–April 22, 1862.
The New Orleans Daily Crescent (New Orleans, La.), June 1, 1861–May 22, 1862.
The Ohio Repository (Canton, Ohio), January 1–May 31, 1862.
The Opelousas Courrier/Le Courier des Opelousas (Opelousas, La.), January 4–May 31, 1862.
The Pantagraph (Bloomington, Ill.), June 13, 1861.
The Parke County Republican (Rockville, Ind.), June 5, 1861–May 28, 1862.
The Princeton Clarion (Princeton, Ind.), June 1, 1861–June 1, 1862.
The Republican Banner (Nashville, Tenn.), June 1–October 29, 1861.
The Seneca Advertiser (Tiffin, Ohio), June 7, 1861–May 30, 1862.
The South Western Baptist (Tuskegee, Ala.), June 6, 1861–June 6, 1862.
The Telegraph (Alton, Ill.), September 20, 1861.
The Tiffin Weekly Tribune (Tiffin, Ohio), June 7, 1861–May 30, 1862.
The Van Buren Press (Van Buren, Ark.), June 5, 1861–January 28, 1862.
The Waterloo Courier (Waterloo, Iowa), June 5, 1861–June 4, 1862.
The Weekly Courier (Natchez, Miss.), July 10, 1861–May 28, 1862.
The Whiteside Sentinel (Whiteside, Ill.), December 19, 1861.

ARTICLES IN JOURNALS OR MAGAZINES

Alison, Joseph Dill. "I Have Been Through My First Battle and Have Had Enough War to Last Me." *Civil War Times Illustrated*, Vol. 5, No. 10 (February 1967), pp. 40–46.

Barnett, James, ed. "Some Civil War Letters and Diary of John Lympus Barnett." *Indiana Magazine of History*, Vol. 37 (March 1941), pp. 162–73.

Belcher, Michael F. "Fear in Combat." *Marine Corps Gazette*, Vol. 64 (September 1980), pp. 49–53.

Berwanger, Eugene H. "Western Prejudice and the Extension of Slavery." *Civil War History*, Vol. XII, No. 3 (September 1966), pp. 197–212.

Blakeley, H.W. "The First 24 Hours." *Army*, Vol. 15 (May 1965), pp. 20–21.

Blakewell, A. Gordon. "The Luck of the War Game Sometimes Makes Heroes: The Orderly that was of the Fifth Co. Washington Artillery. Shiloh!" *Illinois Central Magazine*, Vol. 4, No. 4 (October 1915), pp. 18–20.

Broyles, William, Jr. "Why Men Love War." *Esquire*, Vol. 102 (November 1984), pp. 55–65.

Cain, Marvin R. "A 'Face of Battle' Needed: An Assessment of Motives and Men in Civil War Historiography." *Civil War History*, Vol. XXVIII, No. 1 (1982), pp. 5–27.

Capron, Thaddeus Hurlbut. "War Diary." *Journal of the Illinois Historical Society*, Vol. XII (1919), pp. 330–406.

Carpenter, C.C. and Crossley, Geo. W. "Seventh Iowa Volunteers in Civil War Gave Valiant Service. *Annals of Iowa*, Vol. XXXIV, No. 3 (September 1957), pp. 100–11.

Catton, Bruce. "Glory Road Began in the West." *Civil War History*, Vol. VI (1960), pp. 229–37.

Conti, Gerald, "Motivation: What Makes a Fellow Fight?" *Civil War Times Illustrated*, Vol. 33, No. 2 (April 1984a), pp. 18–23.

———. "Seeing the Elephant." *Civil War Times Illustrated*, Vol. 33, No. 4 (June 1984b), p. 19.

Crenshaw, Edward. "Diary of Captain Crenshaw." *Alabama Historical Quarterly*, (Winter 1930), pp. 438–52; (Fall 1939), pp. 261–70; (Spring 1940), pp. 52–71; (Summer 1940), pp. 221–38; (Fall 1940), pp. 365–85.

Dawes, E.C. "First Day at Shiloh: An Eyewitness Account." *Civil War Times Illustrated*, Vol. 7, No. 10 (February 1969), pp. 4–9, 44–48.

Dupuy, Trevor. "Analyzing Trends in Ground Combat." *History, Numbers and War*, Vol. 1, No. 2 (Summer 1977), pp. 77–83.

Ellis, Richard N. "The Civil War Letters of an Iowa Family." *Annals of Iowa*, 3rd Series, Vol. 39, No. 8 (Spring 1969), pp. 561–86.

Glover, Amos. "Diary." *Ohio State Archaelogical and History Quarterly*, Vol. 44 (1935), pp. 258–72.

Harris, Boyd. M. "A New Army Emphasis on Leadership: Be, Know, Do." *Military Review*, Vol. 43, No. 2 (February 1983), pp. 62–71.

Hays, John Bowen. "An Incident of the Battle of Shiloh." *Tennessee Historical Magazine*, Vol. 9 (1925–26), pp. 144–55.

Houston, Sam, Jr. "Shiloh Shadows." *Southwestern Historical Quarterly*, Vol. 34 (1930–31), pp. 329–33.

Jessup, Lewis B. "The 24th Indiana at Shiloh." *The National Tribune Scrapbook*, Vol. 3 (n.d.), pp. 158–59.

Kohn, Richard H. "The Social History of the American Soldier: A Review and Prospectus for Research." *American Historical Review*, Vol. 86, No. 3 (June 1981), pp. 553–67.

Lathrop, Barnes F. "A Confederate Artilleryman at Shiloh." *Civil War History*, Vol. 8, No. 4 (1962), pp. 373–85.

Laurie, Clayton. "Two-Sided Adventure." *Civil War Times Illustrated*, Vol. 24, No. 4 (June 1985), pp. 40–47.

Long, J.M. "A Seventeen Year Old Texas Boy at Shiloh." *Blue and Gray*, Vol. 1 (1893), pp. 278–79.

McBride, George W. "My Recollection of Shiloh." *Blue and Gray*, Vol. 3 (1894), pp. 8–12.

———. "Shiloh, After Thirty-Two Years." *Blue and Gray*, Vol. 3 (1894), pp. 303–10.

McDonough, James L. "Glory Can Not Atone: Shiloh—April 6–7, 1862." *Tennessee Historical Quarterly*, Vol. 35, No. 3 (1976), pp. 279–95.

Mahon, John K. "Civil War Infantry Assault Tactics." *Military Affairs*, Vol. 25, No. 2 (Summer 1961), pp. 57–68.

———, ed. "The Civil War Letters of Samuel Mahon, Seventh Iowa Infantry." *Iowa Journal of History*, Vol. 51 (1953), pp. 233–66.

Marsh, Nelson L. "Bloody Shiloh." *Official United States Army Magazine*, Vol. 30 (April 1975), pp. 43–49.

Martin, David G. "Data File." *Strategy and Tactics*, No. 89 (November–December 1981), p. 22.

Maslowski, Pete. "A Study of Morale in Civil War Soldiers." *Military Affairs*, Vol. 34 (December 1970), pp. 122–26.

Moore, Robert T. "A Letter of R.T. Moore, August 22, 1861; and a letter of William T. Moore, April 21, 1862." *Alabama Historical Quarterly*, Vol. 23 (1961), pp. 300–302.

Mott, Charles R., Jr., ed. "War Journal of a Confederate Officer [W.H. Mott]." *Tennessee Historical Quarterly*, Vol. 5, No. 3 (September 1946), pp. 234–47.

Nixon, Liberty Independence. "An Alabamian at Shiloh: The Diary of Liberty Independence Nixon." *Alabama Review*, Vol. 11 (April 1958), pp. 144–55.

Olney, Warren. "The Battle of Shiloh: With Some Personal Reminicences." *The Overland Monthly*, Vol. 5 (1885), pp. 577–89.

———. "Shiloh as Seen by a Private Soldier: Paper Read before the California Commandery of the Military Order of the United States, May 31, 1889." *War Paper*, No. 5 (1889), pp. 1–26.

Porter, William Clendenin. "War Diary of W.C. Porter." *Arkansas Historical Quarterly*, Vol. 11 (1952), pp. 286–314.

Prescott, W.J. "Combat." *Army*, Vol. 15 (December 1965), pp. 38–42.

Robertson, James I., Jr., ed. " 'Such is War': the Letters of an Orderly in the 7th Iowa Infantry." *Iowa Journal of History*, Vol. 58 (1960), pp. 321–56.

Rogers, William J. "William P. Rogers Memorandum Book." *West Tennessee Historical Society*, Vol. 9 (1955), pp. 59–92.

Rogers, William P. "Diary and Letters of William P. Rogers." *Southwestern Historical Quarterly*, Vol. 332, No. 4 (April 1929), pp. 259–99.

Roland, Charles P. "Albert Sidney Johnston and the Shiloh Campaign." *Civil War History*, Vol. 4, No. 4 (1958), pp. 355–82.

Rudolph, Jack. "Taking Up Arms." *Civil War Times Illustrated*, Vol. 23, No. 2 (April 1984), pp. 8–17.

Ruff, Joseph. "Civil War Experiences of a German Emigrant." *Michigan History Magazine*, Vol. 27 (Spring/Summer 1943), pp. 271–301, 442–62.

Saloman, Herman. "Civil War Diary of Herman Saloman." *Wisconsin Magazine of History*, Vol. 10, No. 4 (1926), pp. 205–10.

Spradlin, Mike, ed. "The Diary of George W. Jones: An Impartial History of Stanford's Mississippi Battery." *Camp Chase Gazette*, Vol. 9 (April 1981), pp. 7–8.

Stephenson, Wendell Holmes and Davis, Edwin Adams, eds. "The Civil War Diary of Willie Micajah Barrow, September 23, 1861–July 13, 1862." *Louisiana Historical Quarterly Reprint*, Louisiana State Library.

Thomas, James W. "An Ohio Corporal's Testament." *Blue and Gray*, Vol. 1 (1893), pp. 307–9.

Thomas, William Candace. "From Shiloh to Port Gibson." *Civil War Times Illustrated*, Vol. 3, No. 6 (October 1964), pp. 20–25.

Thompson, Joseph Dimmit. "The Battle of Shiloh: From the Letters and Diary." Edited by John G. Biel. *Tennessee Historical Quarterly*, Vol. XVIII, No. 3 (1958), pp. 250–74.

Thompson, William Candace. "From Shiloh to Port Gibson." *Civil War Times Illustrated*, Vol. 3, No. 6 (October 1964), pp. 20–25.

Throne, Mildred. "Letters from Shiloh." *Iowa Journal of History*, Vol. 52, No. 3 (July 1954), pp. 235, 235–80.

Wardlaw, Grant. "We Need to Know Man's Behavior Under Combat Stress." *Pacific Defence Reporter*, Vol. 11 (August 1904), pp. 55–57, 67.

Weller, Jac and Gleason, F.W. Foster. "Civil War Tactics." *Ordnance*, Vol. 49 (November/December 1964), pp. 303–6.

Wiley, Bell I. "Home Letters of Johnny Reb and Billy Yank." *Army Information Digest*, Vol. 16 (August 1961), pp. 76–81.

———. "Johnny Reb and Billy Yank." *American History Illustrated*, Vol. 3 (1968), pp. 4–9, 44–47.

———. "Johnny Reb and Billy Yank at Shiloh." *West Tennessee Historical Society Papers* (1972), pp. 5–12.

Williams, T. Harry. "The Return of Jomini—Some Thoughts on Recent Civil War Writings." *Military Affairs*, Vol. 34 (1970), pp. 127–31.

Woolridge, William O. "Combat." *Army Digest*. Vol. 23 (January 1968), pp. 6–11.

BOOKS

Abernathy, Byron R., ed. *Private Stockwell, Jr. Sees the Civil War*. Norman: University of Oklahoma Press, 1958.

Adams, George Worthington. *Doctors in Blue: The Medical History of the Union Army in the Civil War*. New York: Henry Schuman, 1952.

Ambrose, Daniel Leib. *History of the Seventh Regiment Illinois Volunteer Infantry*. Springfield: Illinois Journal Co., 1868.

Ashworth, Tony. *Trench Warfare, 1914–1918: The Live and Let Live System*. London: Macmillan Press, 1980.

Bacon, Alvin Q. *Thrilling Adventures of a Pioneer Boy*. N.p., 186– .

Baird, Nancy Disher. *David Wendel Yandell: Physician of Old Louisville.* Lexington: University Press of Kentucky, 1978.

Barber, Lucius W. *Army Memoirs.* Chicago: J.M.W. Jones, 1894.

Bartlett, Napier. *A Soldier's Story of the War, Including the Marches and Battles of the Washington Artillery.* New Orleans: Clark and Hefeline, 1874.

Barton, Michael. *Goodmen: The Character of Civil War Soldiers.* University Park: Pennsylvania State University Press, 1981.

Battles and Leaders of the Civil War. Vol. I. From Sumter to Shiloh. South Brunswick, N.J.: Thomas Yoseloff, 1956.

Baynes, John. *Morale: A Study of Men and Courage.* London: Cassell, 1967.

Beaumont, Roger A. and Snyder, William P. "The Dimensions of Combat Effectiveness." In *Combat Effectiveness: Cohesion, Stress, and the Volunteer Military.* Edited by Sam C. Sarkesian. Beverly Hills: Sage, 1980.

Bergeron, Arthur W., Jr., ed. *Reminiscences of Uncle Silas [Grismore]: A History of the Eighteenth Louisiana Infantry Regiment.* Baton Rouge: Louisiana State Library, 1981.

Berwinger, Richard; Hattaway, Herman; Jones, Archer; and Still, William N., Jr. *Why the South Lost the Civil War.* Athens: University of Georgia Press, 1982.

Bevens, W.E. *Reminiscences of a Private, Company "G," First Arkansas Regiment Infantry.* N.p., n.d.

Bierce, Ambrose. *Collected Works.* Vol. I. New York: Gorden Press, 1966.

Blalock, Hubert M., Jr. *Social Statistics.* New York: McGraw-Hill, 1960.

Bowman, Thornton Hardie. *Reminiscences of an ex-Confederate Soldier.* Austin, Tex.: Gammel-Stateman, 1904.

Boyd, Cyrus F. *The Civil War Diary of Cyrus F. Boyd, Fifteenth Iowa Infantry, 1861–1863.* Edited by Mildred Throne. Iowa City: The State Historical Society of Iowa, 1953.

Burge, William. *Through the Civil War and Western Adventures.* Lisbon, Iowa: Torch Press, 1907.

Carroll, John W. *Autobiography and Reminiscences.* Henderson, Tenn.: n.p., 1898.

Cherry, Peterson H. *Prisoner in Blue.* Los Angeles: Wetzel Publishing Co., 1931.

Clairborne, John Francis Hamtramck. *A Sketch of Harvey's Scouts formerly of Jackson's Cavalry Division.* Starkville, Miss.: Southern Live-Stock Journal, 1885.

Connelly, Thomas H. *History of the Seventieth Ohio Regiment.* Cincinnati: Peak Bros., 1902.

Connelly, Thomas L. *Army of the Heartland.* Baton Rouge: Louisiana State University Press, 1967.

Coons, John W. *Indiana at Shiloh.* Indianapolis: Indiana Shiloh National Park Commission, 1904.

Crooker, Lucien B. "Episodes and Characters in an Illinois Regiment." In *Military Essays and Recollections: Papers Read before the Commandery of the State of Illinois Military Order of the Loyal Legion of United States.* Edited by M.O.L.L.U.S. Chicago: A.C. McClung, 1891.

Cumming, Kate. *A Journal of Hospital Life in the Confederate Army from the Battle of Shiloh to the End of the War.* Louisville: John P. Norton, 1866.

Cunliffe, Marcus. *Soldiers and Civilians: The Martial Spirit in America, 1775–1865.* Boston: Little, Brown and Co., 1968.

Dew, Charles. *Ironmaker to the Confederacy: Joseph R. Anderson and the Tredegar Iron Works*. Wilmington, N.C.: Broadfoot, 1987.

Dollard, John. *Fear in Battle*. Washington, D.C.: The Infantry, 1944.

Donald, David. "The Confederate as a Fighting Man." In *The Southerner as American*. Edited by Charles Grier Sellers, Jr. New York: E.P. Dutton, 1966.

————. ed. *Why the North Won the Civil War*. New York: Collier Books, 1962.

Downing, Alexander G. *Downing's Civil War Diary*. Des Moines: The Historical Department of Iowa, 1916.

Dugan, James. *History of Hurlbut's Fighting Fourth Division*. Cincinnati: E. Morgan, 1863.

Duke, John K. *History of the Fifty-Third Ohio Volunteer Infantry*. Portsmouth, Ohio: Blade Printing Co., 1900.

Dupuy, R. Ernest and Dupuy, Trevor N. *The Encyclopedia of Military History*. New York: Harper and Row, 1970.

Egbert, Robert L. et al. *The Characteristics of Fighters and Non-Fighters*. Fort Ord, Calif.: Human Research Unit No. 2, 1954.

————. *Fighter I: A Study of Effective and Ineffective Combat Performers*. Washington, D.C.: The George Washington University Human Resources Research Office, March 1958.

Ellis, John. *Armies in Revolution*. New York: Oxford University Press, 1974.

————. *The Sharp End of War: The Fighting Man in World War II*. North Pomfret, Vt.: David and Charles, 1980.

Essame, H. *Patton: A Study in Command*. New York: Charles Scribner's Sons, 1974.

Fleming, Robert H. "The Battle of Shiloh as a Private Saw it." In *Sketches of War History, 1861–1865; Papers Read before the Ohio Commandery of the Military Order of the Loyal Legion of the United States*. Vol. 6. Edited by M.O.L.L.U.S. Cincinnati: R. Clarke, 1888–1908.

Folmar, John Kent, ed. *From that Terrible Field: Civil War Letters of James M. Williams, Twenty-First Alabama Infantry Volunteers*. University: University of Alabama Press, 1981.

Foote, Shelby. *The Civil War: A Narrative*. Vol. I, *Fort Sumter to Perryville*. New York: Random House, 1958.

Fussell, Paul. *The Great War and Modern Memory*. London: Oxford University Press, 1975.

Gabriel, Richard A. and Savage, Paul L. *Crisis in Command: Mismanagement in the Army*. New York: Hill and Wang, 1978.

Ganoe, William A. *The History of the U.S. Army*. New York: D. Appleton, 1942.

Grant, U.S. *Papers of Ulysses S. Grant*. Vol. 5. Carbondale: Southern Illinois University Press, 1973.

————. *Personal Memoirs of U.S. Grant*. New York: De Capo Press, 1982.

Grant, U.S. III. "Military Strategy of the Civil War." In *Military Analysis of the Civil War*. Edited by T. Harry Williams. Millwood, N.Y.: KTO Pres, 1977.

Grinkler, Roy R. and Spiegel, John P. *Men Under Stress*. Philadelphia: Blakiston, 1945.

Grose, William. *The Story of the Marches, Battles and Incidents of the 36th Regiment*

Indiana Volunteer Infantry. New Castle, Ind.: The Courrier Company Press, 1891.

Hancock, John. *The Fourteenth Wisconsin: Corinth and Shiloh*. Indianapolis: Engle, 1895.

Hardee, William Joseph. *Rifle and Light Infantry Tactics*. 2 Vols. Philadelphia: Lippincott, 1855.

Harman, Nicholas. *Dunkirk, the Patriotic Myth*. New York: Simon and Schuster, 1980.

Hart, Ephraim. *History of the Fortieth Illinois Infantry*. Cincinnati: H.S. Bosworth, 1864.

Hasting, Max and Jenkins, Simon. *Battle for the Falklands*. New York: W.W. Norton, 1982.

Hattaway, Herman and Jones, Archer. *A Military History of the Civil War: How the North Won*. Chicago: University of Illinois, 1983.

Hauser, William L. "The Will to Fight." In *Combat Effectiveness: Cohesion, Stress, and the Volunteer Military*. Edited by Sam C. Sarkesian. Beverly Hills: Sage, 1980.

Hazen, W.B. *A Narrative of Military Service*. Boston: Ticknor and Company, 1885.

Hearnden, Patrick J. *Independence and Empire: The South's New Cotton Campaign, 1865–1901*. DeKalb: Northern Illinois University Press, 1982.

Hicken, Victor. *The American Fighting Man*. London: Macmillan, 1969.

Hickenlooper, Andrew. "The Battle of Shiloh." In *Sketches of Civil War History, 1861–1865; Papers before the Ohio Commandery of the Military Order of the Loyal Legion of the United States*. Vol. 5. Edited by M.O.L.L.U.S. Cincinnati: R. Clarke, 1903.

Hobart, Edwin Lucius. *Semi-History of a Boy-Veteran of the Twentieth Regiment Illinois Infantry*. Denver: N.p., 1909.

Holman, T.W. and Starr. N.D. *The 21st Missouri Regiment Infantry Veteran Volunteers*. Fort Madison, Iowa: Roberts and Roberts, 1899.

Holmes, Richard. *Firing Line*. Harmondsworth, UK: Penguin Books, 1986.

Indiana Battle Flag Commission. *Indiana Battle Flags and A Record of Indiana Organizations in the Mexican, Civil and Spanish American Wars*. Indianapolis: Indiana Battle Flag Commission, 1929. *Indiana. Report of the Adjutant General. Vol. II 1861–1865 (Rosters)*. Indianapolis: W.R. Holloway, 1865.

Janowitz, Morris. *Sociology and the Military Establishment*. New York: Sage Foundation, 1959.

Kammen, Michael. *The Machine that Would Go of Itself*. New York: Knopf, 1986.

Keegan, John. *The Face of Battle*. New York: The Viking Press, 1976.

Kellett, Anthony. *Combat Motivation: The Behavior of Soldiers in Battle*. Boston: Kluwer Nijhoff, 1982.

Kerwood, Ashbury L. *Annals of the Fifty-Seventh Regiment Indiana Volunteer Infantry*. Dayton, Ohio: W.J. Shuey, 1868.

Kimberly, Robert L. and Holloway, Ephraim S. *The Forty-First Ohio Veteran Infantry in the War of the Rebellion, 1861–1865*. Cleveland: Smellie, 1897.

Lewy, Guenter. "The American Experience in Vietnam." In *Combat Effectiveness: Cohesion, Stress, and the Volunteer Military*. Edited by Sam C. Sarkesian. Beverly Hills: Sage, 1980.

Linderman, Gerald F. *Embattled Courage*. New York: Free Press, 1987.

Lonn, Ella. *Desertion During the Civil War*. Gloucester, Mass.: Peter Smith, 1966.

Lorenz, Konrad. *On Aggression*. Toronto: Bantam, 1967.

Lynn, John A. *The Bayonets of the Republic: Motivation and Tactics in the Army of Revolutionary France*. Chicago: University of Illinois Press, 1984.

McDonough, James Lee. *Shiloh—in Hell before Night*. Knoxville: University of Tennessee Press, 1977.

McEathron, Alexander. *Letters and Memoirs of Alexander McEathron during the Civil War*. N.p., 1938.

McMurray, William J. *History of the Twentieth Tennessee Regiment Volunteer Infantry, C.S.A.* Nashville: N.p., 1904.

McWhiney, Grady and Jamieson, Perry D. *Attack and Die: Civil War Militia Tactics and the Southern Heritage*. University: University of Alabama Press, 1982.

Mahon, John K. "Civil War Infantry Assault Tactics." In *Military Analysis of the Civil War*. Edited by T. Harry Williams. Millwood, N.Y.: KTO Press, 1977.

Mahon, John K. and Danysh, Romana. *Infantry*. Washington, D.C.: Office of the Chief of Military History, U.S. Army, 1972.

Marshall, Samuel L.A. *Men Against Fire*. New York: William Morrow and Co., [1947] 1966.

Mitchell, Reid. *Civil War Soldiers: Their Expectations and Their Experiences*. New York: Viking Peguin, 1988.

Moran, Charles Lord. *The Anatomy of Courage*. London: Constable, 1966.

Morris, Desmond. *The Naked Ape*. Toronto: Bantam, 1969.

Moskos, Charles C. *The American Enlisted Man*. New York: Russell Sage Foundation, 1970.

Newton, James K. *A Wisconsin Boy in Dixie*. Madison: University of Wisconsin, 1961.

Official Records, War of the Rebellion, Series I. Vol. X, Part I. Washington, D.C.: U.S. War Department, 1880.

Patrick, Joseph M. *Civil War Memoirs Written by a Participant in It*. Enid, Okla.: Drummond and Patrick, 191–.

Patrick, Robert Dranghon. *The Secret Diary of Robert Patrick*. Baton Rouge: Louisiana State University Press, 1959.

Payne, Edwin Waters. *History of the Thirty-Fourth of Illinois Infantry*. Clinton, Iowa.: Allen, 1902.

Peterson, Harold L. *The Treasury of the Gun*. New York: Golden Press, 1962.

Reid, Whitelaw. *Ohio in the War: Her Statesmen, her Generals, and her Soldiers; Vol. II, the History of her Regiments and Other Military Organizations*. Cincinnati: Moore, Wilstach and Baldwin, 1868.

Richardson, F.M. *Fighting Spirit. A Study of Psychological Factors in War*. London: Leo Cooper, 1978.

Russ, Martin. *The Last Parallel: A Marine's War Journal*. New York: Rinehart and Co., 1957.

Shattuck, Gardiner, H., Jr. *A Shield and Hiding Place: The Religious Life of the Civil War*. Macon, Ga.: Mercer University Press, 1987.

Sledge, E.B. *With the Old Breed: At Peleliu and Okinawa*. Novato, Calif.: Presidio Press, 1981.

Starr, Steven Z. *Union Cavalry in the Civil War*. 3 Vols. Baton Rouge: Louisiana State University Press, 1981.

Stillwell, Leander. *The Story of A Common Soldier of Army Life in the Civil War, 1861–1865*. N.p.: Franklin Hudson, 1920.

Stouffer, Samuel L. et al. *The American Soldier: Vol II: Combat and Its Aftermath.* Princeton, N.J.: Princeton University Press, 1949.

Sullins, D. *Recollections of an Old Man*. Bristol, Tenn.: King Printing, 1910.

Sword, Wiley. *Shiloh: Bloody April*. New York: Morrow, 1974.

Vail, D.F. *Company K, of the 16th Wisconsin, at the Battle of Shiloh*. N.p.: N.p., 1897.

Van Creveld, Martin L. *Fighting Power: German and U.S. Army Performance, 1939–1945*. Westport, Conn.: Greenwood Press, 1982.

Vandiver, Frank E. *Plowshares into Swords; Josiah Gorgas and Confederate Ordnance*. Austin: University of Texas Press, 1952.

Van Doren Stern, Philip, ed. *Soldier Life in the Union and Confederate Armies*. New York: Bonanza Books, 1961.

Watkins, Samuel R. *Co. Aytch: A Confederate Soldier's Memoirs*. New York: Collier Books, [1881–2] 1962.

Watson, Peter. *War on the Mind: The Military Uses and Abuses of Psychology*. New York: Basic Books, 1978.

Weigley, Russell F. *Eisenhower's Lieutenants*. Vol. I. Bloomington: Indiana University Press, 1981.

Wesbrook, Stephen D. "The Potential for Military Disintegration." In *Combat Effectiveness: Cohesion, Stress, and the Volunteer Military*. Edited by Sam C. Sarkesian. Beverly Hills: Sage, 1980.

Wheeler, Richard, ed. *Voices of the Civil War*. New York: Thomas Y. Crowell, 1976.

Wiley, Bell I. *The Life of Billy Yank*. Baton Rouge: Louisiana State University Press, 1978a.

———. *The Life of Johnny Reb*. Baton Rouge: Louisiana State University Press, 1978b.

Williams, T. Harry. "The Military Leadership of North and South." In *Why the North Won the Civil War*. Edited by David Donald. New York: Collier Books, 1962.

Williams, Thomas J. *An Historical Sketch of the 56th Ohio Volunteer Infantry*. Columbus, Ohio: The Lawrence Press, 1899.

Wilson, Edmund. *Patriotic Gore: Studies of the Literature of the Civil War*. Boston: Northeastern University Press, 1984.

Woodruff, George H. *History of Battery D, First Artillery, McAllister's Battery*. N.p., 1876a.

———. *Fifteen Years Ago*. Joliet, Ill.: J. Goodseed, 1876b.

Wright, Charles. *A Corporal's Story: Experiences in the Rank of Company C, 81st Ohio Vol. Infantry*. Philadelphia: State Historical Society, 1887.

Wright, Henry H. *A History of the Sixth Iowa Infantry*. Iowa City: State History Society of Iowa, 1923.

Young, Jesse Bowman. *What a Boy Saw in the Army*. New York: Hunt and Eaton, 1894.

Index

The University of Illinois Press
is a founding member of the
Association of American University Presses.

———————————————

University of Illinois Press
1325 South Oak Street
Champaign, IL 61820-6903
www.press.uillinois.edu